The Island of World Peace

The Island of World Peace

The Jeju Massacre and State Building in South Korea

Gwisook Gwon

ROWMAN & LITTLEFIELD
Lanham • Boulder • New York • London

Published by Rowman & Littlefield
An imprint of The Rowman & Littlefield Publishing Group, Inc.
4501 Forbes Boulevard, Suite 200, Lanham, Maryland 20706
www.rowman.com

86-90 Paul Street, London EC2A 4NE

British Library Cataloguing in Publication Information Available

Library of Congress Cataloging-in-Publication Data Available

ISBN 9781538145692 (cloth : alk. paper) | ISBN 9781538145708 (epub)

♾™ The paper used in this publication meets the minimum requirements of American National Standard for Information Sciences—Permanence of Paper for Printed Library Materials, ANSI/NISO Z39.48-1992.

Contents

Acknowledgments   vii

Introduction   ix

Chapter 1: Beginning: Postcolonial Aspirations for a New State   1

Chapter 2: State Violence: The Jeju Massacre   21

Chapter 3: Reintegration 1: The South Korean State and the Korean
        War   49

Chapter 4: Reintegration 2: Jeju Marines as Ghost Busters   71

Chapter 5: Reconstruction: Jeju Wise Mother, Good Wife on the
        Island of Working Women   91

Chapter 6: Reconciliation: The Jeju 4.3 Peace Park   119

Conclusion: The Island of World Peace   135

Bibliography   157

Index   171

About the Author   185

Acknowledgments

This book was made possible with the help of many individuals and institutions that provided intellectual, financial, and emotional support. First of all, I owe an enormous debt to members of the international academic project Beyond the Korean War. In particular, I would like to express my special thanks to the project director, Heonik Kwon, who offered me a great opportunity to participate in this project and stimulated my intellectual progress. I also owe an enormous debt of gratitude to fellow advisory members of the project who offered intellectual inspiration and emotional encouragement, such as Bruce Cumings, Nan Kim, Seong-bo Kim, Seong-nae Kim, Christina Klein, Steven Lee, Myung-lim Park, Mark Selden, Jeong-ran Yoon, and the late Marline Young. Mark Selden inspired me to pursue my research and helped me to develop and expand my ideas throughout the writing process. Steven Lee provided invaluable suggestions on the framework and details of the chapters, while Nan Kim helped me strengthen the book proposal and develop arguments throughout. Finally, Jeong-ran Yoon particularly encouraged me not to give up on writing the book during some of the more difficult phases.

I would also like to extend my deepest gratitude to my colleagues who provided intellectual inspiration and constructive feedback on various drafts the book. Man-hyeong Lee especially helped me develop the framework of the manuscript and articulate specific arguments throughout. Keun-sik Jung, Eun-sil Kim, and You-joung Kim provided insightful feedback on entire chapters of early drafts. Finally, Brendan Wright also helped me with the flow and structure of the book draft amid his own busy schedule.

I owe my deepest debt to numerous interviewees, especially Jeju marine veterans, women survivors of Jeju 4.3, and activists of the advocacy movement of Jeju 4.3. The Jeju marine veterans willingly shared their memories of the Korean War and invited me to their commemorative events. Women interviewees also shared their stories of the Jeju massacre, the Korean War, and the postwar period. The activists, meanwhile, provided me with pertinent details of the advocacy movement and transitional justice processes. Without all these interviewees and individuals, this manuscript would not have been completed.

A work such as this also depends on the generosity of many institutions. I would like to thank the Academy of Korean Studies (AKS-2010-DZZ-3104) for generous financial support. I would also like to thank both the Department of Sociology and the Research Institute for the Tamla Culture at Jeju National University for offering office space and library services. I would also like to thank Susan McEachern, Katelyn Turner, and Ashley Dodge, acquisitions editors, and Franny DeAtley, production editor, at the publishers, for supporting the book production processes. I would like to extend my thanks to two anonymous reviewers of the work who provided substantive and valuable suggestions to improve the manuscript. I would like to also thank Gloria Chang and Tom Wells for the best proofreading and editorial support. Finally, I am grateful to my family members, especially my late mother-in-law Shin Eun-hee; my husband, Yang-ho Hyun; and my son, Su-wan, who all provided steady support and encouragement over the past ten years.

I would like to dedicate this book to people of Jeju who underwent the horrors of Jeju 4.3 and the Korean War.

Introduction

The Jeju 4.3 Peace Park is located on Jeju Island, 130 kilometers (80.8 miles) south of the Korean Peninsula (map i.1). Officially opened in 2008, it was constructed by the South Korean government in response to demands by Jeju residents that the truth finally be told about the deadliest recognized civilian massacre in modern Korean history and hopes from the victims' families that historical justice be served. When visitors first arrive in the Jeju 4.3 Peace Memorial Hall at the park, they encounter *Baekbi*, the "Unnamed Monument" (figure i.1). The monument is a long, rectangular, gray granite slab, which is uncharacteristically placed sideways on the floor. The text in Korean next to it reads: "Someday we will carve the name of Jeju 4.3 in this monument and then erect it."

The monument has no name or inscription for a reason. The Jeju 4.3 Peace Park is a national memorial museum and park, but there is still no accepted definition of the massacre among state officials, scholars, or even Jeju people themselves. The text continues: "Jeju 4.3 has been referred to as a resistance, an uprising, a rebellion, or an incident thus far, but it still does not have a proper historical definition." Visitors might wonder, "Why were so many Jeju people killed?" "Why does Jeju 4.3 lack an official term?" and "What should a proper definition of Jeju 4.3 be?"

Definitions remain elusive, but thanks to the tireless work of activists, we now have a fuller picture of the grim events. Referred to as Jeju *Sasam* or Jeju 4.3 after the uprising that broke out on April 3, 1948, on Jeju Island, the events were a series of violent clashes between local communist insurgents on the one side and the newly installed dictatorial South Korean government that the Americans supported on the other. The brutalities continued throughout the Korean War (1950–1953) and officially ended on September 21, 1954. The cumulative violence featured indiscriminate killing, forced relocation, torture, wholesale detention, rampant sexual violence, and countless other atrocities and human rights violations. Between twenty-five and thirty thousand unarmed civilians—or about 10 percent of Jeju's residents—were killed

Figure i.1.   Baekbi, the "Unnamed Monument"Map i.1. Map of Jeju Island (Reprinted from The Massacres at Mt. Halla: Sixty Years of Truth Seeking in South Korea by Hun Joon Kim, published by Cornell University Press. Copyright © 2014 by Cornell University. Used by permission of the publisher.)

on the island.[1] The mass killings were principally carried out by counterinsurgency forces but also by insurgents. Visceral acts of killing and physical violence, however, are only part of the story. More than forty thousand Jeju people fled to Japan to escape the killings,[2] and by the end of the massacre, 91,732 people—almost half of those who had remained on Jeju—had become refugees, with 39,285 homes being completely destroyed.[3] Some 134 dong (a subdivision of a village) where completely wiped off the map of Jeju as the houses of the displaced residents were burned down and the survivors were scattered.[4]

If human were displaced, so was the history of the atrocity. For most of its postwar period, the Jeju massacre was kept hidden from the public through anticommunist propaganda that legitimated the suppression of communists on the basis of both the 1948 National Security Law and the Anti-Communism Law of 1961, which allowed the state to punish people who opposed its anticommunist policies. However, after decades of silence, an advocacy movement on behalf of Jeju victims began in the 1980s during the broader movement for democratization and civil and political rights in South Korea.

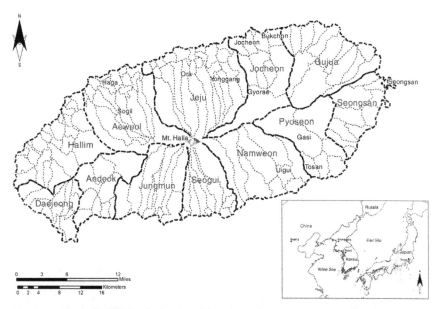

Map i.1.   Map of Jeju Island (Reprinted from The Massacres at Mt. Halla: Sixty Years of Truth Seeking in South Korea by Hun Joon Kim, published by Cornell University Press. Copyright © 2014 by Cornell University. Used by permission of the publisher.)

Jeju residents fought for restorative justice by advancing a counternarrative to the state's official history of Jeju 4.3, one that focused on recognition of the victims' sufferings. Their efforts resulted in the Special Act for Investigation of Jeju 4.3 and Restoration of the Honor of Victims in 2000. As a consequence, the official report in 2003 by the Jeju 4.3 National Committee for the Investigation of Truth (Jeju 4.3 National Committee), established by the Kim Dae-jung government (1998–2003), replaced the public narrative of a "communist rebellion" with one highlighting "civilian sacrifices." Moreover, President Roh Moo-hyun (2003–2008) officially apologized for state violence as president of South Korea on the basis of the official report in that year. In 2005, he declared Jeju an "Island of World Peace" to sublimate the tragedy of Jeju 4.3 into reconciliation and coexistence and eventually contribute to world peace. Finally, in 2008, the Jeju 4.3 Peace Park was created to commemorate those who died or disappeared as a consequence of the Jeju 4.3 events. It has since become an important site for the collective memory of the massacre and is visited by South Koreans and people from other countries.

This book examines the history of Jeju 4.3 and its aftermath from the outbreak of violence to the construction of the Jeju 4.3 Peace Park through the lens of the state-building process of South Korea. The concept of the state is contentious, but here I use sociologist and historian Charles Tilly's definition of "relatively centralized, differentiated organizations, the officials of which more or less successfully claim control over the chief concentrated means of violence within a population inhabiting a large, contiguous territory."[5] As Tilly's definition makes clear, violence is central to the state-building process—a key insight for understanding South Korean history and the Jeju 4.3 incident's place in it. While South Korea is now recognized as a wealthy democratic nation-state that is renowned for its popular culture, it has experienced a complex, and often traumatic, process of state building from its inception. The history of Jeju 4.3 and its aftermath is an illustration of the state-building process of South Korea. Jeju's people experienced violent state formation, their incorporation into the anticommunist state in the post-4.3 period, and the establishment of state-led truth commissions about Jeju 4.3 with the arrival of democracy.

The concept of state building is also contentious, but this study defines it as a long-term internal process of forming a legitimate, stable, and sustainable state that involves national security, national identity, economic development, and political democracy.[6] Scholars who have studied state building in South Korea argue that the national division and the establishment of two separate governments on the Korean peninsula during the early Cold War had a profound influence on setting key goals of state building in South Korea.[7] After the state makers formed a government amid violent repression against political leftists and dissenters, they sought for legitimacy, national security, national identity, and financial stability. The Korean War was a watershed of state building in terms of national security, legitimacy, and national identity. In postwar South Korea, the Rhee Syng-man (1948–1960) and Park Chung-hee (1961–1979) regimes gave an impetus to economic development and capitalist modernization while encouraging voluntary participation of people, particularly women. A long-term struggle for democracy on the basis of economic growth and the expansion of the liberal middle class helped to reach democratic governance by the end of the 1980s. Following the end of military rule, South Korean regimes have moved on to democratic consolidation, a more advanced stage of state building. Jeju 4.3 and its aftermath both shaped and was shaped by these processes.

This emphasis on state building over the *longue durée* builds on an already rich historiography on the Jeju 4.3 events while also addressing critical lacunas in the existing literature. The majority of previous studies of the history of Jeju 4.3 focused on the causes and the historical background of the uprising and counterinsurgency campaign. With the release of the U.S. military and government documents in the 1980s, academic work on Jeju 4.3 emerged. John Merrill, the author of "The Cheju-do Rebellion," addressed the local, national, and international context of the uprising and counterinsurgency operations.[8] Bruce Cumings, the author of *The Origins of the Korean War*, regarded Jeju 4.3 as a precursor to the Korean War,[9] noting how a strong political leadership on Jeju and the U.S. military government in South Korea worked to produce the conflict.[10] Recently, Jeju 4.3 studies in North America have reexamined the background of the uprising and counterinsurgency operations. Military historians such as Kyeongho Son remarked on the role of local communists and the left-leaning South Korean Labor Party in the course of Jeju 4.3.[11] Meanwhile, Su-kyoung Hwang examined how a power struggle among local communist rebels, civilians, the U.S. military government, and the South Korean government created violence on Jeju, while Brendan Wright focused on the relationship between state violence and the formation of the South Korean state within a broader context of "politicidal" violence.[12]

South Korean scholars have also played an instrumental role in furthering our understanding of the 4.3 violence. After the movement for democratization in the late 1980s in South Korea, South Korean scholars explored alternative interpretations to the official history of "communist rebellion."[13] For example, scholars such as Ko Chang-hun emphasized the Jeju people's resistance against the suppression of the U.S. military government and the division of the country,[14] while others, such as Heo Ho-joon, interpreted the counterinsurgency operations as a political genocide.[15] In response, Ko Mun-seong and other conservative scholars have stressed the responsibility of communist rebels for the massacre.[16]

Recently, studies throughout the globe have addressed the truth-seeking and reconciliation processes connected to 4.3. Kim Jong-min explored the role of local journalism, academic circles, and the development of democracy in the truth-seeking process.[17] Hun Joon Kim, who wrote the only monograph about Jeju 4.3 in English, chronicled the persistent local activism that laid the foundation for the truth commission process.[18] Meanwhile, both Heonik Kwon and Myung-lim Park explored the role of local initiatives and the moral and political solidarity of Jeju people in achieving reconciliation.[19]

Despite this often exemplary work, these studies have largely overlooked three crucial points. First, they did not fully describe how and why the newborn state adopted strong repression measures or reintegration policies at different points throughout the six and a half years of the incident. From this vantage point, it is important to note that the armed conflicts took place over the critical period of state formation in South Korea. Though some scholars, such as Heo and Wright, addressed the relationship between the mass killing by the regime and the birth of South Korea, they did not clearly discuss histories following the 1948–1949 mass killings, including the mobilization of islanders during the Korean War. In these works, the analysis of state building is limited to the phenomenon of mass violence rather than the total 4.3 process. Second, and related to this, studies have largely ignored the post-4.3 history during the authoritarian years. The massacre ended on September

21, 1954, when the authorities ordered the reopening of Mt. Halla on Jeju Island and the displaced residents returned to their villages. However, the truth-seeking process started in the end of the 1980s. Previous works have largely overlooked these intervening years, which are crucial to understanding of the state-building process. Though Wright has narrowly focused on the activism during the 1960–1961 period,[20] the broader dynamics between state and society during the authoritarian decades have been left unexplored. Finally, the existing studies have not fully accounted for the active involvement of the South Korean state in the transitional justice process. Though scholars such as Kim Jong-min and Hun Joon Kim addressed mature democracy as a key factor in establishing the truth commissions, the studies did not further look into the state's agency in intervening in the attempted resolution of historical conflicts.

This book therefore contributes to a better understanding of the history of Jeju 4.3 in relation to state building in South Korea and is likewise one of a few attempts to explore post-4.3 history from this integrated perspective. This emphasis on state building is foundational for understanding postwar history on Jeju Island as the island has been directly implicated in core facets of South Korean state building, such as the foundation of the anticommunist state, development, and democratization. For example, Jeju was the only region in the southern portion of Korea where large populations rose in an armed uprising and also boycotted the 1948 general election to object to the creation of South Korea (officially the Republic of Korea). This means that the Jeju 4.3 events occurred during the critical period of the establishment of anticommunist South Korea. Due to this history of opposition, Jeju was a community that was particularly targeted by the national identity building and economic policies of the dictatorial and authoritarian regimes in the postwar period. Since South Korea transformed to a democracy in the late 1980s, the South Korean government has launched various transitional justice measures to investigate past human rights violations. The investigation of the truth of Jeju 4.3 has generally been acknowledged as the most successful among the cases in South Korea. In other words, Jeju has vividly experienced the state-building process of South Korea from its creation to a mature democracy.

This book first looks at how and why Jeju experienced mass violence in the early postliberation period. I examine the establishment of the People's Republic of Jeju formed before the creation of South Korea, which I see as a foundational feature of the Jeju 4.3 uprisings. Immediately following Korea's liberation from Japan's thirty-five-year colonial rule on August 15, 1945, local political leaders voluntarily organized their own committees, called "People's Committees," to maintain peace and security both on Jeju Island and throughout the Korean peninsula. These committees ultimately supported the Committee for the Preparation for Korean Independence (shortly to be renamed the Korean People's Republic), which was an interim government that worked toward the construction of a new Korean state. On Jeju, the left-leaning People's Committee effectively exerted its political influence on the island until early 1948.[21] The committee and its aligned leftist forces resisted its suppression by the U.S. military government, eventually rising in an armed insurgency in the spring of 1948. The first chapter therefore examines the establishment of the Jeju People's Committee, its activities, and its relationship with the U.S. military government. It also supplements this institutional analysis by examining the island's tradition of rebellion and tight kinship system, which both contributed to the nature of the resistance during the Jeju 4.3 events.

Chapter 2 explores the civil war between the insurgency group that had established the People's Republic of Jeju and the newly born anticommunist South Korean state and its American patron. Here the focus is principally on state violence. Even before the outbreak of the uprising, the U.S. military government and its aligned Korean authorities perceived Jeju as an "Island of Reds" and targeted political leftists. However, the most concentrated mass killing of the whole duration of the events occurred in the winter of 1948–1949, just after the establishment of the Rhee Syng-man government (1948–1960), also known as the First Republic of Korea. About 70 percent of the deaths of children and elderly took place during this period. This chapter investigates the newly established government's adoption of deadly policies, including the declaration of martial law. It also explores how the counterinsurgency forces expanded the boundary of their targets through the implementation of policies at the local level. It concludes with a discussion of how the Korean culture of guilt by association escalated and justified the violence. Overall, this chapter demonstrates the thorough connections that existed between the establishment of the South Korean state and the violence on Jeju.

In the second section of the book, the focus shifts to social history post-4.3 through an analysis of the stories of Jeju soldiers and women between the 1950s and 1970s. Fundamentally, the post-4.3 social history reflects the South Korean state's assimilation policies for converting survivors of the massacre into loyal anticommunist subjects, on the one hand, and the islanders' struggle for incorporation into the state, on the other. After the mass murder in the winter of 1948–1949, the South Korean state began to reintegrate the island's population into its citizenry. A crucial event in shaping this process was the Korean War, which was a watershed for South Korean state building. While the Rhee regime attempted to remodel young Jeju people during the war, Jeju soldiers sought to incorporate themselves into the state by proving their worth as "loyal and brave," despite the stigma of coming from the "Island of Reds." The three thousand Jeju marines, the first recruits on Jeju, became heroic figures throughout both the island and the mainland. They were accorded the moniker "Invincible Marine Corps" and given commendations for "admirable service by superhumans" by Rhee Syng-man.

To contextualize this phenomenon, chapters 3 and 4 describe the process of military enlistment with a particular focus on the Rhee government's establishment of mass organizations to monitor the population. The chapters recount the means through which the Jeju recruits were transformed into patriotic marines, including their disciplined physical training, their internalization of the military mind-set, the formation of their group identity and group solidarity, and the creation of an imagined national community that the marines were willing to die for. The chapters also discuss the role of the U.S. military, including its military training and ideological propaganda, in the marines' transformation. I argue that Jeju 4.3, including the stigmatization of Jeju Islanders as communists, is essential for explaining why the Jeju marines became known as the most virulently conservative, anticommunist, and pro-American battalion among all South Korean troops.

Gender likewise played a role in the post-4.3 project of national identity building. The government viewed the regulation of women's labor and sexuality as critical to rebuilding South Korea following the end of the war. The Rhee government's sanctioned ideology of "Wise Mother, Good Wife," which was a legacy of Confucianism in Korea and Japanese colonialism, dictated that women sacrifice themselves for their children and families to serve the state. The Park Chung-hee regime (1961–1979) further reshaped this gender ideology to mobilize women in national economic development, emphasizing aspects of female labor participation. Given its gender ratio in the early postwar period, Jeju became a focal point for the operations of this gendered ideological mobilization. Indeed, due to the sustained massacre of young males during the 4.3 episode, Jeju had the lowest male-female ratio in South Korea following the Korean War[22]—seventy-nine males for every one hundred females—which essentially rendered Jeju a "woman's island." Due to this imbalance, Jeju women were a primary labor force until the early 1980s, particularity in agriculture and fisheries. As a result, female minds and bodies became central sites for the production of and contestations over anticommunist ideology. Chapter 5 consequently explores how these gendered ideological operations were practiced on Jeju during the Rhee and Park regimes.

Concretely, I examine the different attitudes toward the Wise Mother, Good Wife ideology among various socioeconomic classes of women on Jeju and its effects on them during the Rhee and Park regimes. During the Rhee years, women of elite social status readily accepted the female ideal, while ordinary Jeju women only embraced the idea of woman as the family provider during men's absence, as per tradition. Throughout the Park years, similar but more complex dynamics emerged between Jeju women and the prevailing gendered state ideology. Jeju women were widely portrayed as a national symbol of Korean working women while they participated in the regime's economic development and modernization projects. However, at the same time, they resisted their extreme labor burden and the destruction of their indigenous belief system. In other words, even in the authoritarian and patriarchal climate of South Korea, Jeju's women exercised considerable agency over how they were incorporated into the postwar state.

In the final section of this book, I examine the process of reconciliation of the Jeju 4.3 incident in relation to the history of state building. Given the scale of brutality that was unleashed on Jeju's population, it is dramatic that the South Korean state acknowledged its own past wrongdoings and presided over the resolution of 4.3's historical conflicts. In this sense, the process of transitional justice by the national government reflects the state's transformation into a democracy. Chapter 6 therefore explores the state's intervention in the reconciliation process through an analysis of the Jeju 4.3 Peace Park, a symbolic site for 4.3's reconciliation. The chapter investigates how the state has played a mediating role in conflicts between the state and the victims and their families, and between groups with different memories of the events and agendas, from the first planning stage in 2000 to the present. It also discusses how the state has attempted to redirect the narrative of Jeju 4.3 to peace and human rights for future generations. I argue that the Jeju 4.3 Peace Park is an expression the state's attempt to legitimize itself as a mature democracy and peace builder in South Korea.

This development, however, has not been without its contradictions and disappointments. This work therefore concludes with a discussion of the limitations of the state-led truth-seeking and reconciliation procedures. It investigates the discord that exists between the purpose of the Jeju 4.3 Special Act and the actual selection of real victims, and the underrepresentation of the Jeju women's history at the Jeju 4.3 Peace Park. The shortcomings of state-mediated reconciliation have consequentially necessitated other forms of reconciliation at the level of society. With this in mind, I also explore cases of reconciliation among Jeju residents where the state was not active enough to intervene. In addition, I discuss a key political conflict on the island that reveals the tensions within Jeju's branding as an "Island of World Peace." Two months after the declaration of Jeju as the Island of World Peace, a political battle with roots in the Jeju 4.3 events was fought over the construction of a new South Korean naval base on Jeju. From the inception of the construction of the naval base (which was completed in 2016), the antibase residents and their supporters challenged the compatibility of the base with the notion that Jeju was an Island of World Peace. This final section discusses how the national government has sought to navigate these political and historical tensions.

These ongoing contradictions and tensions within the state-building process reveal that the history of Jeju 4.3 is a route for understanding key features of the state-building process in South Korea. From the inception of the South Korean state through to the contemporary moment, Jeju Island and its people have been enmeshed within the broader threads of South Korea's state-building process. This has often been a difficult past, where the shadow of mass violence has loomed over the island's population, influencing the ways the people of Jeju have forged their relationship with the state. Coercion and repression have structured much of this. However, as will be revealed in these pages, islanders often adapted to their conditions strategically, in turn acquiring a certain purchase over their ongoing relationship to the state. Among other things, this is a reflection of Jeju's long history of ambivalence and resistance toward the mainland state.

A NOTE ON SOURCES

This book is based on personal interviews, local and national newspaper reports, the official report of the Jeju 4.3 National Committee, testimonies and oral histories of Jeju 4.3 survivors, and memoirs of military veterans. I drew especially from the official report of the Jeju 4.3 National Committee, published in 2003, as it is the most reliable source about Jeju 4.3.[23] The investigation team of the national committee did an exceptional job of securing evidence from both domestic and overseas sources, including South Korean military and government documents and U.S. military documents.[24] It also systematically selected and recorded the testimonies of more than five hundred witnesses.[25]

I also relied extensively on testimonies and oral histories of the survivors for this book, particularly in chapters 2, 3, and 5. Advocacy organizations and individual activists have been committed to collecting those materials since the beginning of the advocacy movement in the late 1980s, and a great number of materials have accumulated. Among them, the Jemin Ilbo 4.3 Reporting Team alone conducted interviews with about seven thousand survivors and participants. Additionally, the Jeju 4.3 Research Institute collected the oral histories of one thousand survivors between 2004 and 2008 and, from among those, published 235 people's stories in sixteen volumes between 2010 and 2015.[26]

This book, particularly chapters 3 and 4, is also based on memoirs of Jeju marine veterans published by their own independent veteran association—the Third and Fourth Groups of Korean Marine Veterans Association—individual editors, or individual veterans. These memoirs present official stories about their war experiences, but they also present valuable information and memories previously unknown to the public. I also collected news reports published between 1945 and 1980 pertaining to the uprising, Jeju soldiers, and Jeju women.[27]

Finally, I conducted personal interviews with marine veterans, survivors, activists, and other Jeju residents to obtain their alternative experiences and previously unspoken memories. My fieldwork on the massacre began in the late 1990s, but I did the bulk of it between 2012 and 2013. With the exception of their testimonies on their experiences in battles, the research on Jeju marines is relatively new and personal interviews are an important source of information regarding their motivations for enlistment and alternative war stories. I conducted interviews with not only male marine veterans but also females. Some 126 female marines performed military duties, including communication and management, in Jinhae, a naval base in the mainland, for a year. Initially, I started my interviews with twelve veterans, including three women, whom I randomly selected out of a list of veterans provided by the office of the veterans association. I then conducted interviews with two additional veterans, one male and one female, through the help of Jeju 4.3 activists who had gathered some of their oral histories about the events and the war.[28]

In addition, I had the opportunity to conduct informal interviews with veterans from all over the country who participated in the Mt. Dosol Battle Memorial Festival in Yanggu in Gangwon Province for three days in June 2012 and at the sixty-second anniversary of the Incheon Landing Operation in Incheon for two days in September 2012. During these two trips, I conducted in-depth interviews with two female veterans who shared a room with me in both places. I also conducted informal interviews with another eleven veterans, including two females. I also had three more informal interviews with one male and two female veterans during a one-day trip to the Jeju Defense Command of the Korean Marine Corps in April 2013. During these three trips, I observed how these veterans commemorated the battles they had participated in. After the trips, I conducted an in-depth interview with one male veteran whom I met in Incehon. In January 2020, I resumed conducting interviews with marine veterans to find alternative voices I might have overlooked. With the help of the same activists who introduced me to the two veterans in 2012 and an individual editor of collected memoirs of Jeju veterans, I conducted interviews with six additional male veterans. In sum, I conducted thirty-seven interviews with marine veterans (twenty-seven with male veterans; ten with females).[29]

To capture the political circumstances after the outbreak of the war, postwar women's experiences, the attempts at reconciliation among Jeju people, and the construction process of the Jeju 4.3 Peace Park, I also conducted interviews with army veterans, Jeju women, bereaved family members, activists, and other Jeju residents throughout my research. In addition, I participated in and observed diverse commemorative events of Jeju 4.3 during this project.

The interviewees were mostly around eighty years old, with some as old as ninety. However, many retained highly detailed memories of Jeju 4.3 and provided compelling testimony about it. I asked one of the marine veterans in a 2012 interview, "How can you remember that far back?" and he said, "I can remember all the details of the war experiences because those were my first shocking moments."[30] These kinds of recollections are representative examples of "flashbulb" memories—durable, detailed, and encoded in long-term memory—that were mostly formed in their late adolescence and early adulthood and became part of their generational identity.[31]

In this book, all Korean names are given with the family name first, except those of scholars who published their writing in English. In these cases, I have used the given name first, followed by the family name. Throughout the work, I have used the Revised Romanization of Korean system for the romanization of Korean names and terms.

NOTES

1. National Committee for the Investigation of the Truth about the Jeju 4.3 Incident (hereafter, Jeju 4.3 National Committee), *The Jeju April Third Incident Investigation Report*, trans. Jeju 4.3 Peace Foundation (Jeju: Jeju 4.3 Peace Foundation, 2013), 455.

2. Bruce Cumings, "American Responsibility and the Massacres in Cheju Conference on Overcoming the Past: Healing and Reconciliation—Cheju and the World in Comparison," *World Environment and Island Studies* 6, no. 4 (2016): 205.

3. Jeju 4.3 National Committee, *Jeju April Third Incident Investigation Report*, 623.

4. Jeju 4.3 Peace Foundation, *Jeju 4.3 sageon chuga jinsang josa bogoseo 1* [The Jeju April Third Incident Additional Investigation Report, vol. 1] (Jeju: Gak, 2019), 633. This investigation report updated information on damages of the massacre since the 2003 official report by Jeju 4.3 National Committee.

5. Charles Tilly, "War Making and State Making as Organized Crime," in *Bringing the State Back*, ed. Peter Evans, Dietrich Rueschemeyer, and Theda Skocpol (Cambridge: Cambridge University Press, 1985), 170.

6. Gregg Brazinsky, *Nation Building in South Korea: Koreans, Americans, and the Making of Democracy* (Chapel Hill: University of North Carolina Press, 2007); Choong Nam Kim, "State and Nation Building in South Korea: A Comparative Historical Perspective," *Review of Korean Studies* 12, no. 1 (2009): 121–50; Jung Ho Park and Young Hag Kim, "A Study on the Influence of Land Institution on State-Building in South Korea: Human Resources," *Land Use Policy* 69 (2017): 106–11.

7. Brazinsky, *Nation Building in South Korea*, 23–25; Kim, "State and Nation Building in South Korea, 133; Jung Han Kim and Jeong-Mi Park, "Subjectivation and Social Movements in Post-colonial Korea," in *The History of Social Movements in Global Perspective: A Survey*, ed. Stefan Berger and Holger Nehring (London: Palgrave Macmillan, 2017), 301–2.

8. John Merrill, "The Cheju-do Rebellion," *Journal of Korean Studies* 2 (1980): 139–97.

9. Bruce Cumings, *The Origins of the Korea War*, vol. 2: *The Roaring of the Cataract, 1947–1950* (Seoul: Yeoksa Bipyeongsa, 2002), 251.

10. Cumings, *Roaring of the Cataract*, 250–59; Bruce Cumings, "The Question of American Responsibility for the Suppression of the Chejudo Uprising," paper presented at the Conference to Celebrate the 50th Anniversary of the April 3, 1948, Chejudo Rebellion, Tokyo, March 14, 1998.

11. Kyeongho Son, "The 4.3 Incident: Background, Development, and Pacification, 1945–1949" (PhD diss., Ohio State University, 2008).

12. Su-kyoung Hwang, *Korea's Grievous War* (Philadelphia: University of Pennsylvania Press, 2016), 26–58; Brendan Wright, "Civil War, Politicide, and the Politics of Memory in South Korea, 1948–1961" (PhD diss., University of British Colombia, 2016).

13. Until democratization in South Korea in the late 1980s, studies of Jeju 4.3 focused on guerrilla warfare and counterinsurgency operations as a part of military history. For example, Institute for Military History Compilation, Ministry of National Defense (MND), *Hangukjeonjaengsa 1: Haebanggwa geongun* [The Korean War History 1: Liberation and Foundation of the Armed Forces] (Seoul: Institute for Military History Compilation, Ministry of National Defense (MND), 1967), 437–51; Jeong-gon Kim, *Hangukjeonggwa nodongdang jeollyak* [The Korean War and the South Korean Labor Party's Strategy] (Seoul: Bakyeongsa, 1973), 142–72. Exceptionally, in 1963, Kim Bong-hyun and Kim Min-ju, who were involved in the uprising and escaped to Japan, addressed the uprising as a national unification movement and anti-imperialist movement from the leftist perspective. Bong-hyun Kim and Min-ju Kim, *Jejudo inmindeurui 4.3 mujang tujaengsa* [A History of the Jeju People's 4.3 Armed Struggle] (Osaka: Munusa 1963).

14. Chang-hun Ko, "4.3 minjung hangjaengui jeongaewa seonggyok [The Process and Characteristics of the 4.3 People's Uprising]," in *Haebang jeonhusaui insik 4* [A View of the History of the Pre/Post-Liberation Periods, vol. 4], ed. Jang-jip Choi (Seoul: Hangilsa, 1989), 245–340; Myung-lim Park, "Jejudo minjung hangjaeng-e gwanhan yeongu" [A Study on the Jeju 4.3 Popular Uprising] (MA thesis, Korea University, 1988); Han-gwon Yang, "Jejudo 4.3 pokdongui baegyeong-e gwanhan yeongu" [A Study on the Historical Background of the Jeju 4.3 Rebellion] (MA thesis, Seoul National University, 1988); Jeong-sim Yang, *Jeju 4.3 hangjaeng: Jeohanggwa apeumui yeoksa* [The Jeju 4.3 Uprising: A History of Resistance and Pain] (Seoul: Seonin, 2008); Chan-sik Park, *4.3gwa Jeju yeoksa* [4.3 and the History of Jeju] (Jeju: Gak, 2008), 169–223.

15. Ho-joon Heo, "Jeju 4.3 hangjanggwa jenosaideu" [The Jeju 4.3 Uprising and Genocide], *4.3gwa Yeoksa* [4.3 and History] 4 (2004): 178–215; Ho-geun Choi,

Jenosaideu: Haksalgwa eunpyeui yeoksa [Genocide: History of Massacres and Cover-up] (Seoul: Chaeksesang, 2005), 356–406; Seong-nae Kim, "Gukgapong-nyeokgwa yeoseong cheheom" [Women's Experiences of State Violence], in *Dongasiaui pyounghwawa ingwon* [Peace and Human Rights in East Asia], ed. Jeju 4.3 Research Institute (Seoul: Yeoksa Bipyeongsa, 1999), 154–72; Gwisook Gwon, "Daeryanghaksarui sahoesimni: Jeju 4.3 sageonui haksal gwajeong" [Sociopsychology of Genocide: The Process of Massacre during the Jeju 4.3 Incident], *Hanguk Sahoehak* [Korean Journal of Sociology] 36, no. 5 (2002): 171–200.

16. Mun-seong Ko, *Jeju saramdeurui seorum* [The Sorrows of Jeju People] (Jeju: Sinamunhwasa, 1991); Nam-su Choi, *4.3 jinsang* [The Truth of 4.3] (Jeju: Wolgan Gwangwangjeju, 1988); Seo-dong Park, *Yeongwonhan urideurui apeum, 4.3* [Our Never-Ending Pains of Life, 4.3] (Jeju: Wolgan Gwangwangjeju, 1990); Association of Bereaved Families Engaging in Fact-Finding Research concerning Jeju 4.3, eds., *4.3ui jinjeonghan huisaengjaneun!* [Who Are the Genuine Victims of 4.3?] (Jeju: Sinmyeong, 2015).

17. Jong-min Kim, "4.3 ihu 50nyeon" [Fifty Years after 4.3], in *Jeju 4.3 yeongu* [A Study on the Jeju 4.3], ed. Jeju 4.3 Research Institute (Seoul: Yeoksa Bipyeongsa, 1999), 338–424.

18. Hun Joon Kim, *The Massacres at Mt. Halla: Sixty Years of Truth Seeking in South Korea* (New York: Cornell University Press, 2014).

19. Heonik Kwon, *After the Korean War: An Intimate History* (Cambridge: Cambridge University Press, 2020), 156–67; Myung-lim Park, "Towards a Universal Model of Reconciliation: The Case of the Jeju 4.3 Incident," *Journal of Korean Religions* 9, no. 1 (2018): 105–30.

20. Brendan Wright, "Raising the Korean Dead: Bereaved Family Associations and the Politics of 1960–1961 South Korea," *Asia-Pacific Journal: Japan Focus* 13, issue 41, no. 2 (2015): 1–19.

21. Cumings, *Roaring of the Cataract*, 252.

22. According to national statistics, the average sex ratio nationwide was 100.03 in 1955 (National Archives of Korea, http://theme.archives.go.kr/next/populationPolicy/statisticsPopup_02.do), while the ratio was 79 on Jeju in 1953. Man-geun Bu, *Gwangbok Jeju 30nyeon* [The Thirty-Year History of Jeju after Korea's Liberation] (Seoul: Munjosa, 1975), 116.

23. The English edition is now uploaded to the section of the Jeju 4.3 Archive on the homepage of the Jeju 4.3 Peace Foundation (http://www.43archives.or.kr/).

24. Jeju 4.3 National Committee, *Jeju April Third Incident Investigation Report*, 52–59. The committee published their collection of these documents.

25. Ibid., 60–62. The team also closely examined and validated the materials and produced the final report after six months of research and deliberations over the first draft prepared by participating institutions, groups, and individuals. Jeju 4.3 National Committee, *Hwahaewa sangsaeng: Jeju 4.3 wiweonhoe hwaldong baekseo* [Reconciliation and Coexistence: White Paper on the Activities of the Jeju 4.3 National Committee] (Seoul: Jeju 4.3 National Committee, 2008), 100–102.

26. The Jeju 4.3 Peace Foundation participated in the publication as a coeditor in 2010 and 2011. The Jeju 4.3 Peace Foundation and the Jeju 4.3 Research Institute

published four volumes of the oral histories in 2010 and 2011. The Jeju 4.3 Research Institute alone published twelve volumes of those between 2013 and 2015. For more details, see Jeju 4.3 Research Institute, ed., *Eotteoke hyeongsaga geomsareul* [How Dare a Detective Arrest a Prosecutor] (Jeju: Jeju 4.3 Peace Foundation, 2015), 9–10.

27. I am indebted to the Jeju 4.3 National Committee, which published their collection of news items of local and national newspapers regarding Jeju 4.3. (The sourcebook of newspapers is now assessable in the Jeju 4.3 Archive, http://43archives.or.kr /data/ncws/list.do.) However, their selection largely missed news reports, particularly regarding Jeju women, so I searched for the missing ones. I was able to collect relevant news reports in national newspapers through the internet, but I visited the Jeju Public Library in Jeju City in January 2013 to collect relevant news items in *Jeju Sinbo*, the only local newspaper, published between 1946 and 1959. The site item "News Library" in Naver (a popular portal site Korean people currently use) provides articles of major national newspapers published between 1920 and 1999 (https:// newslibrary.naver.com/search/searchByDate.nhn).

28. The interviews were semistructured. I developed some interview questions about such topics as their memories of the massacre, enlistment motivation, and war experiences, but I was flexible and proceeded based on their responses.

29. Most informal interviews at the commemorative events took less than thirty minutes but were very focused. Two interviews with female veterans among the informal interviews lasted more than four hours over several meetings. These interviewees were all cooperative, and so I conducted several follow-up interviews with them via telephone and email. Most other interviews typically took about two hours in a single session, although several interviews took more than four hours over two to four meetings. Most interviews, except those at commemorative events, were conducted in the subjects' homes, offices, or other comfortable locations such as cafés.

30. Interview with Moon Chang-hae on April 26, on Jeju.

31. Martin Conway, "The Inventory of Experience: Memory and Identity," in *Collective Memory of Political Events*, ed. James Pennebaker, Dario Paez, and Bernard Rime (Mahwah, NJ: Lawrence Erlbaum, 1997), 21–45.

Chapter 1

Beginning: Postcolonial Aspirations for a New State

The outbreak of political violence on Jeju Island is inextricably tied to the postliberation struggle to achieve autonomous rule at both the local and national levels. Immediately following the Japanese surrender in August 1945, local political activists attempted to form their own People's Republic on the basis of the People's Committee (PC) on Jeju Island.[1] A number of scholars and sources indicate that this was the dominant political group on the island from 1945 to 1948. According to Cumings, the Jeju PC, which first emerged in August 1945, effectively exerted its political influence on the islanders until early 1948.[2] Grant Meade, a U.S. military government officer in 1945, wrote in his book, "The Jeju People's Committee was the only political party in the island and the only organization acting like a government."[3] The available evidence strongly suggests that this organization was autonomous of outside communist influence. John Hodge, the commander of the U.S. occupying forces, reported to the American Congress in October 1947 that Jeju was "a truly communal area that is peacefully controlled by the People's Committee without much Comintern influence."[4] The survivors of Jeju 4.3 likewise said that the Jeju PC was "a grassroots, autonomous, and effective administrative institution" for local people.[5]

This chapter examines the efforts at mobilizing the postcolonial desire to make a new Korean state on the island and the ways through which the Jeju PC built a well-functioning organization that achieved popular support. It also considers the U.S. military government's late intervention in weakening the authority of the committee, which was a harbinger of future chaos. I begin, however, with a discussion of the island's tradition of appropriation and resistance—the historical legacies of which contributed to solidifying postliberation Jeju's sense of independence.

A TRADITION OF APPROPRIATION AND RESISTANCE

Jeju is an extinct volcanic island, dominated by Mt. Halla, the highest mountain (1,950 meters, 6,398 feet) in South Korea. Due to its geographical isolation from the mainland, Jeju had its own distinctive culture, thick dialect (which only Jeju Islanders could understand), tight kinship community, deeply rooted indigenous beliefs, and other unique everyday customs, which influenced its tendency for self-determination. Jeju's historical experiences with outside powers also produced a culture of resistance. Jeju Island itself developed originally as an independent polity, "Tamla," for roughly one thousand years before it came under the control of the mainland Goryeo Dynasty in AD 1105. Suffering an invasion from Mongolia in 1231, Jeju was directly controlled by the Mongols for close to a century. Later, Jeju became a district of the Joseon Dynasty (1392–1910), but it was treated as an internal colony. Jeju was used as a prison for political exiles, and it suffered considerably from meeting the demands of excessive taxes and tributes. The burdens were so heavy that many men escaped from the island even after the Departure Prohibition Order in 1629 (which lasted for about two hundred years). However, the majority of Jeju's people tended to protest rather than flee their homeland.

Toward the end of the Joseon period, Jeju had six peasant rebellions, all of which were against corrupt officials and excessive taxes.[6] The last of these rebellions, the 1901 Rebellion of Lee Jae-su, left a deep impression on the islanders and is often regarded as a precursor to the Jeju uprising.[7] In 1899, a tax official was dispatched from the central government and began to arbitrarily collect taxes to increase state revenues. The level of taxation was egregious as taxes were imposed on virtually everything on the island, including trees and chickens.[8] At the same time, the Catholic Church's violence against the Jeju locals grew after two French priests came to the island in 1899. Jeju converts on the island did most of the collection of taxes, while also seizing the other resident's property and therefore depriving the peasants of the right to cultivate their own land. The converts also tied up and beat the other residents and raped many women, but they were not arrested due to the Catholics' power of extraterritoriality. Jeju people exploded with anger when the Catholics destroyed village shrines and interrupted shamans' exorcisms and Confucian rituals.[9] After the local people failed in appealing to their governor for a peaceful solution, they decided to organize an armed revolt to protest the abuses, and Lee Jae-su, a slave in government, became their leader. The rebellion lasted for about two months, leaving 350 Catholics dead.[10] The rebellion was quelled, and Lee was executed in October 1901. However, from that moment onward, Jeju natives have remembered him as a hero who resisted foreign invasion against them and their culture.[11] The rebellion strengthened an already existing tradition of separatism and resistance to outside interferences, on one hand,[12] while reinforcing the mainlanders' images of Jeju as a prison for political exiles and a place of revolts, on the other hand. This shared history of suspicion would later haunt the island.

Beyond this history of estrangement from the mainland, Jeju villagers traditionally had strong bonds of community through marriage and collective work, which lent the island a remarkable degree of cohesion. Unlike mainlanders, Jeju people searched for their children's spouses in their own village or neighboring villages. It was common that a villager was another villager's relative. When I moved to a seaside village of Jeju in 1993, I was surprised that many villagers seemed to be a relative of my husband's grandfather (who had five siblings) or grandmother (who had nine siblings). The solidarity of the kinship system was well maintained by performing ancestral ceremonies together with the kinship members. In a broad sense, a Jeju village was a network of kinship communities. Further, due to their natural environment, Jeju people collectively worked through communal livestock farms or fishing grounds. This sense of communal obligation persists. In my village, female divers still share a communal fishing ground while working together and obeying rules of collection and sale of their products. In addition, Jeju people usually had labor cooperatives among neighbors, kinship members, and friends to carry out a big family or village event, such as wedding ceremonies, the building of homes, or the making of village roads. They also had traditional private funds among themselves to prepare for expensive purchases such as sedan chairs for the bride, bowls for ancestor ceremonies, and funeral biers, which further solidified their relationships. This deep cultural reservoir provided fertile grounds for socialist and liberationist ideologies in the post-1945 period.

POPULAR SENTIMENT IN POSTCOLONIAL JEJU

Jeju's experiences during the colonial period added a specific political character to these latent tendencies toward independence and solidarity. Indeed, the colonial period was a critical factor in forming the formidable PCs on Jeju. During these years, Jeju had an unusual connection with Japan compared to any other region on the mainland of Korea. The Japanese colonial government launched a regular passenger ship between Jeju and Osaka in 1918 to supply the area with labor to fuel various modernization drives. Driven by prospective opportunities and rural displacement, Jeju people moved to Japan to work in the factories in Osaka, where industries such as textile production and mining were flourishing.[13] The result was a substantial migration of the island's population over the next decades: throughout the colonial period, roughly two hundred thousand Jeju people moved back and forth between Jeju and Osaka, and by the middle of the 1930s, the number of Jeju people who were living in Japan had already reached about fifty thousand—a quarter of the total population of the island.[14] In historical terms, this represented a profound shift as Jeju had long been on the periphery of the mainland during the Joseon Dynasty. Now, however, Jeju was integrated into the migratory core of the colonial state, where many islanders had contact with modern Japanese industries, mass organizations, the school system, and even political ideologies.

Jeju migrants in Japan became politicized through this process. Encouraged by the Russian Revolution of 1917, young islanders became influenced by socialism and communism as active strategies of national liberation.[15] Many of these activists joined the Communist Party of Japan, which had declared its support for the national independence of Korea, and they participated in high-risk missions for national independence.[16] The number of Jeju native activists at Osaka according to the Japanese police authorities reached about three hundred as of August 1932.[17] Many of these activists were arrested for spying or distributing documents. Underground activities, however, were not the only forms of resistance, as Jeju migrants in Japan also resisted national discrimination in their workplaces by organizing consumer clubs and labor unions for the interests of Koreans. These activities often resonated because Koreans only received half the wages of Japanese workers. In addition to labor organization, they also learned the importance of cultural activism in the realms of education and media. They supported their children's education in Japan and brought their siblings and offspring to Japan for a higher-quality education.[18] Migrants also played a key role in publishing a Korean newspaper, called *Minjungsibo* (People's Newspaper), in 1935 in Osaka.[19] The newspaper aimed to provide information about the improvement of living conditions for Korean migrants in Japan and to raise national consciousness. The cumulative result of this process was profound: when they returned home at the time of liberation, Jeju migrants were no longer typical peasants, and many had become modernized political subjects.[20] In particular, many of the youth were educated and radical, aspiring to make an independent socialist country.

Migrants were not the only agents of political action during the colonial period. On Jeju, local people also resisted national discrimination. Between 1931 and 1932, almost all female divers in northeastern Jeju protested the exploitation of their labor by the Japanese-controlled fishery union. The uprising started as a struggle for fair compensation but soon transformed into an anti-Japanese struggle. The fishery union had prohibited female divers from selling their own products and set up a standard price for the benefit of a few authorized merchants and union members. The local people in the region, including young people, ordinary farmers, and fishermen, cooperated in the struggle.[21] The historical memory of this struggle still animates the collective identity of many islanders and is tellingly honored as an example of Jeju's tradition of resistance in the Jeju 4.3 Peace Memorial Hall at the Peace Park.

In addition, young leftist intellectuals who migrated to Japan and returned home encouraged a national independence movement throughout Jeju. They organized the Jeju *Yacheika* in 1927, a subgroup of the Communist Party of Korea, formed in Seoul in 1925, and the Jeju Youth Union in 1928, a provincial-level left-wing youth association.[22] The two organizations attempted to instill national consciousness in villagers by establishing peasant unions and opening night schools, public lectures, and other events. The Jeju *Yacheika* also supported the female divers' struggle. These colonial-era acts of organization and resistance had substantial consequences in the postliberation period. The leaders of the two organizations participated in building the PCs and leftist organizations on Jeju just after Korea's liberation,[23] and one of them, Oh Dae-jin, became the chair of the provincial-level committee.

Traumas and hardships that were accumulated throughout the Second World War likewise played a role in radicalizing the population. For example, the colonial government mobilized Korean youths, including Jeju Islanders, in the Japanese military and industry. Across the country, over one million Korean men were conscripted as forced laborers or soldiers, and tens of thousands of women were forced to serve as sex slaves, or "comfort women," for the Japanese army. Approximately thirty thousand Jeju young people were also sent to Sakhalin, coal mines in Hokkaido, the South Sea Islands, or other sites to support the war.[24] In local villages, these dislocations could have profound consequences. For instance, in a village of Gujwa-myeon (town), some twenty-five young people between eighteen and thirty years old, including three young girls, were conscripted, according to the villagers.[25] It is possible that the girls were sent to the comfort stations to be raped and sexually enslaved.[26] In addition, Jeju residents aged between sixteen and sixty were forced to build defense fortifications throughout when Japan fortified the whole island to protect the Japanese mainland as the last bulwark for fighting against America in early 1945.[27] Jeju residents had to build military airfields, construct fire signal positions on the tops of mountains, and dig tunnels under inhumane working conditions.[28] According to their testimonies, they suffered from hunger, severe cold, physical punishment, and overwork.[29] Further, Jeju people were forced to provide war supplies, including grain, livestock, and even brassware for ancestor worship. The forced labor and delivery of war supplies gave Jeju residents tremendous difficulties. These combined experiences raised considerable resentments against the colonial government and pro-Japanese factions in Jeju society.[30]

FORMATION OF THE PEOPLE'S REPUBLIC OF JEJU

Liberation on Jeju

When Korea was liberated from colonial rule on August 15, 1945, Jeju had ideal conditions to establish stronger PCs compared to the mainland. First of all, Jeju retained an organized political force for the foundation of the committees and other independent organizations. While about sixty thousand Japanese soldiers left the island, by November 1945 according to the U.S. army's reparation program, the same number of Jeju people had returned. With this, Jeju's population increased from 220,000 to 280,000 within a year following liberation. In particular, the returnees were no longer traditional peasants or laborers. The returnees from Japan had national consciousness and organizing experiences, and those from the South Sea Islands had combat experiences.[31] This was an unprecedented change in the quantity and qualitative character of the population on Jeju. As a result, Jeju had many experienced people to effectively organize and operate PCs, branches of political parties, and youth associations.

Second, Jeju was able to retain a wide range of supporting groups for the PCs through school education. Jeju residents launched an enthusiastic campaign aimed at setting up elementary schools in every village and middle schools in every town immediately following the collapse of colonial rule.[32] Not only educated returnees from Japan but also local community leaders initiated the establishment of these schools. Buoyed by the popular support of Jeju residents, forty-four elementary schools and ten middle schools were newly constructed between liberation and the end of 1947 on the island.[33] Accordingly, the number of elementary school students sharply increased from twenty thousand to thirty-eight thousand, and the number of middle school students also remarkably increased more than tenfold, from three hundred to 3,600, for the period.[34] Jeju had already ranked as the most highly educated population in the southern Korea as of 1947. Indeed, when Cumings compared the percentage of graduates from elementary schools or higher in males fifteen years and over among fifteen counties in southern Korea in 1947, he found that the figure in the northern part of Jeju was 35.7 percent, the highest among the counties. This figure was 9 percent higher than that in the second highest county, Changwon, which stood at 26.7 percent.[35]

The schools provided an occasion for some educated returnees from Japan to be teachers. The teachers, mostly key members of the PCs, tried to instill national consciousness and social awareness in students. The middle school students, mostly aged between thirteen and seventeen, became more progressive and composed a new reservoir of support for the PCs and their aligned leftist organizations. For example, in February 1947, a thousand middle school students boycotted the import of American confections to prevent "America's colonization of Korea."[36]

Finally, Jeju peasants, who constituted the majority of Jeju's population, had a strong sense of solidarity. Due to a policy of divide and rule by the colonial government, only 16.5 percent of peasants on the mainland were independent farmers in 1947.[37] Korean tenants on the mainland struggled against exploitation by landlords and supervisors and rack rent throughout the 1920s and the 1930s. However, there were no similar struggles on Jeju as the island had a comparatively low rate of tenancy. Over 70 percent of peasants were independent farmers in 1946, though most of them owned small-sized farms.[38] Furthermore, Jeju farmers usually undertook fishery activities as an additional source of livelihood, weakening the landlord-tenant relationship. This low rate of tenancy, coupled with a weak landlord structure, helped enrich the power of the Jeju PC.[39]

Establishment of the Jeju People's Committee: Background

The Jeju PC started from the Jeju branch of the Committee for the Preparation of Korean Independence (CPKI), the interim government.[40] Immediately after liberation, renowned political leaders such as Yeo Un-hyeong and Ahn Jae-hong established the CPKI to maintain law and public order until the construction of a new Korean state. The CPKI declared the name of the country as the Korean People's Republic (KPR) on September 6, just before the U.S. Army entered Korea. The KPR declared the establishment of a completely unified nation, the eradication of any reactionary forces and legacies of Japanese colonialism, and the liberation of the democratic public as its founding ethos. It had wanted to express Korea's capacity for self-government and aspiration for independence, lest the Americans or pro-Americans have other plans.[41]

Upon hearing the news of the establishment of the CPKI, Korean people throughout the peninsula formed CPKI branches and associated self-governing committees. The speed with which these branches were set up, along with their scale, is indicative of wide-spread support from Koreans. Almost overnight, 145 CPKI branches sprang up in cities, towns, and counties.[42] The CPKI branches focused on maintaining public order and taking over administrative functions in provinces. By the end of September, the majority of them had renamed themselves as People's Committees to support the KPR.[43] Many indigenous communists likely played a key role in organizing branches of the CPKI and the KPR, but students, demobilized soldiers, local village elites, and even former colonial officials worked to organize them.[44] In addition, nearly all levels of local associations, including peasant unions, workers' unions, women's groups, and youths, supplemented the PCs.[45] The organization of local PCs rapidly spread even into the smallest villages in Korea, and the number of township-level committees reached 2,244 (1,680 in the South and 564 in the North) by November 1945.[46] Cumings saw the phenomenon as "a political *movement*" that "would no doubt represent a degree of rural political organization and participation unmatched in Korea before or since."[47] In addition to maintaining public order and taking over local governance, PCs attempted to punish "national traitors" or former Japanese collaborators, including local government officials, the police, and landlords, while also moving to nationalize major industries owned by the Japanese.[48] The PCs received a wide degree of support from the public and governed roughly half of all counties in the South at one point.[49] The Jeju People's Committee was an example of them.

The Jeju branch of the CPKI at the provincial level was formed in Jeju-eup (currently Jeju City) on September 10 by about one hundred people who represented each town and county. An executive team was also created the same day. The executive members, including the chair, Oh Dae-jin, were elected by recommendation of the participants.[50] The branch claimed to be the Jeju PC on September 22,[51] but it had autonomy from the mainland central body. The Jeju PC decided to struggle for an independent unified country, the elimination of the vestiges of Japanese colonialism and international fascism, and the development of democracy.[52] The organizational structure of the Jeju PC then spread to each village throughout the island.[53]

However, the U.S. military government, which had been installed in the southern portion of Korea the day after the arrival of the U.S. Army, adopted anticommunist policies from its initiation, in turn empowering rightist groups and suppressing these grassroots state-building efforts. The military government did not acknowledge the political authority of the KPR, and the commanding general of the United States Armed Forces in Korea (USAFIK), John Hodge, judged the KPR as a "communist regime set up before our arrival."[54] With this suspicion, the U.S. military government declared itself the only legitimate power while restoring the preexisting colonial bureaucracy at the expense of the KPR. It employed former pro-Japanese collaborators and colonial police officers, provoking nationwide frustration. In particular, it filled the highest posts, including the head of the Supreme Court and the chief of police, with colonial elites or members of the Korean Democratic Party (led by Song Jing-woo and Kin Seong-su), an extremely conservative party.[55]

Yeo Un-hyeong, who organized the KPR, finally left the KPR in November, thus weakening its power. Hodge announced again through a broadcast in December 1945 that the KPR was an illegal government. Although members of the KPR transferred to the Democratic People's Front, an alliance of leftist organizations established in February 1946, the KPR lost its influence as a provisional government. The U.S. military government also outlawed the PCs in December 1945 because it saw the committees as left leaning and threatening the power of the military government.[56] Most PCs in the mainland began to lose their influence in provinces from that point on. However, the Jeju PC had a relatively friendly relationship with the military government until the time that the U.S. military government granted the island, which had been a subordinate administrative unit of South Jeolla Province, autonomous provincial status in August 1946.[57] The U.S. military government preferred to ignore Jeju because of the island's geographical isolation, its lack of transportation networks, and the belief among the American occupation that the Jeju PC was politically moderate.[58] Because of its autonomy, the Jeju PC was effectively able to continue constructing its own form of political organization on the island.

Establishing a De Facto Government on Jeju: Organizational Activities of the Jeju People's Committee

The Jeju PC entrenched its power by extensively organizing its structure and performing a full range of activities. The former leaders of the anti-Japanese activities took the lead in organizing the Jeju branch for the CPKI and the KPR, but these committees initially included a diverse membership, regardless of their ideological orientation. Almost everyone except for the pro-Japanese factions participated in the committees at the level of town and county.[59] However, the Jeju branch of the Communist Party of Korea virtually directed the Jeju PC after it was formed in early October 1945.[60] The role of Korean communists in the KPR and local PCs is clear, though their degree of control or particular agenda is open to debate. The Communist Party of Korea (led by Park Heon-yeong), which was restructured after liberation, actively participated in or supported the KPR. The leaders of the Jeju PC, including the chair, Oh Dae-jin, established the Jeju branch of the Communist Party of Korea and covertly used the Jeju PC as a mass organization even as they implemented moderate policies until early 1947.[61]

The Jeju PC established a systematic and extensive organizational structure. It had a central committee, county and town committees, and branches in every village. The central, county, and town committees had a general affairs department, an organization department, a publicity department, an industry department, and an education department.[62] The Jeju PC also organized diverse subgroups that reached people of all levels of society. The Jeju Council of the Korean Democratic Youth League, the core among the subgroups, formed its own branch in all of twelve counties and towns and nearly all of the island's 169 villages.[63] The youth league took the lead in enlightenment activity, such as holding study meetings, lectures, and open debates.[64] The other subgroups included women's leagues, a teachers' guild, a consumers' union, a farmers' cooperative, labor unions, and a cultural association. The Jeju committee published the only local newspaper, *Jeju Sinmun*, on October 1, 1945, to communicate with these networks and the public.[65] Members of these subgroups later helped organize a rally to celebrate the twenty-eighth anniversary of the March First Korean Independence Movement of 1919, and participated in the Jeju 4.3 uprising.

Through its organizational prowess, the Jeju PC began to expand its political and economic power, essentially acting like a government. The first and most prominent activity of the PC was the maintenance of local security. It organized peacekeeping units in towns, counties, and villages, and leaders of the Youth League did the bulk of this work.[66] The security forces aimed at maintaining public order, punishing pro-Japanese collaborators, monitoring Japanese soldiers' sale of their military supplies, and preventing crimes.[67] According to the Jemin Ilbo Reporting Team's research, the peacekeeping units first punished pro-Japanese collaborators by opening a kangaroo court.[68] Some had to flee Jeju after the court's decision. The units also watched Japanese soldiers (who had entered the island at the end of the Second World War and now waited for repatriation) sell their military supplies, including wood, food, medicine, and blankets, to local residents.[69] The Jeju PC saw the military supplies as communal properties of the Jeju people and planned to confiscate them after their repatriation.[70] For example, the PC in Myeongwol village on the northwest side of Jeju succeeded in confiscating military supplies such as dishes and daily necessities and distributed them to the villagers.[71] In addition, the security forces tried to crack down on crimes such as assault and gambling, which the colonial police had previously undertaken.[72]

The Jeju PC also managed properties and industries that the Japanese had previously owned. For example, during the colonial era, Japanese businesspeople had operated seventy-two chemical and manufacturing plants, including a brewery, a pharmaceutical company, a sock factory, canned food factory, and shell button plants on the island.[73] After liberation, a temporary management committee was established in each of these plants to run them. The Industry Department of the Jeju PC took over the management as the committee thought that the plants were also common properties of the Jeju people.[74] With wide support, the PC managed those plants until the U.S. military government took them over in December 1945.[75]

Similar to the PCs on the mainland, the Jeju PC took over local governance in the vacuum caused by the unexpected liberation from Japanese rule. By late September 1945, the PC representatives of counties and towns and of villages succeeded in taking over the administrative tasks in their districts.[76] In some towns and villages, the representatives themselves served as heads of their administrative districts. In other cases where members did not directly rule, the town officials usually consulted with leaders of the PC for important administrative tasks. In nearly every village, the branch office of the PC was used as the village office, indicating clear administrative integration.[77] A former resident of Gimnyeong village said that the PC in his village took charge of the administrative and other tasks in the village.[78] Another resident in Udo, an island off the northeastern coast of Jeju, likewise recalled that the committee in his village was an organization for discussing and solving various problems of the village in order "to live together in peace."[79] As an indication of its ambition, the Jeju PC selected Ahn Se-hun as the governor of the island, though the U.S. military government did not approve of this decision.[80]

Beyond administrative activities, the committees provided a variety of roles related to residents' daily lives. They supplied industrial products and daily necessities to residents, hosted athletic and entertainment contests, and provided education on livestock raising and farming techniques through these subgroups.[81] For example, the consumer union under the PC sold soaps and fertilizers to the residents that the committee members brought from the northern part of Korea.[82] The committee in Hallim village distributed dried sweet potatoes kept in village storage to the residents, and the committee in Sumang village made a village road with the residents and provided education on silkworm breeding and livestock raising to them.[83] These moderate and useful policies received wide support from the public, as indicated by reporting from the *Donga Ilbo*.[84] The popularity of these initiatives was not without political consequence: according to a report written in December 1946 by the American Public Opinion Bureau in the U.S. military government, local rightists were afraid that the committees on Jeju would become stronger.[85]

Buttressing these communal projects was a particularly strong emphasis on educational matters. The critical role of education cannot be overemphasized. For the leaders of the committee, education was seen as a vital tool for the creation of the independent Korea that they desired. The branches themselves in some towns and villages established and operated schools.[86] For example, the branch in Jocheon-myeon established Jocheon Middle School in early 1946 and operated it, while the branch in Daejeong-myeon established Daejeong Middle School in September 1946.[87] The first representative of the branch in Aewol-eup (county) founded Hagui Middle School in November 1945.[88] The PC then educated students through the teachers, who were also members of the committee. Educational leaders formed the nucleus of local left power on the island. For example, the key leaders of the 1948 Jeju uprising, including Kim Dal-sam, Lee Deok-gu, and Kim Dong-hwan, were all teachers at these new middle schools.

The former elementary and middle school students in the villages of Jocheon, Daejeong, and Hagui remembered that their schoolteachers taught socialist theories such as Marx and Engel's *Capital* and Bukharin and Preobrazhensky's *The ABC of Communism* to people as young as elementary students.[89] One former student from the Jocheon Middle School testified that "the school was strongly left leaning. All six teachers including Lee Deok-gu were socialists,"[90] and "most students joined in the Jeju branch of the Communist Party of Korea as a cell. Following an order from the party, I participated in a group meeting where we studied Marxist theories."[91] One former student in Hagui Middle School also said that "the teachers tried to make us build a utopian country. The mimeographed copies of books about historical materialism and dialectic were widely circulated in the school."[92] The PC's educational work appeared successful. The local middle school student union held its own ceremony for the 1947 March First Independence Movement Anniversary at Ohyun Middle School. Over two thousand students and nearby villagers gathered, shouting slogans such as "Let's achieve independence and unification in a spirit of the March First Independence Movement."[93] Many students also participated in the uprising in the following year. According to a former student of Daejeong Middle School, some 450 out of 600 students in the school joined in the uprising.[94]

At the same time, the Jeju PC attempted to educate ordinary residents who had not received any formal school education by opening night schools in every village. The teachers taught them to read and write in Korean while promoting social consciousness and socialist ideals. Night schools included lessens on the "role and circumstances of the propertyless mass" to develop critical thinking skills for ordinary residents.[95] According to historian Jeong-sim Yang, the night schools particularly attracted women because the teachers emphasized the equal rights of women and men and advocated monogamy.[96] One woman who took night classes became involved in the activities of the PC for the following reason: "I liked the slogan, 'Completely eliminate polygamy.' I lived so painfully in the [polygamy] system, so I wanted the next generation to live in a better world."[97] Other women also supported the idea of women's liberation. Almost all woman insurgents in Jocheon-myeon were either widows or concubines who were more likely to oppose the patriarchal system and polygamy.[98] The survivors said that woman insurgents were deeply committed to their work.[99] This emphasis on women's liberation, coupled with the broader progressive politics of the local PCs, meant that for a large number of the island's population their personal fates and that of the People's Republic of Jeju were intertwined. Unsurprisingly, one of the slogans that the armed insurgents published at the time of the uprising was "Absolute defense of the People's Republic."[100]

THE U.S. MILITARY GOVERNMENT'S INTERVENTION

The postcolonial aspiration of political activists on the island began to shatter with the establishment of Jeju as an independent province and the U.S. military government's subsequent adoption of a hard-line policy by the end of 1946. American forces first arrived on Jeju on September 28, 1945, to disarm and repatriate Japanese soldiers, but the local branch of the U.S military government was not established until November 9, 1945, eighty-six days after liberation.[101] During this period, the Jeju PC had already established its organizational structure and subgroups, effectively acting like a government, as discussed above. The Jeju military government started to maintain public order and manage properties that the Japanese had owned, in turn replacing the local PCs as the authority.[102] As in Seoul, the Jeju military government employed former officials and police officers from the colonial era. However, the Jeju military government used the Jeju PCs in administering and maintaining public order and had a cooperative relationship with them for roughly a year.

The U.S. military government granted the island autonomous provincial status in response to demands from the right-wing camp on Jeju and the local branch of the military government.[103] For the local branch, it was easier to deal directly with the central government on most matters than to have to pass through the South Jeolla Province.[104] The new status of Jeju meant that the island would be integrated into the central government, a development that the Jeju PC opposed.[105] According to a former member of Jeju South Korean Labor Party (SKLP), the Jeju PC opposed this shift because "this administrative issue of Jeju Island should be decided by the incoming Korean government that we Koreans would establish in a near future. We disliked that Americans decided it instead of our incoming government."[106] In spite of the opposition from the Jeju PC and a majority of Jeju people, Jeju Island became the ninth province in the south of Korea.

The subsequent changes resulted in the expansion of administrative organizations and the police on the island. Firstly, the police presence expanded from September 1946 as the number of policemen increased to 330 in February 1947, up from 101 at the time of liberation. The establishment of Jeju as a sperate province also led to the presence of a regional regiment of the Korean Constabulary—a proto-national army—on Jeju.[107] With this, the Ninth Regiment was established in November 1946 and began to recruit soldiers among young men on Jeju. By 1948, the number of soldiers had reached four hundred.[108] With this intrusion of rival administrative and coercive power, the Jeju PC now found itself in a serious predicament.

Shifts on the mainland likewise augured poorly for the Jeju PC as the military government focused its policy on "control and internal security" following a series of calamitous events in the fall of 1946.[109] Through the fall, large-scale nationwide strikes and protests against major policies of the U.S. military government, including land reform and rice collection, occurred in all the southern provinces for almost two months.[110] The uprisings began with a massive general strike by railroad workers in late September which quickly spread to all other major industries. After police fired on and killed protesters in Daegu on October 1, a larger peasant uprising broke out and escalated into other cities and districts in the southern provinces. The U.S. military government violently quelled the uprisings by sending in strikebreakers, the police, rightist youth groups, and U.S. troops and tanks, which resulted in 30,500 casualties, including 300 dead and 3,600 missing.[111] Despite the grievances stated above, the U.S. military government saw the Communist Party of Korea as the key director of the uprising.[112] As such, the military government strengthened its policy against communism by suppressing all leftist leaders and organizations and social movements in the South, including Jeju. Although the Jeju PC did not join these uprisings, the hard-line policy further weakened its power.

In response to these developments, the left on Jeju, including the local PCs, began to consolidate and drift more firmly toward the left. The committee's leadership began to transfer to the Jeju branch of the Democratic People's Front under the Jeju South Korean Labor Party (SKLP) in early 1947.[113] The Jeju SKLP was established near the end of 1946 and was connected to the central structure of the SKLP. The leaders of the SKLP wanted to jointly pursue policies such as supporting trusteeship and land reform.[114] While on the mainland the SKLP was an amalgamation of various leftist parties, on Jeju, the Jeju Communist Party of Korea was the only leftist party at the time, and therefore the establishment of the Jeju SKLP was simply a change in monikers.[115] Shortly afterward, on March 1, 1947, this Jeju branch of the SKLP organized a protest against the suppression by the military government as well as the division of Korea, publishing a slogan of "Hand back power to the People's Committee."[116] The shooting incident that resulted from the police's suppression of these protests is generally recognized as the beginning of the 4.3 Incident, as will be discussed in the next chapter.

The March 1 protests and subsequent shooting incident were a regrettable but understandable consequence of the built-up tensions on the island and the polarized political environment. As this chapter has intimated, from the moment of liberation, Jeju's political leadership sought an alternative form of political organization than that which was steadily imposed by the American occupation. Much of this was nurtured by Jeju's long tradition of self-determination, its tightly knit kinship culture, and its particular colonial conditions. As the U.S. military government sought to forge an anticommunist mainland state, the tensions between Jeju's leadership and the occupying authorities became irreconcilable. In this sense, the 1945–1947 period was an ominous prelude to the mass killings that engulphed the island one year later.

NOTES

1. Jeong-sim Yang, "Jeju 4.3, Memories of Massacre and Times of Uprising," in *The Jeju 4.3 Mass Killing: Atrocity, Justice, and Reconciliation*, ed. Jeju 4.3 Peace Foundation (Seoul: Yonsei University Press, 2018), 156–62; Jey Hauben, "People's Republic of Jeju Island, 1945–1946," *Papers, Essays and Reviews* 3, no. 3 (2011): 277.

2. Cumings, *Roaring of the Cataract*, 252.

3. Jeju 4.3 National Committee, *Jeju April Third Incident Investigation Report*, 83.

4. Cumings, *Roaring of the Cataract*, 252.

5. Jeju 4.3 Research Institute, ed., *Ijesa malhaemsuda 1* [Now We Speak Out, vol. 1] (Seoul: Hanul, 1989), 173–75, 187–88; Jeju 4.3 Peace Foundation and Jeju 4.3 Research Institute, eds., *Jigeumkkaji sarajin geosi yongheongeora* [It Is a Miracle That I've Survived] (Jeju: Hangeuru, 2011), 156.

6. Merrill, "Cheju-do Rebellion," 142–48.

7. Hwang, *Korea's Grievous War*, 31–32.

8. Chan-sik Park, *1901nyeon Jeju millan yeongu* [A Study of the Jeju Uprising in 1901] (Jeju: Gak, 2013), 107.

9. Ibid., 113.

10. Ibid., 186.

11. Ibid., 326–32.

12. Merrill, "Cheju-do Rebellion," 148.

13. Jeju 4.3 National Committee, *Jeju April Third Incident Investigation Report*, 80.

14. Ibid., 81; Hauben, "People's Republic of Jeju Island," 279.

15. Dong Choon Kim, "The Social Grounds of Anticommunism in South Korea: Crisis of the Ruling Class and Anticommunist Reaction," *Asian Journal of German and European Studies* 2 (2017): 5–6.

16. Chang-hu Kim, "Jaeiljejuinui hangil undong" [Jeju Islander's Anti-Japanese Movement in Japan], *Jejudosa Yeongu* [Review of Jeju History] 4 (1995): 262–63.

17. Ibid., 261.

18. Jo-hoon Yang, "The Truth of the April 3 Incident and the Role and Responsibility of the U.S.," in *The Jeju 4.3 Mass Killing: Atrocity, Justice, and Reconciliation*, ed. Jeju 4.3 Peace Foundation (Seoul: Yonsei University Press, 2018), 69.

19. Jeju Special Self-Governing Provincial Office of Education, *Geunhyeondae Jeju gyoyuk 100nyeonsa* [The One-Hundred-Year History of (Early) Modern Education in Jeju] (Jeju: Gyeongsin Inswaesa, 2011), 148.

20. Jeju 4.3 National Committee, *Jeju April Third Incident Investigation Report*, 81.

21. Park, *4.3gwa Jeju yeoksa*, 129–65.

22. Ibid., 47–51.

23. Jemin Ilbo 4.3 Reporting Team, *4.3eun malhanda 1* [4.3 Speaks, vol. 1] (Seoul: Jeonyaewon, 1994), 197.

24. Ibid., 45.

25. Ibid., 32–33.

26. Ibid., 33. The conscription of young girls on Jeju Island had been a hot issue since the *Asahi Shimbun* reported the confession of Seiji Yoshida, a self-proclaimed recruitment official in Korea, in 1982. He confessed to kidnapping up to two hundred young girls on Jeju Island and many other girls in the mainland of Korea for comfort stations. His testimony has influenced historians and South Korean and international public opinion, while also provoking controversies. However, on August 5, 2013, the *Asahi Shimbun* announced that after doing additional research on the island, they concluded that the testimony of Yoshida was a fabrication. *Asahi Shimbun*, August 22, 2014.

27. Jeju 4.3 National Committee, *Jeju April Third Incident Investigation Report*, 68–70.

28. Ibid., 70.

29. Seong-yoon Cho, Yeong-im Ji, and Ho-joon Heo, *Ppaeatgin sidae, ppaeatgin sijeol: Jejudo minjungdureui iyagi* [Robbed of Their Era and Time: Stories of the People of Jeju Island] (Seoul: Seonin, 2007).

30. Jeju 4.3 National Committee, *Jeju April Third Incident Investigation Report*, 70.

31. Ibid., 78, 81; Jeju 4.3 Research Institute, *Ijesa malhaemsuda 1*, 180.

32. Jeju 4.3 National Committee, *Jeju April Third Incident Investigation Report*, 120.

33. Ibid.

34. Ibid., 120–21.

35. Bruce Cumings, *The Origins of the Korean War*, vol. 1: *Liberation and the Emergence of Separate Regimes, 1945–1947* (Seoul: Yeoksa Bipyeongsa, 2002), 347.

36. *Jeju Sinbo*, February 10, 1947.

37. Jemin Ilbo 4.3 Reporting Team, *4.3eun malhanda 1*, 50; Cumings, *Liberation and the Emergence of Separate Regimes*, 344–45.

38. Jemin Ilbo 4.3 Reporting Team, *4.-3eun malhanda 1*, 50–51.

39. Cumings, *Liberation and the Emergence of Separate Regimes*, 348–49.

40. Jeju 4.3 National Committee, *Jeju April Third Incident Investigation Report*, 86.

41. Suzy Kim, *Everyday Life in the North Korean Revolution, 1945–1950* (New York: Cornell University Press, 2013), 44.

42. Cumings, *Liberation and the Emergence of Separate Regimes*, 73.

43. Kim, *Everyday Life in the North Korean Revolution*, 44–45.

44. Cumings, *Liberation and the Emergence of Separate Regimes*, 271.

45. Ibid., 270.

46. Kim, *Everyday Life in the North Korean Revolution*, 45.

47. Cumings, *Liberation and the Emergence of Separate Regimes*, 270.

48. Kim, *Everyday Life in the North Korean Revolution*, 44–45.

49. Cumings, *Liberation and the Emergence of Separate Regimes*, 275.

50. Jeju 4.3 National Committee, *Jeju April Third Incident Investigation Report*, 86–87.

51. Ibid., 88.

52. Dong-man Kim, "Haebang jikhu jibang jeongchi yeongu: Jeju jibang geon-gukjunbiwiwonhoe inminwiwonhoeui jojikgwa hwaldong" [A Study on Postlib-eration Local Politics: The Organization and Activities of the Jeju Branch of the Committee for the Preparation of Korean Independence and of the Committee for the Korean People's Republic], *Yeoksa Bipyeong* [Critical Review of History] 14 (1991): 195.

53. Jeju 4.3 National Committee, *Jeju April Third Incident Investigation Report*, 88.

54. Brazinsky, *Nation Building in South Korea*, 15.

55. Ibid.

56. Kim, *Everyday Life in the North Korean Revolution*, 45.

57. Merrill, "Cheju-do Rebellion," 151–52.

58. Cumings, *Roaring of the Cataract*, 252; Ho-joon Heo, *American Involvement in the Jeju April 3 Incident*, trans. David Carruth and Colin Mouat (Jeju: Jeju 4.3 Research Institute, 2021), 65–67.

59. Jemin Ilbo 4.3 Reporting Team, *4.3eun malhanda 1*, 70.

60. Yang, "Jeju 4.3, Memories of Massacre and Times of Uprising," 156.

61. Ibid.

62. Jeong-sim Yang, "Judoseryeogeul tonghaeseo bon Jeju 4.3 hangjaengui bae-gyeong" [Background of the Jeju 4.3 Uprising: With a Focus on Leading Forces], in *Jeju 4.3 yeongu* [A Study on Jeju 4.3], ed. Jeju 4.3 Research Institute (Seoul: Yeoksa Bipyeongsa, 1999), 60–61.

63. Yang, "Jeju 4.3, Memories of Massacre and Times of Uprising," 156–57.

64. Bong-hyun Kim and Min-ju Kim, "Jejudo inmindeurui 4.3 mujang tujaengsa" [A History of the Jeju People's 4.3 Armed Uprising], in *Jeju minjung hangjaeng 1* [Jeju People's Uprising, vol. 1], ed. Arari Research Institute (Seoul: Sonamu, 1988), 207. This is the first book on Jeju 4.3, published in the year 1963 in Japan.

65. Ibid., 208.

66. Jemin Ilbo 4.3 Reporting Team, *4.3eun malhanda 1*, 76.

67. Yang, "Jeju 4.3, Memories of Massacre and Times of Uprising," 157.

68. Jemin Ilbo 4.3 Reporting Team, *4.3eun malhanda 1*, 74.

69. Ibid., 75–76.

70. Ibid.

71. Kim, "Haebang jikhu jibang jeongchi yeongu," 198.

72. Jemin Ilbo 4.3 Reporting Team, *4.3eun malhanda 1*, 72.

73. Yang, "Jeju 4.3, Memories of Massacre and Times of Uprising," 157–58.

74. Ibid.; Kim, "Haebang jikhu jibang jeongchi yeongu," 198.

75. Yang, "Jeju 4.3, Memories of Massacre and Times of Uprising," 158.

76. Ibid.

77. Kim, "Haebang jikhu jibang jeongchi yeongu," 199.

78. Jeju 4.3 Peace Foundation and Jeju 4.3 Research Institute, *Jigeumkkaji sarajin geosi yongheongeora*, 156.

79. Jeju 4.3 Research Institute, ed., *Geuneul sogeui 4.3* [In the Shadows of 4.3] (Seoul: Seonin, 2009), 63.

80. Yang, "Jeju 4.3, Memories of Massacre and Times of Uprising," 158.

81. Ibid.

82. Kim, "Haebang jikhu jibang jeongchi yeongu," 199.

83. Jemin Ilbo 4.3 Reporting Team, *4.3eun malhanda 1*, 72.

84. *Donga Ilbo*, December 21, 1946.

85. Cumings, *Liberation and the Emergence of Separate Regimes*, 346.

86. Jemin Ilbo 4.3 Reporting Team, *4.3eun malhanda 1*, 72.

87. Yang, "Jeju 4.3, Memories of Massacre and Times of Uprising," 158–59.

88. Jeju 4.3 Research Institute, *Ijesa malhaemsuda 1*, 20, 124, 277.

89. Ibid., 56; Jeju 4.3 Research Institute, ed., *Dasi hagui junghagwoneul gieokhamyeo* [Recollecting the Days of Hagui Middle School] (Seoul: Hanul Academy, 2013), 20.

90. Jeju 4.3 Research Institute, *Ijesa malhaemsuda 1*, 47–48.

91. Ibid., 52–53.

92. Jeju 4.3 Research Institute, *Dasi hagui junghagwoneul gieokhamyeo*, 20.

93. Jemin Ilbo 4.3 Reporting Team, *4.3eun malhanda 1*, 263.

94. Ko, *Jeju saramdeurui seorum*, 116.

95. Yang, "Jeju 4.3, Memories of Massacre and Times of Uprising," 160.

96. Ibid., 160–61.

97. Ibid., 161.

98. Jeju 4.3 Research Institute, *Ijesa malhaemsuda 1*, 16–17.

99. Ibid., 17, 44, 105.

100. Un-bang Lee, "4.3 sageonui jinsang" [The Truth of the Jeju 4.3 Incident], in *Ijesa malhaemsuda 1* [Now We Speak Out, vol. 1], ed. Jeju 4.3 Research Institute (Seoul: Hanul, 1989), 218. Lee was the head of Daejeong-myeon branch of the Jeju South Korean Labor Party.

101. Jeju 4.3 National Committee, *Jeju April Third Incident Investigation Report*, 93–94.

102. Ibid., 96.

103. Jeju 4.3 National Committee, *Jeju April Third Incident Investigation Report*, 99.

104. Merrill, "Cheju-do Rebellion," 152.

105. Wright, "Civil War, Politicide, and the Politics of Memory in South Korea," 40.

106. Jemin Ilbo 4.3 Reporting Team, *4.3eun malhanda 1*, 167.

107. Jeju 4.3 National Committee, *Jeju April Third Incident Investigation Report*, 102–3.

108. Ibid., 105–6.

109. Merrill, "Cheju-do Rebellion," 152.

110. For more details about land reform, see Inhan Kim, "Land Reform in South Korea under the U.S. Military Occupation, 1945–1948," *Journal of Cold War Studies* 18, no. 2 (2016): 97–129.

111. Kim, "State and Nation Building in South Korea," 134.

112. Kim, *Massacres at Mt. Halla*, 26.

113. Yang, "Jeju 4.3, Memories of Massacre and Times of Uprising," 162; Merrill, "Cheju-do Rebellion," 151.

114. For details about the trusteeship, see Kim, *Massacres at Mt. Halla*, 22–23.

115. Jemin Ilbo 4.3 Reporting Team, *4.3eun malhanda 1*, 198.

116. Jeju 4.3 National Committee, *Jeju April Third Incident Investigation Report*, 127.

Chapter 2

State Violence: The Jeju Massacre

The precise number of individuals who were murdered or disappeared over the course of Jeju 4.3 remains unknown. The death toll varies depending on the data source and ranges between fifteen thousand and sixty-five thousand.[1] The population of the island at the time of the outbreak of Jeju 4.3 was approximately 280,000, which suggests that a substantial percentage of islanders were wiped out.[2] Hundreds more were mentally and physically abused through torture and other violence. The *Jeju April Third Incident Investigation Report* of 2003 by the Jeju 4.3 National Committee reports that between twenty-five and thirty thousand people on Jeju Island were killed over the six years of the massacre, the majority of whom were unarmed civilians.[3] In comparison, the number of soldiers and police officers who died were estimated to be 162 and 289, respectively.[4] This grim imbalance is indicative of a massive slaughter by any metric. The official number of victims now recognized by the state is roughly half of the total estimate. After a special act to investigate the truth of Jeju 4.3 was enacted in 2000, the Jeju 4.3 National Committee received reports on the victims from their families and identified a total of 14,442 victims as of December 2019.[5] The category of "victims" included those who had died, disappeared, were disabled, or were imprisoned.[6] This discrepancy between the estimated number and the officially registered number is largely due to the fact that by the time of the reports, many families were dead or reticent to report victims among their family members out of fear that they and their children might be accused of being communists.

A further breakdown of the numbers reveals crucial patterns to the violence in terms of victimization, perpetrators, and time line. The proportion of young children less than ten years old among the victims on Jeju was 4.8 percent, and that of the elderly over sixty-years old was 6.9 percent—indicating indiscriminate features of the massacre.[7] However, the proportion of men and women among the victims was 79.1 percent and 20.9 percent,[8] suggesting that men were primary targets. According to the above reports on the victims, the vast majority of the dead—a full 83.6 percent—were killed at the hands of state agents such as the police, the military, and rightist groups, and 16.4 percent were killed by the Armed Resistance Group, who were local communist insurgents.[9] The proportion of victims varied over the duration of the events. In the initial stage of the massacre, from March 1, 1947, to October 10, 1948, 6.6 percent were killed. During the time period of the establishment of the South Korean government, between October 11, 1948, and February 1949, the majority—67.2 percent—were killed. From March 1949 to the end of the massacre in September 1954, meanwhile, 24.0 percent were killed or disappeared.[10] The majority in this last period were victimized immediately following the outbreak of the Korean War. More than one thousand Jeju residents who were on the police blacklist of alleged communists were executed on Jeju by order of the South Korean government, and about 2,900 Jeju people who had been sent to prisons on the mainland in connection with the uprisings did not return home—presumably executed as part of a broader national policy of exterminating potential communist supporters during the early initial North Korean invasion.[11]

These waves of mass killings and executions during the winter of 1948–1949 and the early Korean War suggest that the events were related to the consolidation of the South Korean state. In this chapter, I focus on state violence committed by the newly established Rhee regime and its American supporters and this violence's relation to the creation of the South Korean state. Many Korean scholars, such as Park Myung-lim and Choi Ho-geun, have drawn connections between state violence and the formation of South Korea, but Wright's study is the most comprehensive English-language synthesis.[12] Drawing on the concept of "politicide," he argues that Jeju 4.3 was not an isolated incident that happened on the island. Rather, it was "both constituted by, and constitutive of, larger patterns of mass violence organized by the embryonic ROK [Republic of Korea] National Security State."[13] In other words, he saw Jeju 4.3, and in particular, the mass killing of the winter of 1948–1949, as a part of the South Korean state's systematic eradication of political leftists to establish a stronger state. His study helps explain why the massacre happened, but it does not fully account for the particular ferocity of violence on Jeju 4.3 or the local conditions that gave the incident its specific character over the 1947–1954 period. This chapter therefore explores how and why Jeju experienced such brutal and bloody violence over this period, particularly during the winter of 1948–1949. I begin with the historical background of the uprising in the context of state formation in South Korea.

INVENTION OF THE ISLAND OF REDS: THE
ORIGIN OF THE ANTICOMMUNIST STATE

Protest against the Suppression by U.S. Occupation Forces: The March First Shooting Incident and General Strike

As discussed in the previous chapter, the weaking of the Jeju PC, coupled with broader dissatisfaction with the policies of the U.S. military government, created a volatile situation on Jeju. This reached a boiling point on March 1, 1947, when protests against major political and economic policies of the U.S. military government exploded on Jeju. Utilizing its subgroups, cells, and members of the PCs in counties and towns, the Jeju SKLP organized a rally to celebrate the twenty-eighth anniversary of the March First Korean Independence Movement of 1919.[14] The Jeju SKLP retained an educated leadership, a highly developed organization, and a wide network of politicized supporters, which made it an effective organization for mobilizing resistance.[15] The SKLP clarified their goal of the rally by publishing slogans. The slogans said, "Support the establishment of a democratic provisional government," "Hand back power to the People's Committee," "Abolish all the administrative bodies from the Japanese era," and "Let the people solve the problems of food shortage by themselves."[16]

On that day, an unusually large crowd participated in rallies held in Jeju-eup and ten other counties. Approximately twenty-five to thirty thousand people gathered in Jeju Book Elementary School in Jeju-eup alone, and many other people participated in the ceremony held in those other counties.[17] The brewing political conflict was exasperated by the deteriorating economic conditions on the island. The island's population already suffered from a high unemployment rate due to the many returnees who had been arriving since liberation, an interruption of remittance of money from Japan, and commodity shortages. Moreover, cholera had begun to spread from the spring of 1946, and staple crops, such as barley, millet, and sweet potato, failed that year. Consequently, many residents struggled to ward off starvation.[18] The repeated forcible rice collection by the local police, a major economic policy of the military government, unsurprisingly provoked stronger resentment.[19] The planned demonstrations offered the islanders an outlet for venting their cumulative frustrations.

The ceremony authorized by the Jeju police in Jeju-eup was peacefully ended, but the shooting incident after the ceremony fueled the islander's grievances. The shooting incident happened during an unauthorized parade, which occurred after the rally. The participants marched down the street, and a policeman from the mainland on horseback accidently hit a child who was among the spectators. When nearby people pursued the policeman, the police opened fire on them, injuring eight and killing six people, including an elementary school student and a young mother holding a baby. After the shooting incident, local people protested in front of the Jeju Police Inspection Agency, but the police justified it as an act of self-defense and maintenance of public order. The islanders were enraged once it became known that the policemen who fired had been from the mainland and the victims all had been spectators.[20] In response, the Jeju branch of the SKLP organized a general strike.

The depth of the strike, starting on March 10, was unprecedented in Korean history. Not only students, teachers, and factory workers but also public officials and even some native policemen participated. Public officials in the Jeju Provincial Office joined the strike, and those in other provincial public offices, including radio stations and tax offices, participated in the strike shortly after. Additionally, Jeju native police officers participated in the strike, and as a result, sixty-six policemen were later dismissed. In sum, some 166 organizations and institutions joined the general strike, and the total number of participants was 41,211—a remarkable number given Jeju's modest population.[21] The remnants of the local PCs played a substantial role in coordinating these and other activities. For example, the fundraising campaigns for the victims' families were actively conducted by the leadership of PCs in counties and towns that still existed at the time. As historian Hwang Su-kyoung notes, the rally on March 1 and the general strike intensified the radical attitude among Jeju people against the police and rightist groups on the island.[22]

Response of the U.S. Military Government: Creation of the Island of Reds

After the general strike, the U.S. military government and its allied Koreans began to label Jeju as an island dominated by leftists, which resulted in the adoption of repressive measures and the empowerment of rightist groups. The U.S. military government perceived the general strike as a consequence of the Jeju SKLP manipulating the hostility between the local people and the police to foment resistance.[23] When the military government proposed a policy of eradicating leftists on Jeju, Cho Byeong-ok, the chief of the Korean National Police and key member of conservative Korean Democratic Party, undertook the task. On the day of his visit to the Provincial Office on Jeju on March 14, Cho expressed his determination that the "Jeju people had rebellious ideas" and he could wipe out the entire population "if they got in the way of the foundation of the state."[24] Choi Gyeong-jin, deputy head of the National Police Agency, made a comparable remark two days before Cho's visit, when he reported at a press conference in Seoul that "about 90 percent of Jeju people are tinged with left-wing ideology."[25] Both Cho's and Choi's comments vividly illustrate that even before the start of the 1948 uprising, Jeju was characterized as an Island of Reds, where the islanders might "get in the way of the foundation of the state."

Cho immediately dispatched about four hundred police officers from the mainland who actively searched, arrested, and tortured the local people. The number of arrested reached 2,500 in just over one year. The scale of repression was so severe that the jails in Jeju became overcrowded. According to a U.S. inspection team, "thirty-five prisoners were crowded in a cell, approximately ten by twelve feet."[26] Many young people fled to Japan to escape the roundup.[27] At this stage, the military government's repressive measures fueled Jeju resident's resistance, in turn worsening the situation. For example, in March 1948, a month before the outbreak of Jeju 4.3, three detainees were killed by torture, which served as an immediate trigger for the uprising.[28]

Meanwhile, the U.S. military government adopted a strategy for supporting rightists to suppress the leftist force on Jeju, which magnified the residents' resentments. The military government appointed Yoo Hae-jin, an extreme rightist from North Jeolla Province, as a new governor in April 1947. He dismissed the public employees in all administrative bodies who were involved in the general strike and filled the majority of those vacancies with extreme anticommunists from the North. Moreover, Governor Yoo and some agents of the U.S. Counterintelligence Corps (CIC) who had arrived on Jeju after the March First Shooting Incident moved to organize rightist youth groups.[29] The CIC had been working on mobilizing youths in the southern portion of Korea since its inception in September 1945.[30] Among these groups, the Jeju branch of the Daedong Youth Corps was established in September 1947 through uniting twenty-two right-wing young men's associations. The youth corps' membership was about one thousand as of November 1947.[31] This youth group made clear that it supported Rhee Syng-man's political line and assisted the police in their duties during Jeju 4.3. As such, it later became a target of the insurgents. The agents of CIC also supported the Jeju branch of the Northwest Youth Association whose members arrived on Jeju just after the March First Shooting Incident.[32] The Northwest Youth Association (NWYA), or *Seobukcheongnyeondan*, was composed of refugees who had fled from North Korea's 1946 land reform, religious oppression, and other communist policies. The association was already known as by far the most violent among the rightist youth groups.[33] The total membership of the Jeju branch of the NWYA was 760 before the outbreak of Jeju 4.3. The members demonized Jeju by calling it "little Moscow"[34] and committed acts of terror against local people upon their arrival. The military government tolerated and supported the brutality of the members as a part of its own anticommunist policies.[35] Kim Ik-ryeol, commander of the Ninth Regiment on Jeju during the incipient phase of the uprising, regarded their brutality and atrocities as a main cause of the outbreak of Jeju 4.3.[36] Many survivors and my interviewees confirmed this.[37] In response to this combination of youth terror and institutional repression, the local branch of the SKLP prepared an armed uprising against their oppression and the division of Korea.[38]

The international political situation around the time further triggered the armed uprising. Starting in 1947, the Truman administration reoriented its foreign policy to contain Soviet geopolitical expansion by adopting the Truman Doctrine in March 1947 and the Marshall Plan (officially the European Recovery Program) in June 1947. Because the administration had asked Congress to authorize massive economic assistance for Greece, Turkey, and other nations of Europe, the extension of the U.S. military in South Korea became a financial liability.[39] Moreover, the United States–Soviet Joint Commission (which was established to organize a system of Korean government in December 1945) had already reached an insurmountable deadlock.[40] As an exit strategy, the Truman administration passed the Korean issue to the newly formed United Nations Temporary Commission on Korea in September 1947, and due to Soviet boycotts, only the southern portion of Korea was poised to hold elections under the observation of the United Nations on May 10, 1948.[41] As the U.S. military government moved toward the construction an anticommunist state in the South, the Jeju SKLP was becoming marginalized.

A Challenge to the Creation of South Korea: The Jeju 4.3 Uprising

On April 3, 1948, around 350 local communists lit a torch to signal their uprising at every parasitic volcano around Mt. Halla. They attacked twelve of twenty-four provincial police stations and the residences of key rightists, killing twelve and injuring twenty-five.[42] The local insurgents or the Armed Resistance Group (*mujangdae*) belonged to the Jeju branch of the SKLP.[43] However, the Seoul central headquarters of SKLP did not order or support the insurgency.[44] The Jeju SKLP had key advantages in the early fighting as it had already established a highly developed organizational structure that linked to every county, town, and village.[45] At the height of the uprisings, the SKLP mobilized around four thousand armed insurgents, though they had little battle experience and few arms: twenty-seven rifles, three pistols, twenty-five grenades, seven smoke shells, and bamboo spears.[46] As the historian Su-Kyoung Hwang notes, the organizational reach of the SKLP made the guerilla struggle highly durable in the early period of the armed uprising.[47]

The Armed Resistance Group, generally known as the People's Liberation Army, or Mountain People, made the goal of their uprising clear through the leaflets distributed to local policemen and citizens. The leaflet distributed to citizens stated the following: "Dear citizens, parents, brothers and sisters! Today, on April 3, your sons and brothers have stood up with arms in hand. We oppose the country-selling separate elections to the death, and have risen up in order to liberate the people, unify the fatherland, and achieve independence."[48] The leaflet distributed to policemen included the same themes— uprising against suppression coupled with support for national unification and anti-American struggle.[49] With this, the insurgents now directly challenged the establishment of South Korea.

Hovering over this phase was the shadow of the People's Republic. The leaders of the Armed Resistance Group appeared to defend the defunct People's Republic. Surviving insurgents recall that they had drawn the flag of the People's Republic in their camp[50] and said that their leaders often told followers that a fair and egalitarian utopia would be created in the near future through the uprising.[51] According to ordinary residents, they saw the insurgents hang the flag on their village hill at the time of the May 10 election.[52] Though there are only a few testimonies, some insurgents appeared to be deeply committed to the People's Republic. One woman leader recalled that fellow insurgents cried, "Hurray for the People's Republic," three times as they were searched and shot dead in the mountains by the counterinsurgents.[53] One survivor remembered that "a young woman arrested by the police never asked for quarter, and she said that 'I will shout hurrah for the People's Republic even if I die.' She actually did until she was shot."[54] Another survivor also said that a woman activist cried, "Hurray for the People's Republic," three times on a snowy day in Jocheon village before being executed by the counterinsurgents.[55] The counterinsurgency forces likewise understood the implications of fighting for the People's Republic. In some cases, the members of the suppression forces demanded that the insurgents or ordinary civilians (whom they had arrested) shout hurray for the People's Republic before executing them.[56] In other words, both the insurgents' commitment to the People's Republic and the counterinsurgency forces' weaponization of these politics contributed to the scale and character of the fighting.

In response to the uprising, the U.S. military government and the Korean police authorities began to delineate the boundary of outsiders from the embryonic state. The U.S. military government first perceived the uprising as an issue of public order because armed revolts had occurred nationwide due to the confrontation between the pro- and anti-unilateral election camps. As such, it sought to quickly repress the uprising by strengthening the police force. Within two days of the outbreak, the military government established the Jeju Emergency Defense Headquarters under the Jeju Police Inspection

Agency and rushed about one hundred police officers from South Jeolla Province to Jeju. Cho Byeong-ok, who perceived Jeju as an Island of Reds, reported in a press conference in Seoul on April 6 that the insurgency was organized by "communist traitors to the country."[57] He again broadened the target to political leftists rather than simply the insurgents. He asked Moon Bong-je, the chair of the NWYA, to send five hundred members to Jeju and appointed those members as combat police officers without proper training. These were the first combat police officers in Korean history and were given a legal right to exercise violence.[58] These police officers and other members of NWYA who were later dispatched became key actors in the bloody massacre, indiscriminately killing, torturing, and infringing on human rights against the people of Jeju.[59]

At the same time, the U.S. military authorities ordered Commander Kim Ik-ryeol to have peace negotiations with the insurgents in order to make them surrender.[60] The negotiations, however, were contradictory. The parties reached an agreement on April 28, but at the same time, the U.S. military government took strong measures to terminate the insurgency before the May 10 election. Consequently, on May 6, Kim Ik-ryeol was replaced by the hard-liner Colonel Park Jin-gyeong, who was more amicable to the U.S. military government's strong repressive measures.

From the outbreak of the insurgency, the Korean police authorities constructed the boundaries of their targets. The enemy from the vantage point of the police was clear. Kim Jeong-ho, the commander of the Jeju Emergency Defense Headquarters, identified them in a public notice two days after the insurgency began: the primary targets were the rioters, or *pokdo*, who had attacked police stations and rightists, and the secondary targets were their supporters.[61] Initially, some signals toward moderation were indicated as Commander Kim also declared, "I will try to do my best to protect good citizens who followed the rioters blindly."[62] Ten days later, however, the "they" was redefined in a warning by Commander Kim and extended to include all leftists, particularly members of the SKLP.[63] Therefore, in less than two weeks, the boundary between the "they" and the "we" had been reset in terms of political ideology rather than riotous behavior. Even leftists who had not supported the insurgency were now excluded from what historical sociologist Helen Fein identifies as the "universe of moral obligation."

Fein argues that in contexts of extreme polarization, "the common conscience is then limited to one's own kind, members of one's class, excluding the other class from the *universe of obligation*—the range of persons and groups toward whom basic rules or 'oughts' are binding."[64] The "we" are the people who "must be taken into account, to whom obligations are due, by whom we can be held responsible for our actions.[65] It is therefore legitimate to attack the 'they' because they are outside the universe of obligation and the 'we' do not have moral obligations to them. The sociologist William Gamson adds to this point by noting that the exclusion is 'a continuous, multi-dimensional variable' rather than a dichotomy," and the targets of mass killing are not "merely outside the most basic universe of obligation; offenses against them are explicitly encouraged, rewarded and sanctioned by regimes."[66] Though the counterinsurgency forces did not launch the mass execution operation against leftists on Jeju at this stage, this construction and reconstruction of the boundaries of enemy contributed to justifying and escalating violence in the subsequent counterinsurgency operations in the 1948–1949 winter.

Despite the hardening of the suppression tactics, the insurgents rallied enough people to boycott the May 10 election that the election results in two of the three electorates on Jeju were declared invalid since a majority of the people did not vote. The residents had climbed up a nearby parasitic volcano prior to the election and stayed there until the election ended.[67] Around the election day, Jeju-eup and towns in northern Jeju such as Jocheon, Gujwa, Aewol, and Hallim were almost empty.[68] This represented a remarkable achievement as Jeju was the only region in the South that boycotted the election. From the military government's perspective, Jeju people were challenging its authority at the height of the Cold War and its plan of establishing a separate government in the South. The U.S. occupation forces therefore began to adopt a stronger counterinsurgency operation throughout the island in the wake of the boycott.

The military government sent the hard-liner Colonel Brown as the U.S. commander on Jeju on May 20. As soon as he arrived on Jeju, he declared that "I am not interested in the cause of the uprising. My mission is to repress it."[69] Brown judged that about 80 percent of Jeju residents were implicated in the communist protests, and he engineered an even stricter counterinsurgency operation "to quell the situation in about two weeks."[70] To facilitate this, a large number of police officers and soldiers were dispatched from the mainland. The number of police officers increased from five hundred at the time of the uprising to nearly two thousand as of July 1948.[71] The number of soldiers also increased from eight hundred just before the outbreak of the uprising to about four thousand as of early June 1948.[72] Moreover, Colonel Park Jin-gyeong, a new regiment commander on Jeju, suggested that the entire Jeju people could be excluded from the boundary of the universe of obligation. As he stated in his inauguration, "In order to suppress a riot, it is fine if 300,000 Jeju people are victimized."[73] Following Brown's direction, Colonel Park indeed executed an operation to search the whole area of mountain villages "from the west to the east" to identify local leftists.[74] The number of arrested alleged communists reached six thousand in a month. Most of the arrested were unarmed civilians, in particular young men.

Separating leftists from noncommunist residents proved difficult to the constabulary from the mainland. Both wore the same Jeju traditional work uniform, or *garot*, cotton clothes dyed with persimmon, and spoke the same dialect. The troops also noticed that those who were farmers by day could change into resisters by night.[75] This confusion, coupled with the extreme ideological polarization, expanded the boundary of the "they" to include large categories of young men, many of whom were not engaged with the insurgency. Witnesses reported that young men were often brutally beaten, arrested, tortured, and even executed on the spot without any reasons.[76] As a result, the proportion of young people in their twenties among the victims was 41 percent, and those in their late teens was 10.4 percent.[77]

However, at this stage, the constabulary acknowledged this problem of separating the insurgents and leftists from civilians and attempted to protect civilians until the coming winter. At the end of May, the constabulary announced a statement that the "majority of them [those arrested] were civilians who had been forced to cooperate with the rebels."[78] Meanwhile, the national newspapers appealed to the authorities to protect civilians.[79] *Yangminjeung*, or identification cards for good people, were issued as a result. The constabulary began to give these cards to people, including those arrested, who passed an examination of identity guarantee.[80] While these may have ostensibly been designed to protect noncombatants, they functioned as credentials of membership in the boundary of nationhood. Though at this point Jeju civilians narrowly belonged to the "we" category in the emerging national state, this status was tenuous at best.

THE WINTER MASSACRE AND THE ESTABLISHMENT OF THE ANTICOMMUNIST SOUTH KOREA

The Republic of Korea was founded on August 15, 1948, and Rhee Syng-man was elected its first president by a legislature that emerged from the May 10 election. The Rhee regime, however, rested on a very weak foundation from its inception. It lacked financial and human resources to properly operate a government, while the division of country presented it with a lack of legitimacy.[81] Soon after the regime took office, moreover, it was faced with a series of internal and external challenges to its authority, capability, and legitimacy. The Rhee regime, nevertheless, took advantage of the challenges to suppress political leftists and opponents and build a stronger anticommunist state.[82] A key result was the winter massacre on Jeju.

Concerning the external threats, the Rhee government had to deal with an imminent withdrawal of American troops. Under the Truman Doctrine and Marshall Plan, the U.S. Army in Korea started to withdraw in September

1948. The loss of the American military presence was potentially catastrophic as the Rhee government almost completely depended on U.S. support.[83] As such, it sought to postpone the withdrawal while asking for military drills and equipment to solidify the regime.[84] However, military and economic aid that had been promised by the United States proceeded slowly, and the U.S. Army decided to completely withdraw its troops by the end of that December. While the withdrawal was eventually postponed to June 29, 1949, this nevertheless presented the Rhee government with a crisis.[85]

No less daunting were the internal challenges presented to the regime as it was confronted with pressures from various oppositional forces who pushed for the punishment of collaborators and for land reform. The regime was based on an alliance between Japanese collaborators, landlords, and the colonial police, whom most Korean people regarded as national traitors since liberation. On September 1, 1948, the Antinational Activist Punishment Law was passed by the National Assembly to punish pro-Japanese groups, and subsequently the Special Committee for Investigating Antinational Activities was formed, threatening Rhee's political base.[86] In addition, most respected conservative leaders, such as Kim Gu and Kim Gyu-sik, still did not acknowledge the separate government and called for the United Nations to help unify the two Koreas.[87]

To make matters worse, the underground election for the foundation of communist government in the North put the regime in a more difficult situation. The central SKLP organized a secret election to elect 1,080 representatives of the South before the general election in the North for the founding of the state on August 25. According to a U.S. intelligence report, about 25 percent of the rural population might have voted, although many people redundantly voted under the pressure of the SKLP.[88] North Korea, officially the Democratic People's Republic of Korea, claimed that 77 percent of the population in the South and 85 percent of Jeju population participated in the general election.[89] Six representatives of Jeju, including Kim Dal-sam, the commander of the Armed Resistance Group, managed to leave the island and attended the staged general election in the North.[90]

Under these internal and external crises, Rhee utilized anticommunism to rally his political base while leveraging South Korea's place in the postwar global order to increase American support. While the United States planned to withdraw its troops in South Korea, it also attempted to build a bulwark against communism, largely due to Korea's symbolic position in the Cold War. According to Wright, "political success and the military viability of the southern state became critical tests for the credibility of the US as a global superpower."[91] Instead of maintaining a military presence, the United States adopted a strategy of empowering the South Korean army to reduce its economic burdens.[92] The gestation of this policy was in 1946 when the U.S.

occupation forces created the Korean Constabulary of about forty thousand soldiers. Following the establishment of the First Republic, the United States dispatched a military advisory group to train the Korean soldiers to be a formal army.[93] President Rhee and his fellow politicians appeared to understand the place of South Korea in the America's postwar global order.[94] In the midst of the winter massacre, Rhee spoke plainly at a cabinet meeting on January 21, 1949, that "although the United States recognized the importance of South Korea . . . they will increase aid only if we eradicate the aftermath of incidents in Jeju and South Jeolla Province. It is demanded to show the dignity of law by repressing extorters and insurgents harshly."[95] In other words, as Wright argues, the suppression campaigns on Jeju were "an integral element of Rhee's calculated statecraft of positioning himself as a reliable stalwart in the US' global struggle against communism."[96]

On October 11, 1948, the suppression campaign started. This was symbolized by changes in the administrative structure of the counterinsurgency campaign. The General Headquarters of the South Korean military established the Jeju Defense Headquarters, which replaced the Jeju Emergency Defense Headquarters that had been under the Jeju Police Inspection Agency. This replacement meant that the Rhee government no longer perceived the insurgency as a matter of public order but rather as a national security threat that had to be managed by the military. Technically, however, the commanding general of the U.S. Army retained the authority to exercise overall operational control of the Security Forces of South Korea until the U.S. Army withdrawal, in accordance with the Executive Agreement between South Korea and the U.S. Concerning Interim Military and Security Matters on August 24, 1948.[97]

The Jeju Defense Headquarters prepared for a full-fledged counterinsurgency operation to round up the insurgents. Central to this was a wave of increases of police, right youth, and soldiers from the mainland. The Rhee government had already sent roughly eight hundred police officers from Seoul to Jeju at the end of August, and again a large number of police officers were moved from the mainland to Jeju in early September.[98] For a swift operation, hundreds of police officers again arrived to strengthen the police power in February 1949 at the height of the massacre.[99] A large number from NWYA had also arrived on Jeju in early October.[100] Specifically, President Rhee himself sent more than one thousand members of the NWYA to work as police officers or soldiers in November and December 1948.[101] Through the regrouping of regiments, more soldiers also arrived on Jeju, while all of Jeju's native soldiers left to the mainland by December 29, 1948.[102] The huge influx of police, soldiers, and extreme anticommunists resulted in more civilians being excluded from the universe of moral obligation and increased polarization between the mainlanders and the islanders.

Beyond the specific ideological context, latent tensions between mainlanders and islanders fueled the conflict. Mainlanders had long perceived Jeju natives as rebellious and looked down on them, while islanders also had a tradition of autonomy. The old generation on Jeju who are now over eighty years old still call anyone from anyplace in the mainland "mainlander" or "son of a mainlander."[103] (The mainlanders usually identify themselves with their hometown or the place they currently live.) The polarization was reinforced by the islander's noticeable accent and clothes, which marked them as distinct. These geographic and cultural differences helped narrow the universe of moral obligation.

The all-out counterinsurgency operation started with the establishment of the free-fire zone, announced in a public notice on October 17, 1948. The commander of the Jeju Defense Headquarters, Song Yo-chan, declared in this notice: "The Army are going to purge impure elements that broke the peace of Jeju Island and threatened the residents to try to violate national sovereignty according to the supreme order of the government. . . . The Army imposes the quarantine on the area further inland than five kilometers from the coastline of Jeju Island. . . . Those who defy the quarantine . . . will be recognized as rioters and be shot to death."[104] Anybody in the free-fire zone could be excluded from the universe of obligation unless proven to be part of the "we." The measure was extreme, to say the least.

To make matters worse, the Yeosu-Suncheon (Yeosun) revolt by leftist soldiers broke out two days later on October 19. The revolt was a serious challenge of the legitimacy of the newborn state, leaving a major mark on the counterinsurgency operation on Jeju. The leftist soldiers stationed at Yeosu, which totaled about two thousand, refused to dispatch reinforcements to Jeju as ordered by Rhee and staged a revolt against their government. The aim of the revolt, according to them, was to obtain "the real independence of Korea" because the Rhee government under American control had partitioned the country.[105] The soldiers soon occupied Yeosu, the neighboring town of Suncheon, and the surrounding areas. The Rhee government brutally suppressed the revolt. On October 25, it declared martial law in the region and sent government forces to suppress the rebels. The forces targeted not only the soldiers but also the sympathizers and many of the civilians of Yeosu, while burning down houses in the region and indiscriminately firing mortars.[106] The revolt was defeated on October 27, two days after the declaration of martial law. The number of houses burned in the region as of December 1948 was 2,766, according to a report by the minister of social affairs,[107] and the number of casualties was 11,131, according to a November 1949 report by the South Jeolla Province authorities.[108]

After the suppression of the Yeosun revolt, the Rhee government carried out more aggressive and deadly policies to promptly eliminate leftists on Jeju in the name of national security. Perhaps most dramatically, President Rhee declared martial law in November on Jeju.[109] Commander Song and Jeju residents alike understood it as an exceptional law that permitted the troops to execute anyone without legal process.[110] The Rhee regime also passed a national security law against communism in December 1948 at the height of the massacre on Jeju, and anyone deemed a communist was considered an offender. Under the protection of the national laws, the state agents established a free-fire zone, forced the displacement of villagers, and carried out search-and-destroy missions to ferret out communist suspects.

These dramatic developments must be understood in the broader context of the relationship between violence and state building. Tilly argues that state agents and allies "regularly employ violence as they pursue their own ends," and they enjoy "legal rights—even legal obligations—to use violent means on behalf of governments."[111] He also argues that governmental sponsorship, such as law, strongly affects the character and intensity of collective violence in any regime.[112] Likewise, Herbert Kelman remarks that even an act of atrocity takes place "under explicit instructions from the authorities to engage in acts of torture, or in an environment in which such acts are implicitly sponsored, expected, or at least tolerated by the authorities."[113] The events on Jeju vividly confirm Tilly's and Kelman's judgements. After the enactment of martial law on Jeju, the residents were more obedient to the army, and the boundary of the "they" expanded further, in turn justifying horrific mass violence. Many survivors of the massacre attribute the indiscriminate killing and the brutality to the declaration of martial law.[114] The judgement of survivors is supported by brutal empirical facts: about 70 percent of the deaths of children and the elderly and the worst atrocities took place during this period from October 1948 to February 1949.

U.S. observers at the time confirmed an indiscriminate slaughter. According to a secret U.S. report, counterinsurgency forces killed everyone they rounded up without verification that they were actually insurgents.[115] The Ninth Regiment, stationed on the island at the time, executed "indiscriminate tactics" in November and December 1948, though "there was a period of relatively little rebel activity."[116] Moreover, the regiment launched "a new wave of guerrilla terrorism"[117] or "the severest repression operation"[118] over the course of the massacre in that December before its replacement because the troops had "the desire to set a high standard of observation and a good record of achievements for their successor."[119] U.S. observers also reported that the Second Regiment, which succeeded the Ninth, often "summarily executed large numbers" of the people of coastal villages "without benefit of trial" during January and February 1949.[120] In addition, the members of NWYA who had been dispatched to Jeju in December 1948 by order of President Rhee demonstrated their "violent anti-communism" over the winter.[121] As a result,

Jeju 4.3 was one of "the most brutal, sustained, and intensive counterinsurgency campaigns in postwar Asia," as Cumings notes.[122]

During the scorched-earth counterinsurgency operation, villagers who lived in mountainous areas were victimized the most often. In order to destroy shelters and supply routes, the military adopted strategies of mass displacement of the villagers. This was accomplished by setting houses on fire prior to giving an evacuation order.[123] However, in most cases, the order was not conveyed to all of the villagers. As a result, the villagers who did not flee frequently died of indiscriminate shooting by the suppression forces, starvation, or frostbite during the winter. Displaced persons who were fortunate enough to survive the initial onslaught were often forcibly detained in camps and deemed family members of the rebels, when in fact they were mostly hapless victims. Gasi, Sangcheon, Sinheung, and Taeheung were among the villages targeted by these strategies. Some 134 *dong* (a subdivision of a village), including around three thousand households, even disappeared from the map of Jeju, thus etching into Jeju's charred landscape the expanded boundary of exclusion.[124]

In the case of Gasi village, troops randomly shot thirty villagers, including children and the elderly, on the grounds of providing a base for the insurgents in November 1948.[125] A man and wife in their sixties hastily fled to a nearby cave with their two grandchildren, a three-year-old and a one-year-old. However, the troops threw a hand grenade at the cave when they heard a child's crying. A week later they ordered the villagers to evacuate to Pyoseon, a nearby seaside village, and detained them in the Pyoseon Elementary School. In the end of December, the forces gathered the detainees at the playground of the school and identified families with members who had disappeared. They then executed seventy-six villagers on the spot. The victims were mostly aged over sixty. According to one survivor, the soldiers only covered the dead bodies with soil, and it took a year before the victims' families and villagers could bury the bodies in the ground. A survivor identified the dead body of his father by his tobacco pipe.[126]

The forces even targeted detainees in the camp and refugees who had escaped from the armed conflicts. Around fifty local elites, working in law, education, media, public office, and private firms, were detained in the Jeju Agriculture School in the fall of 1948. The soldiers in the Ninth Regiment began to execute the detainees from October but massacred the majority of them to achieve a good record when the regiment was replaced with the Second Regiment at the end of 1948.[127] The military also killed refugees who had escaped to woods and caves in the mountains after their houses were reduced to ashes. For example, the forces killed about one hundred villagers in Yonggang who had escaped to the woods nearby in February 1949.[128] They killed some thirty-six residents of Eoeum and nearby villages in Billemot cave in January 1949.[129] According to one survivor, a policeman killed his cousin, who was only a seven-month-old baby, by flinging the baby onto the rocky ground.[130] Similar killings took place at Banmot cave in Seonheul and Darangshi cave in Sehwa at the end of 1948.

The forces further expanded the boundary of the national enemy by making lists of potential enemies that included family members of those who had disappeared, been shot, had fled the violence, or been named by residents who had been tortured. Survivors remember placement on the lists as tantamount to a death warrant.[131] The forces' search-and-destroy missions attempted to gain confessions from villagers and sometimes to trap them into cooperating with the rebels. For example, in December 1948, around 150 villagers in the northern county of Jocheon confessed that they had cooperated with the rebels after being promised by soldiers that it would save their lives. Instead, they were all murdered.[132] Soldiers also disguised themselves as rebels and asked villagers to collaborate with them. The disguised soldiers often forced villagers to cooperate—then shot anyone who did. The troops regarded anyone who was tricked as the enemy. In this sense, strategies of entrapment dovetailed the terroristic violence.[133]

Revenge likewise contributed to expanding the boundary of "the rioters" to include citizens. In Uigui village, the counterinsurgency troops captured and killed eighty residents wandering around the mountainous area after four of their comrades were killed by the insurgents in January 1949.[134] The worst case of revenge occurred on January 17, 1949, in Bukchon village, where over three hundred villagers were summarily executed. They were shot after two soldiers were attacked by the rebels, and only the family members of the police or the army living in the village were spared. Some one hundred members of the village who had been evacuated to a neighboring village were killed shortly afterward, indicating a methodological nature to these supposed acts of revenge.[135] The disproportionate revenge was also manifest in the villages of Sumang, Hanman, Namwon, and Wimi as unarmed civilians were massacred with impunity.[136]

The troops even went after members of the allied Civilian Guard (*minbodan*), which was established in August 1948 to support the police.[137] According to survivors, after attacks by insurgents, the troops would often brutally torture those members who had stood sentry at the villages, forcing them to confess to cooperation with the insurgents.[138] Some members of the Civilian Guard were tortured to death or executed as retaliation when the forces were killed. Furthermore, the forces often mobilized members of the Civilian Guard in their attacks on insurgents (including on residents of their own villages) but did not trust any Jeju resident unless they were sure of their allegiance. Almost everyone was seen as a communist and excluded from the universe of obligation—even if they were integrated into the counterinsurgency apparatus.

A typical act of retaliation by the counterinsurgency forces was the public execution of civilians, a policy that was utilized by the Joseon state but carried out on a mass scale by the emerging anticommunist government. In the villages of Moseulpo,[139] Oedo, and Hagui, government forces summoned all villagers to public sites and executed family members of those who had eluded the forces' forceful displacement from the mountain villages. They shouted, "Watch this!"[140] In Hagui village, police officers stripped two women in front of the villagers and impaled them with a spear until they died. One eyewitness recounted, "The policemen forced us to watch the killing. It would have been much easier to watch an execution by gun. I could not bear to look at the dreadful sight of an execution with a spear."[141] The purpose here was quite plainly to sow maximum terror, and the survivors called the public executions *gwangwang chongsal*, meaning "execution as sightseeing."[142]

Dehumanizing and sadistic violence was central to the enterprise. "They were not human beings!" survivors of the Jeju 4.3 often said about those offenders.[143] Members of the NWYA were particularly notorious for engaging in indiscriminate killing, torture, sexual violence, and other merciless acts against Jeju residents.[144] For example, the police chief of Samyang Police Station, a member of the NWYA who was dispatched in December 1948, thrust his gun into a pregnant woman's vagina after heating the gun in a stove in February 1949.[145] Another member of the association made female members of the Civilian Guard puncture the stomachs of their fellow villagers, including relatives, with a spear after being attacked by rebels in Jocheon.[146] The NWYA members in the Samyang Police Station were known to say, "I cannot help killing one or more a day. Otherwise, I lose my appetite."[147] However, placing the blame solely on the individuals obscures the range of perpetrators as the U.S. military government and the rightist factions supported and encouraged the members' violence throughout the ordeal.[148] Historian Monica Kim also argues that the members' "very brutal, very public acts of violence were integral to the anti-communist politics practiced and developed on the southern half of the Korean peninsula in the post 1945 era."[149] In this sense, these acts of sadism cannot be severed from the broader process of early Cold War state building.

Though a larger number of men were killed, many survivors recall that it was women who suffered some of the worst indignities. Indeed, women were subjected to unique forms of gendered violence, such as forced marriage, rape, gang rape, molestation, torture, and other types of violence. The police were so notorious for keeping sexual servants that there was even a saying: "If a widow is pretty, then she must be a second wife of the police."[150] (The Jeju villagers commonly used the term "second wife" in these cases, but they were actually sexual servants.) One villager reported that his sister became the seventh sexual servant of a policeman under death threat.[151] This practice of sexual slavery could often have the effect of destroying families as some women were forced to leave their husbands and children to be a sexual servant of a police officer.[152] Unmarried women, meanwhile, were particularly vulnerable and sometimes had to marry a police officer or soldier in order to save their families. When the women refused, "the soldiers arrested them and confined them as leftists. These women had no other choice than to follow the soldier's demands."[153] Unsurprisingly, members of the NWYA were notorious for this kind of violence. According to my interviewees, the members threatened to shoot the family members of their victims.[154] The members mostly craved teachers or daughters of wealthy families for their brides due to their social and economic stability. Beyond forced marriages, rape was also frequent. Tak Seong-nok, a military captain, was perhaps the most notorious serial rapist on the island. Tak raped and also forcibly made many women his sexual servants when he became bored or dissatisfied.[155] Tak was hardly the only sexual predator in the security forces. A police officer in Gimnyeong named Noh, for example, raped virtually any woman who lacked the protection of a man, such as unmarried women and widows.[156] These are two of the most notorious individuals, but the practice was widespread. Indeed, villagers in Gimnyeong and other villages testified that policemen and soldiers stationed in their village routinely called widows and "pretty unmarried women" into their residence to sexually abuse them.[157] These gender-specific forms of violence were more durable than the mass killings. In March 1949, the indiscriminate killing sharply declined when only 250 rebels remained and the military launched a program of amnesty for about twenty thousand refugees who had escaped in the mountains.[158] However, these oppressions against women continued until the outbreak of the Korean War in June 1950.

If the above descriptions of gendered violence reveal the traumas that Jeju's women endured throughout the suppression campaign, they also shed light on the character of early South Korean state building. Anthropologist Seong-nae Kim, a pioneer of Jeju 4.3 and gender studies, interpretated state violence against Jeju women as a representation of the "bodies of the reds."[159] The "body of the red," according to her, is the place where "the fear of communism and desire for conquering it can be 'felt and seen' and becomes, therefore, a part of the spectacle of performance in the violent politics of anticommunism."[160] Elaborating on Kim's argument, Jieun Chang addresses that the mass rapes on Jeju were not a sexual assault but "a state tactic to marginalize and alienate, by sexual means, the entire Jeju citizens."[161] As Chang remarks, Jeju's people were located "outside the protection of law and outside the boundary of the civil/national community,"[162] and abuses against them were justifying by any means. In this sense, early state building in South

Korea was an embodied and gendered phenomenon—catastrophically waged on the violated bodies of Jeju's women.

THE ISLAND OF REDS AND THE
GUILTY IN KOREAN SOCIETY

In the last chapter, I argued that the violence of the South Korean state-building process was augmented by the communal structure of Jeju, which in turn impacted the relationship between islanders and the nascent anticommunist state. At the height of the violence in 1948–1949, this played out in horrific ways as the strong solidarity networks of marriage, communal work, kinship, and social gatherings meant that virtually any member of a village was personally connected with the insurgents in some form or another. This tight network interacted with the Korean tradition of guilty by association (*yeonjwaje*) and resulted in escalating the violence in the politically volatile context.

Since the Jeju 4.3 events, anticommunist Koreans in the South have used the term *ppalgaengi*, "commies" or "the reds," to refer to communists, who they believe merit punishment. The rightists first used the term in September 1945 to belittle the extreme leftists.[163] By the election on May 10, 1948, supporters of Rhee Syng-man, many of whom were former pro-Japanese collaborators, were using the term to tarnish their political opponents and paper over their own dubious history.[164]

However, prior to the use of the term "commie" or "the reds" becoming ubiquitous in South Korea, nomenclatures such as "the rioters" and "the guilty" had similar cultural meanings in Korean society. During the Jeju massacre, the term "the guilty" was often used in distinguishing those outside the universe of moral obligation. Both the counterinsurgency troops and Jeju residents used it rather than "rioters," "leftists," or "the reds." The term was so widely accepted that even today survivors ask the question, "Why did they kill those who were not guilty?" indicating that they have internalized the term and its implied moral judgement.[165]

This phenomenon has a historical pedigree. Historically, in Korean political culture, the concept of guilt was applied to those trying to overthrow the regime or the state. During the Joseon Dynasty, which profoundly influenced Korean political and social culture as it lasted for five hundred years, being guilty of attempting to overthrow the regime was the worst crime imaginable. Thus, the guilty had to be banished from society or eliminated. The application of this form of guilt was deeply hierarchical as the state had the power to decide the standard for guilt and the appropriate level of punishment, while the severity and scope of punishment were a demonstration of the regime's power and supremacy. Therefore, to punish the guilty was considered an act of loyalty to the regime.

Moreover, the guilty included not only people accused of a crime against the state but their family members, who were guilty by association and were potentially subject to the same punishment. If someone was judged guilty of subverting the dynasty, the family lines of their father, mother, and spouse were to be executed to eliminate any offspring. This extreme form of punishment usually occurred when a new regime overthrew the ruling party; it was a demonstration of its legitimacy and power.[166] The law of guilt by association (*yeonjwaje*) was abolished in 1894 at the end of the Joseon Dynasty but was revived under Japanese colonial rule, and it was officially practiced by authoritarian Korean governments until South Korea's democratic transition in 1987.[167]

Consequently, the tradition of applying the term "the guilty" to those who engage in violence against the state was deeply ingrained by the time of the Jeju 4.3 uprisings. In the context of politicized violence, this had horrendous consequences. One former policeman stated that "everybody was guilty and could be killed at any time," referring to the population of Jeju.[168] In this cultural and political matrix, violence necessarily expanded exponentially as the number of "the guilty" naturally increased, and punishment of them was legitimized. The definition of guilt used by the counterinsurgency troops was ambiguous, to say the least, but the punishment was not.[169]

Family members of the guilty were the first group after the rebels to be excluded from the in group. Family members of the insurgents, fugitives, and the executed were primarily tortured or killed, in line with the established culture of punishment. If men were absent, women were often victimized in their place.[170] According to survivors, the third cousin in the family lines of the father, mother, and spouse of the rebels was widely known as the cut-off point of guilty family members.[171] However, the boundaries were porous enough to theoretically include any relative. For example, one member of the army declared that all relatives of the guilty, no matter how distant, should be executed.[172] The above-discussed January 17, 1949, massacre in Bukchon village was the most vivid example of this. According to a survivor's testimony, soldiers ordered immediate family members all the way to the third cousin in the family lines of both parents of the rebels to assemble and executed them as revenge for their comrades' deaths.[173] The killings did not pose a moral dilemma to the troops partly because they had internalized a tradition of violence and punishment through their culture.

These intimate and indiscriminate massacres represent the most extreme violence and cruelty of the state-building project on Jeju Island. The local communists under the Jeju SKLP protested the creation of South Korea. In response, the newborn state and its American supporters thoroughly retaliated against their challengers to secure their ideological legitimacy and build a stronger state. Under the government's explicit support, its agents expanded the boundary of the national enemy into ordinary civilians at the local level, resulting in about 10 percent of Jeju's population being killed and countless more traumatized and displaced. In the wake of this catastrophic violence, the remaining survivors' place in the new political order was tenuous.

NOTES

1. According to a U.S. Embassy document and the *New York Times* in 1949, the death toll was fifteen thousand. However, *Jeju Sinbo*, a local newspaper, estimated in 1960 that the death toll was actually sixty-five thousand. The South Korean government reported in September 1949 that 29,702 had died, while the North Korean government said in January 1950 that more than thirty thousand had been killed. See Jeju 4.3 National Committee, *Jeju April Third Incident Investigation Report*, 451–53; Bruce Cumings, "American Responsibility," 205.

2. Jeju 4.3 National Committee, *Jeju April Third Incident Investigation Report*, 454.

3. Ibid., 455.

4. Jeju 4.3 Peace Foundation, *Jeju 4.3 sageon*, 633.

5. Ibid., 68–71.

6. Ibid., 66–71. Among the victims identified by the committee, 71.9 percent had been killed, 25.0 percent had disappeared, 1.1 percent had been disabled, and 1.9 percent had been imprisoned. The Jeju 4.3 Special Act of 2000 defined victims of Jeju 4.3 as those who died, disappeared, or were permanently injured as a result of the events. In a revised act in 2007, political prisoners of Jeju 4.3 were also included.

7. Ibid., 88.

8. Ibid.

9. Jeju 4.3 Peace Foundation, *Jeju 4.3 sageon*, 85. This figure is estimated after excluding the deaths (3.3 percent) who were either killed by unidentified persons or died from disease or starvation.

10. Ibid., 89.

11. Park, *4.3gwa Jeju yeoksa*, 297–308.

12. Myung-lim Park, "Minjujuui, iseong, geurigo yeoksa yeongu: Jeju 4.3gwa hanguk hyeondaesa" [Democracy, Reason, and a Study of History: Jeju 4.3 and Modern History of Korea], in *Jeju 4.3 yeongu* [A Study on Jeju 4.3], ed. Jeju 4.3 Research Institute (Seoul: Yeoksa Bipyeongsa, 1999), 444–48; Choi, *Jenosaideu*, 377–89; Seong-nae Kim, "Sexual Politics of State Violence: On the Cheju April Third Massacre of 1948," in *Traces 2: Race Panic and the Memory of Migration*, ed. Meagan Morris and Brett de Bary (Hong Kong: Hong Kong University Press, 2001), 259–91; Gwon, "Daeryanghaksarui sahoesimni," 177–85; Wright, "Civil War, Politicide, and the Politics of Memory."

13. Wright, "Civil War, Politicide, and the Politics of Memory," 35.

14. Jeju 4.3 National Committee, *Jeju April Third Incident Investigation Report*, 126.

15. Merrill, "Cheju-do Rebellion," 196.

16. Jeju 4.3 National Committee, *Jeju April Third Incident Investigation Report*, 127.

17. Ibid., 130.

18. Ibid., 118–19.

19. Kim, "Land Reform," 117.

20. Jeju 4.3 National Committee, *Jeju April Third Incident Investigation Report*, 136.

21. Ibid., 142.

22. Hwang, *Korea's Grievous War*, 34.

23. Jeju 4.3 National Committee, *Jeju April Third Incident Investigation Report*, 148.

24. Ibid., 149–50.

25. Ibid., 150.

26. "Report of Special Investigation—Governor Ryu, Hai Chin of Cheju-do Island," March 11, 1948, Report of Special Investigation by Lt. Col. Lawrence A. Nelson, United States Army Military Government in Korea, in Jeju 4.3 National Committee, ed., *Jeju 4.3 sageon jaryojip 9: Miguk jaryo pyeon 3* [Jeju 4.3 Incident Sourcebook, vol. 9: U.S. Documents, vol. 3] (Seoul: Geumseong Munhwasa, 2003), 330.

27. Jeju 4.3 National Committee, *Jeju April Third Incident Investigation Report*, 154–55; interviews with Ko Chang-seon and Bae Gwang-si, residents in Hagui village, on June 28, 2020, on Jeju.

28. Ibid., 186–88.

29. Ibid., 180–81.

30. Monica Kim, *The Interrogation Rooms of the Korean War: The Untold History* (Princeton, NJ: Princeton University Press, 2019), 56, 222–31.

31. Jeju 4.3 National Committee, *Jeju April Third Incident Investigation Report*, 176–78.

32. Ibid., 143.

33. Kim, *Interrogation Rooms of the Korean War*, 222–31.

34. Headquarters of United States Army Forces in Korea (hereafter, Hq. USAFIK), *G-2 Periodic Report*, no. 693, November 25, 1947, in Jeju 4.3 National Committee, ed., *Jeju 4.3 sageon jaryojip 7: Miguk jaryo pyeon 1* [Jeju 4.3 Incident Sourcebook, vol. 7: U.S. Documents, vol. 1] (Seoul: Geumseong Munhwasa, 2003), 291.

35. Kim, *Interrogation Rooms of the Korean War*, 236.

36. Kim Ik-ryeol left behind memoirs. Ik-ryeol Kim, "4.3ui jinsil" [The Truth of Jeju 4.3], in *4.3eun malhanda 2* [4.3 Speaks, vol. 2], ed. Jemin Ilbo 4.3 Reporting Team (Seoul: Jeonyaewon, 1994), 286–87.

37. Jeju 4.3 Research Institute, *Eotteoke hyeongsaga geomsareul*, 84; Seong-chan Oh, ed., *Hallaui tonggoksori: Jeju daehaksarui jeungeon* [The Wailing of Halla: Testimonies about the Jeju Massacre] (Seoul: Sonamu, 1988), 106; interview with Bu Chang-ok on April 12, 2012, on Jeju.

38. Jeju 4.3 National Committee, *Jeju April Third Incident Investigation Report*, 206–7.

39. Kim, *Massacres at Mt. Halla*, 26.

40. Merrill, "Cheju-do Rebellion," 155–56.

41. Hope May, "The United States, the United Nations and the Jeju April 3rd Incident: A Story of Responsibility," in *The Jeju 4.3 Mass Killing: Atrocity, Justice,*

and Reconciliation, ed. Jeju 4.3 Peace Foundation (Seoul: Yonsei University Press, 2018), 37–42.

42. Two policemen were missing. Jeju 4.3 National Committee, *Jeju April Third Incident Investigation Report*, 219.

43. Jemin Ilbo 4.3 Reporting Team, *4.3eun malhanda 2*, 103–4.

44. Jeju 4.3 National Committee, *Jeju April Third Incident Investigation Report*, 206–7.

45. Ibid., 114–15, 231–35.

46. Jeju 4.3 National Committee, *Jeju April Third Incident Investigation Report*, 203; Hwang, *Korea's Grievous War*, 39.

47. Hwang, *Korea's Grievous War*, 38–39.

48. Merrill, "Cheju-do Rebellion," 167.

49. Jeju 4.3 National Committee, *Jeju April Third Incident Investigation Report*, 212.

50. Jeju 4.3 Research Institute, *Ijesa malhamsuda 1*, 88.

51. Ibid., 87, 91; Jeju 4.3 Research Institute, ed., *Ijesa malhaemsuda 2* [Now We Speak Out, vol. 2] (Seoul: Hanul, 1989), 220.

52. Jeju 4.3 Research Institute, *Ijesa malhamsuda 1*, 105.

53. Gyeong-in Yang, *Seonchangeun eonjena naui moksieotda: Yeoseonghaebangui kkumeul kkun Jeju 4.3 yeoseong undonggaui saengae* [I Always Led the Others When Singing in a Team: The Life of a Jeju 4.3 Female Activist Who Dreamed of Women's Liberation] (Seoul: Eunhaengnamu, 2022), 58.

54. Jeju 4.3 Research Institute, *Ijesa malhamsuda 1*, 105.

55. Ibid., 44.

56. Ibid., 88.

57. *Seoul Sinmun*, April 7, 1948.

58. Dae-sik Lim, "Jeju 4.3 hangjaenggwa u-ik cheongyeondan" [The Jeju 4.3 Uprising and the Rightist Youth Association], in *Jeju 4.3 yeongu* [A Study on Jeju 4.3], ed. Jeju 4.3 Research Institute (Seoul: Yeoksa Bipyeongsa, 1999), 232–33.

59. Jemin Ilbo 4.3 Reporting Team, *4.3eun malhanda 4* [4.3 Speaks, vol. 4] (Seoul: Jeonyaewon, 1997), 147–48.

60. For more details about the peace negotiation, see Kim, "4.3ui jinsil," 273–357.

61. Jemin Ilbo 4.3 Reporting Team, *4.3eun malhanda 2*, 61–62.

62. Ibid., 61.

63. Ibid., 64.

64. Helen Fein, *Imperial Crime and Punishment* (Honolulu: University of Hawaii Press, 1977), 7.

65. Ibid.

66. William Gamson, "Hiroshima, the Holocaust, and the Politics of Exclusion," *American Sociological Review* 60 (1995): 3–4.

67. Jeju 4.3 Research Institute, *Ijesa malhamsuda 1*, 118–19; Yang, "Jeju 4.3, Memories of Massacre and Times of Uprising," 163.

68. Jemin Ilbo 4.3 Reporting Team, *4.3eun malhanda 2*, 217–20.

69. Jeju 4.3 National Committee, *Jeju April Third Incident Investigation Report*, 271.

70. Cumings, "American Responsibility," 205; Ho-joon Heo, "Jeju 4.3e isseoseoui minganin haksal nolli" [Logics of Civilian Massacre Perpetrated during Jeju 4.3], *4.3gwa Yeoksa* [4.3 and History] 8 (2008): 127.

71. Jeju 4.3 National Committee, *Jeju April Third Incident Investigation Report*, 279.

72. Jemin Ilbo 4.3 Reporting Team, *4.3eun malhanda 3* [4.3 Speaks, vol. 3] (Seoul: Jeonyaewon, 1995), 147.

73. Ibid., 275–76.

74. *Hyeondae Ilbo*, June 3, 1948.

75. Jeju 4.3 Research Institute, ed., *Jeju 4.3 jaryojip II: Migukmuseong jejudo gwangye munseo* [Jeju 4.3 Sourcebook II: The U.S. State Department Documents Related to Jeju Island] (Jeju: Gak, 2001), 109.

76. Jemin Ilbo 4.3 Reporting Team, *4.3eun malhanda 3*, 35, 78.

77. Jeju 4.3 Peace Foundation, *Jeju 4.3 sageon*, 88.

78. *Donga Ilbo*, June 5, 1948.

79. *Chosun Ilbo*, June 5, 1948; *Chosunjoongang Ilbo*, June 6, 1948; *Seoul Sinmun*, June 11 and June 12, 1948.

80. *Chosun Ilbo*, June 4, 1948; Jemin Ilbo 4.3 Reporting Team, *4.3eun malhanda 3*, 142–45.

81. Choong Nam Kim, "State and Nation Building in South Korea: A Comparative Historical Perspective," *Review of Korean Studies* 12, no. 1 (2009): 137.

82. Wright, "Civil War, Politicide, and the Politics of Memory," 67.

83. Kim, "State and Nation Building in South Korea," 139.

84. Jeju 4.3 National Committee, *Jeju April Third Incident Investigation Report*, 308–9.

85. Ibid., 309.

86. Ibid., 307.

87. Ibid., 308.

88. Merrill, "Cheju-do Rebellion," 177.

89. Ibid.

90. Kim, *Massacres at Mt. Halla*, 34.

91. Wright, "Civil War, Politicide, and the Politics of Memory," 68.

92. Ibid., 68–69.

93. Brazinsky, *Nation Building in South Korea*, 24.

94. Wright, "Civil War, Politicide, and the Politics of Memory," 69.

95. Jeju 4.3 National Committee, *Jeju April Third Incident Investigation Report*, 361. As Rhee expected, the United States increased military and economic aid to South Korea in March 1949. As communist insurgency exploded in Jeju and Yeosu in South Jeolla Province, Americans debated the South Korean government's capacity for maintaining national security. As a result, in March 1949, the Truman administration adopted National Security Council 8/2 to enhance the South Korean security forces. The United States spent fifty-six million dollars to implement a national security program in South Korea by June 1949. According to Brazinsky, the U.S. funding was ultimately used in wiping out the insurgents who remained in Jeju and South Jeolla. For more details, see Brazinsky, *Nation Building in South Korea*, 24.

96. Wright, "Civil War, Politicide, and the Politics of Memory," 69.

97. Jeju 4.3 National Committee, *Jeju April Third Incident Investigation Report*, 314–20.

98. Ibid., 327–28.

99. Ibid., 385.

100. Ibid., 327–30.

101. Ibid., 336.

102. Ibid., 379–82.

103. For more details, see Chul-in Yoo, *Munhwaillyuhakjaui jagi minjokji: Jejudo* [An Autoethnography Written by a Cultural Anthropologist: Jeju Island] (Seoul: Minsokwon, 2021), 19–23.

104. *Chosun Ilbo*, October 20, 1948.

105. George Katsiaficas, *Asia's Unknown Uprisings Volume 1: South Korean Movements in the 20th Century* (Oakland: PM Press, 2012), 98–99.

106. Ibid., 101–3; Mu-yong Kim, "Yeosu-Suncheon sageon jinabeul wihan daehang guerilla jakjeongwa minganin huisaenghwa jeollyak" [Counterguerilla Operations and Civilian Victimization Strategies during the Suppression of the Yeosu-Suncheon Incident], *Yeoksa Yeongu* [Journal of History] 31 (2016): 268–70.

107. Kim, "Yeosu-Suncheon sageon," 274.

108. Yeong-il Lee, "Yeo-Sun sageon jinsanggyumyeongwiwonhoeui siljewa gwaje" [The Reality and Challenge of Commission for the Investigation of the Truth of the Yeosu-Suncheon Incident], paper presented at the Symposium to Celebrate the 68th Anniversary of the Yeosu-Suncheon Incident, Yeosu, October 21, 2016.

109. The declaration of martial law was authorized by Brigadier General Roberts, the chief of the Provisional Military Advisory Group in South Korea. For more details, see Jong-min Kim, "Early Cold War Genocide: The Jeju 4.3 Massacre and U.S. Responsibility," *Korea Policy Institute*, April 4, 2020, https://www.kpolicy.org/post/early-cold-war-genocide-the-jeju-4-3-massacre-and-u-s-responsibility).

110. Jeju 4.3 National Committee, *Jeju April Third Incident Investigation Report*, 352–53.

111. Charles Tilly, *The Politics of Collective Violence* (Cambridge: Cambridge University Press, 2003), 19.

112. Ibid., 19–20.

113. Herbert Kelman, "The Policy Context of Torture: A Social-Psychological Analysis," *International Review of the Red Cross* 87 (2005): 125–26.

114. Jeju 4.3 National Committee, *Jeju April Third Incident Investigation Report*, 347–48.

115. Hq. USAFIK, *G-2 Periodic Report*, No. 1097, April 1, 1949, in Jeju 4.3 National Committee, *Jeju 4.3 sageon jaryojip 7*, 361–62.

116. Ibid., 362.

117. Ibid.

118. Jeju 4.3 National Committee, *Jeju April Third Incident Investigation Report*, 382.

119. Hq. USAFIK, *G-2 Periodic Report*, No. 1015, December 17, 1948, in Jeju 4.3 National Committee, *Jeju 4.3 sageon jaryojip 7*, 344–45.

120. Hq. USAFIK, *G-2 Periodic Report*, No. 1097, April 1, 1949, in Jeju 4.3 National Committee, *Jeju 4.3 sageon jaryojip 7*, 362.

121. Ibid., No. 1005, December 6, 1948, 342; Jeju 4.3 National Committee, *Jeju April Third Incident Investigation Report*, 383–85.

122. Cumings, *Liberation and the Emergence of Separate Regimes*, 349.

123. Jemin Ilbo 4.3 Reporting Team, *4.3eun malhanda 5* [4.3 Speaks, vol. 5] (Seoul: Jeonyaewon, 1998), 243–49.

124. Jeju 4.3 Peace Foundation, *Jeju 4.3 sageon*, 123–31.

125. Jeju 4.3 National Committee, *Jeju April Third Incident Investigation Report*, 490–92.

126. Ibid., 492.

127. Ibid., 474.

128. Ibid., 496–99.

129. Ibid., 499–501.

130. Jeju 4.3 Research Institute, ed., *Billemotgul, geu kkeuteomneun eodum sogeseo* [Billemot Cave, in That Never-Ending Darkness] (Seoul: Hanul Academy, 2013), 40.

131. Jemin Ilbo 4.3 Reporting Team, *4.3eun malhanda 5*, 158–59, 210–11, 236–37.

132. Jeju 4.3 National Committee, *Jeju April Third Incident Investigation Report*, 375.

133. *Jemin Ilbo*, May 21, 1999.

134. Jeju 4.3 National Committee, *Jeju April Third Incident Investigation Report*, 392–93.

135. Ibid., 393.

136. Jemin Ilbo 4.3 Reporting Team, *4.3eun malhanda 5*, 131.

137. Jeju 4.3 National Committee, *Jeju April Third Incident Investigation Report*, 343–47.

138. Ibid., 285–87.

139. Jeju people have commonly called the two southwest villages of Hamo and Sangmo, Moseulpo.

140. Jeju 4.3 National Committee, *Jeju April Third Incident Investigation Report*, 374–75; Jeju 4.3 Research Institute, *Billemotgul*, 131.

141. Jeju 4.3 Research Institute, *Billemotgul*, 176–77.

142. Jemin Ilbo 4.3 Reporting Team, *4.3eun malhanda 5*, 322.

143. Jemin Ilbo 4.3 Reporting Team, *4.3eun malhanda 3*, 83; Jemin Ilbo 4.3 Reporting Team, *4.3eun malhanda 4*, 394–95; Jeju 4.3 Research Institute, ed., *Garib-angeuro gieokhaneun yeoldu sal sonyeoneui 4.3* [A Twelve-Year-Old Boy's Memory of Jeju 4.3 Left in Mimeograph] (Seoul: Hanul Academy, 2015), 178–82.

144. Jeju 4.3 National Committee, *Jeju April Third Incident Investigation Report*, 383–85.

145. Ibid., 511.

146. Jeju 4.3 Peace Foundation and Jeju 4.3 Research Institute, ed., *Saneseodo museopgo araeseodo museopgo geunyang sallyeogoman* [We Just Tried to Survive, Scared of Both Guerillas in the Mountain and Counterinsurgents Sent by the Government] (Jeju: Hangeuru, 2011), 261–63.

147. Jeju 4.3 National Committee, *Jeju April Third Incident Investigation Report*, 510–11.

148. Bong-jin Kim, "Paramilitary Politics under the USAMGIK and the Establishment of the Republic of Korea," *Korea Journal* 43, no. 2 (2003): 310–13.

149. Kim, *Interrogation Rooms of the Korean War*, 231.

150. Jeju 4.3 Peace Foundation and Jeju 4.3 Research Institute, *Saneseodo museopgo araeseodo museopgo*, 286.

151. Jeju 4.3 Research Institute, *Eotteoke hyeongsaga geomsareul*, 69.

152. Jeju 4.3 Peace Foundation and Jeju 4.3 Research Institute, *Jigeumkkaji sarajin geosi yongheongeora*, 102.

153. Interview with Lee Yeon-hwa, a female veteran of the Korean Marine Corps, on September 16, 2012, in Incheon.

154. Interview with Ko San-seok, a local female elite during the 1950s and the 1960s, on February 7, 2013, on Jeju; interview with Kim Jin-hyeon, another local female elite during the period, on March 30, 2013, on Jeju; interview with Kang Il-hwa, a former elementary school teacher, on April 18, 2012, on Jeju.

155. Jeju 4.3 National Committee, *Jeju April Third Incident Investigation Report*, 475.

156. Jeju 4.3 Peace Foundation and Jeju 4.3 Research Institute, *Saneseodo museopgo araeseodo museopgo*, 24.

157. Jeju 4.3 Research Institute, ed., *4.3gwa yeoseong: Geu saranaen naldeurui girok* [Jeju 4.3 and Women: A Record of the Hard Days They Went Through] (Jeju: Gak, 2019), 243; Jeju 4.3 Peace Foundation and Jeju 4.3 Research Institute, *Saneseodo museopgo araeseodo museopgo*, 232–35.

158. Jeju 4.3 National Committee, *Jeju April Third Incident Investigation Report*, 401–8.

159. Kim, "Sexual Politics of State Violence," 273.

160. Ibid., 271.

161. Jieun Chang, "National Narrative, Traumatic Memory, and Testimony: Reading Traces of the Cheju April Third Incident, South Korea, 1948" (PhD diss., New York University, 2009), 1997.

162. Ibid., 185.

163. Seong-hyeon Kang, "'Aka'-wa 'ppalganengi'ui tansaeng: Jeok mandeulgiwa bigungminui gyebohak" [The Birth of "Aka" (meaning Reds in Japanese) and "Ppalgaengi" (the Reds): The Making of the Enemy and the Genealogy of Those Unqualified as Good Citizens], *Sahoewa Yeoksa* [Society and History] 100 (2013): 255.

164. Ibid., 256.

165. Jemin Ilbo 4.3 Reporting Team, *4.3eun malhanda 4*, 420; Jemin Ilbo 4.3 Reporting Team, *4.3eun malhanda 5*, 145; Jeju 4.3 Peace Foundation and Jeju 4.3 Research Institute, ed., *Galchiga galchi kkollaeng-i kkeuneomeogeotda hal subakke* [A Cutlassfish Eats Up the Other Cutlassfish's Tail] (Jeju: Hangeuru, 2010), 140.

166. Yeong-beoum Kim, "Yeonjwajeui yeoksajeok jeongaewa geu uimimang: Joseon sidaereul jungsimeuro" [The Historical Process of the Guilt-by-Association System and Its Semantic Network in the Joseon Dynasty], in *Sahoesa yeonguui*

irongwa silje [Theory and Practice in Social History Studies], ed. Korean Social History Research Group (Seoul: Munji Publishing, 1990), 324–47.

167. Jae-woo Sim, "Joseon sidae yeonjwajeui silsang" [The Reality of the System of Guilt by Association in the Joseon Dynasty], *Hanguk Munhwa* [Korean Culture] 55 (2011): 87–112; Kim, *Massacres at Mt. Halla*, 90. In fact, the 1980 Constitution of the Republic of Korea had abolished the system. This institutional practice, however, essentially persisted until the democratic transition in 1987. In accordance with the democratic force's demand, the 1987 Constitution included the same article on the abolition of this practice as was in the 1980 Constitution.

168. Jeju 4.3 Documentary Production, *Yueon* [Will], dir. Dong-man Kim, 1999.

169. Dong Choon Kim, *Jeonjaenggwa sahoe* [War and Society] (Seoul: Dolbegae, 2000), 78.

170. For more details, see Brendan Wright, "Kinship Killings, Taesal and Biologized State Violence during the Korean Civil War," *Journal of Genocide Research* (October 2021): 1–15.

171. Jeju 4.3 Peace Foundation and Jeju 4.3 Research Institute, *Saneseodo museopgo araeseodo*, 245; Center for Supporting Those Related to the Jeju April 3 Incident and Jeju 4.3 Research Institute, eds., *Jaeiljejuin 4.3 jeungeon chaerokjip* [A Collection of Testimonies of Jeju 4.3 from Jeju Natives in Japan] (Jeju: Center for Supporting Those Related to the Jeju April 3 Incident and Jeju 4.3 Research Institute, 2003), 26–27.

172. Jemin Ilbo 4.3 Reporting Team, *4.3eun malhanda 5*, 207.

173. Jeju 4.3 Peace Foundation and Jeju 4.3 Research Institute, *Saneseodo museopgo areseodo museopgo*, 244–45.

Chapter 3

Reintegration 1: The South Korean State and the Korean War

Concurrently with the mass killings on Jeju, the newly established the Republic of Korea devoted its efforts to constructing its own imagined national community. In the ideological arena, the Rhee government advocated the state doctrine of the "One People Principle" (*Ilminjuui*), which sought to forge a coherent national identity and instill ideological cohesion among South Korea's citizens. To facilitate this endeavor, the government utilized law, media, and various other tools within the state apparatus. In particular, it established national mass organizations to regulate, educate, discipline, or convert its population. This chapter examines how the Republic of Korea utilized these methods and institutions to assimilate Jeju Islanders into the national community in the wake of the winter massacre. Specifically, it examines the process of military recruitment for achieving these ends.

From the war's inception, troop shortages plagued South Korea's military, and over the course of the war, the Rhee government devised a series of laws that evolved into a system of conscription. When the Korean War started on June 25, 1950, with the sudden and full-scale attack by the North Korean military, South Korea was not able to mobilize people under its existing national Military Service Law of August 6, 1949. Because quotas had been reached, the law was not technically in effect.[1] Therefore, the South Korean government declared a state of emergency across the country, with the exception of the South Jeolla Province, on July 8, 1950, and issued the Special Act for the draft by presidential emergency order on July 26, 1950.[2] After the Incheon Landing in the middle of September 1950, the South Korean government gradually developed a drafting system through major acts of law: the Act on the Establishment of National Defense Army on December 21, 1950; the revision of the Military Service Law on May 25, 1951; and the creation of a conscription system on August 25, 1951.[3] Throughout the three years of fighting, the war against North Korea was an enormous challenge for South

Korea, with great human losses. Indeed, only a week after the war began, nearly half of the ninety-eight thousand South Korean soldiers were killed, captured, injured, or missing.[4] The Ministry of Defense therefore needed to quickly recruit as many people as it could. Existing mass organizations, especially youth organizations, played a key role in achieving this.

Since the end of 1948, the Rhee Syng-man government had established numerous organizations for surveillance and control that the Ministry of Defense used to recruit new soldiers while surveilling potential internal enemies. In the initial phase of the war, one of these groups, the National Student Corps, became the fastest organizer of the volunteer army. For example, about seven hundred students formed the Student Volunteer Army in Daejeon in South Chungcheong province by July 4, 1950. The members of the Daehan Youth Association, a right-wing organization established in December 1948, were likewise influential. They primarily helped maintain public order, but President Rhee also ordered the association to organize the defense corps for every region in South Korea and to collect information about potential internal enemies.[5]

In these chaotic weeks, the Ministry of Defense, through the regular police and military police, forcibly drafted any young men on the street or in refugee camps.[6] The drafting was usually done with a simple evaluation: if a man was tall enough to carry a rifle on his shoulder, he was recruited. To help keep numbers high, the Special Act for the Draft mandated one recruit per one hundred households. However, recruitment became arduous when by the end of July 1950 the North Korean military occupied the whole of South Korea except for Jeju and a part of Gyeongsang Province on the southeast mainland. Faced with these shortages, in early August, President Rhee established the Female Volunteer Army to make up for the shortage of troops.[7] According to a statement released by Kim Hyeon-suk, who took charge of organizing and training the female army, the Female Volunteer Army was designed to support the military in the areas of administration, nursing, and communication. A highly gendered and patriotic pitch was made for recruits, as women were presented as taking the place of "cowardly men who tried to evade recruitment."[8] The army authorities succeeded in recruiting five hundred women in that part of Gyeongsang Province, and Shin Seong-mo, the minister of defense, hosted the enlistment ceremony for the first group of the female army on September 4.[9] The government continued mobilizing women throughout the war, and the total number of female soldiers, including volunteer armies, marines, fliers, nurse officers, and student volunteers, was estimated to be 2,400 over the course of the war.[10]

For the South Korean marines, Jeju was the most advantageous region remaining for the recruitment of young people, including women, because marines had been stationed there since December 1949. Unlike other regions, on Jeju there was no need for random, coercive drafting in the streets. When the authorities began to recruit soldiers with public notices in the middle of July, about three thousand young men who were primarily members of the Daehan Youth Association and middle school students rushed to join the marines.[11] A total of 126 women, schoolteachers, middle school students, and other young women also joined the marines. The South Korean army soon began to recruit on Jeju, and about ten thousand men, all of whom were aged between sixteen and twenty-eight, joined the army by October 1950.[12] The motivations for joining were complex as always, but they were primarily driven by a desire to escape the horrific violence of the Jeju massacre and motivated by a new national identity promoted by President Rhee. In other words, both coercive and constructive aspects of the state-building process influenced their decision to join.

NATIONAL IDENTITY FORMATION

As previously intimated, when the Korean War started, the ideology of anti-communism was already well established on Jeju Island. It was imprinted on people as equivalent to life itself, particularly after the intense armed conflicts between October 1948 and February 1949. Jeju people were haunted by the fear of being killed by the counterinsurgency forces, who decided who was or was not a communist and, therefore, who lived and who died. Anybody could be killed, including sympathizers, relatives, and neighbors of the insurgents. The declaration of martial law on Jeju by President Rhee in November 1948 dramatically heightened their fears. Jeju residents correctly understood martial law to provide legal justification for the execution of communists or suspected communist without a trial, and indeed summary killing increased considerably after the enactment of the law.

At the national level, codification of anticommunism into state law culminated with the National Security Act in December 1948, which specified that anyone who participated in left-wing organizations or supported these organizations was a threat to South Korea's national security.[13] For example, it was made illegal to "praise, encourage, disseminate or cooperate" with any antistate group or "create or spread false information which may disturb national order."[14] As a result, the police arbitrarily interpreted violations of the law so loosely that the number of people found in violation reached an astonishing 118,621 nationwide only one year after its enactment.[15] The punishment for violating the act was severe, ranging up to life imprisonment. The act was therefore a cudgel for enforcing ideological discipline throughout South Korea.

The Korean War was a watershed in the formation of South Korean national identity. In South Korea, the material and institutional form of state building preceded a distinct form of national community. To fill this void, the Rhee government propagated *Ilminjuui*, or the One People Principle, to forge a coherent national identity in South Korea. To create "a new people" for the new South Korean government, the Rhee regime pushed the ideal of a homogeneous, single Korean people on the basis of one blood lineage. President Rhee proclaimed in his book *Ilminjuui gaesul*, or *Outline of One People Principle*, that the Korean people were "one people" that shared the same blood and history.[16] According to An Ho-sang, the minister of education and principal theoretician of One People Principle, the same bloodline of one people "is natural and inevitable," as in one family, and thereby "one people should share sour and sweet, cry and laugh, and death and life all together."[17] Rhee and An emphasized overcoming differences of class, status, region, and gender in pursuit of homogeneity and unity for the South Korean people.[18] They argued that "communism had split the one Korean people into two," and so "the followers of One People Principle should destroy communism to unify two Koreas into one people."[19]

In July 1949, a year before the outbreak of the Korean War, the Ministry of Education linked loyalty to the state to anticommunism by launching a national campaign called *Uriui maengse*, or Our Pledge. The three lines of the pledge were:

> We, sons and daughters of the Republic of Korea, should defend the country by sacrificing our lives.
>
> We should overthrow communist invaders by unifying ourselves as a whole with steely determination.
>
> We should unify North and South Korea by waving the South Korean national flag at the summit of Mt. Baekdu.

The ministry ensured that all books, including school textbooks, included this pledge and made every student recite it.[20] An Ho-sang declared, "One people who are the same in the blood lineage and the destiny should be the same in thought and deed."[21] If it were not, he argued, the result would be the "destruction of one nation because one people come to have two destinies and are divided and split."[22] The One People Principle had been reconstructed to refer to both the same blood lineage *and* the same ideas.[23] The South Korean nation meant a community of new people who possessed the same ideas, beyond the unitary bloodline. The One People Principle worked as a vital tool for excluding nonconformists and antistate groups from the national community.[24] An Ho-sang argued that "one people (Korean people) should have one nation (Korea) and protect the nation. If one people were spilt, one people should desperately defend it, following the One People Principle."[25] He added that "some who split our people are evils and some others who sit on their hands in that situation are also evils. Therefore, we must thoroughly eradicate the rebellious and destructive elements who split our people from outside and inside the country."[26] The Rhee government, based on the idea, violently repressed the dissents and antistate groups as "evils," regardless of their blood. After the suppression of the Yeosu-Suncheon incident, one loyal officer of the Rhee government said that "the bastards against the heavenly way do not belong to our people."[27] President Rhee also proclaimed that the dissenters should be ostracized not only from the national community but also from the human world for national security.[28]

The One People Principle was utilized to generate loyalty to President Rhee and increase support for stamping out communism in the South. President Rhee delivered a special message about the One People Principle in December 1949: "The aim of the One People Principle is to develop the spirit of democracy through the overthrow of communism. The sense of anti-communism leads to promoting national security and freedom for the people. . . . I ask for unity of our loyal people in order to strengthen democracy in this country."[29] In public lectures, statements to the media, and presidential messages, South Korea's ruling elite called both loyalty to Rhee and anticommunism a "solemn obligation."[30] The fight against communism and patriotism were sold as two sides of the same coin. When the Korean War broke out, the South Korean government utilized the One People Principle in mobilizing its people.

ESTABLISHMENT OF SURVEILLANCE SYSTEMS TO FIGHT COMMUNISM

The process of ideological inculcation was mirrored by the creation of a dense and interlocking network of surveillance structures that served to further the reach of the state. To monitor the population, the government built circular panopticons for housing on Jeju, which maximized the surveillance power of the police and military. In December 1948, the military ordered Jeju residents to build stone walls around villages near the coast, not only to prevent attacks by the rebels but also to help keep tabs on civilians who lived in the villages.[31] Islanders were mobilized into participating in their own surveillance as all Jeju people, including pregnant women, children, and the elderly, were forced to work on the construction of the walls for two months.[32]

By January, the stone walls around the villages extended for 120,000 meters (74.6 miles), reminding the villagers of the Great Wall of China.[33]

The panoptic style of building was first designed by the English philosopher Jeremy Bentham as a structure for prisons in the late eighteenth century. It had a tower at the center, from which it was possible to see every cell in the structure, though people in the cells could not tell when they were being watched. The novel structures built on Jeju resembled this architecture. In Hamdeok village in northern Jeju, a castle-like wall two and half meters high was built around the village, with four main gates around the village and a number of small gates in between the main ones.[34] A guard post at the front gate was built on elevated ground. In Nakseon of Seonheul village in northern Jeju, a square-shaped wall at least three meters high and one meter wide was built around the village, and a trench two meters deep was dug around the wall and thorns were placed in it (figure 3.1).[35] The total length of the wall was about five hundred meters (1,640 feet), and the area inside the wall was around fifteen thousand square meters (3.7 acres).[36] Inside the wall of each village, villagers who had been forcibly displaced from the mountainous area of Jeju populated by rebels resided in newly built mud huts. In Nakseon, about 250 households from the mountainous area nearby resided inside the

Figure 3.1 Stone wall in Nakseon of Seonheul Village (Source: Jeju 4.3 Peace Foundation)

wall for six years until the end of Jeju 4.3.[37] With walls around each village, Jeju civilians were confined inside and constantly monitored by the police.

Michel Foucault, the French philosopher and social theorist, argued that an individual in a panoptical building, including prisons, insane asylums, and schools, internalizes the regulations of those holding power by being observed constantly. The constant surveillance acts as a control mechanism, and the inmates internalize prescribed behaviors and obedience to the rules of the observer or those in power.[38] On Jeju, the mechanisms in place for imposing obedience were vast and severe. Jeju's villagers, including members of the rightist Daehan Youth Association, stood as sentry at the village gates in shifts under the timetables of the police.[39] In Nakseon, forty villagers stood as sentry at nine guard posts in a five-hour shift during the night.[40] Brutal punishments were administered for failures to comply with the rules. For example, one woman was never able to walk properly following a brutal beating for being late.[41] A further layer of the surveillance was added as a pass card was required to leave and reenter the village when the villagers farmed or did other work outside their residences. Even students were inspected whenever they went to school.[42] At times, this could work to strain familial bonds. One marine veteran said that his brother, his only remaining family member, was not able to see him off at the time of his enlistment because of the strict rules restricting people's movements.[43] The intensity of these forms of surveillance appears to have worked. After the village walls were built on Jeju, attacks by the rebels on the counterinsurgency forces decreased, and the villagers inside the walls were no longer suspected of supporting the rebels. The villagers had become more obedient to the counterinsurgency forces through fear and forced participation. This helped fuel enlistment in the military.

THE PROCESS AND MOTIVATIONS FOR ENLISTMENT

The South Korean army and navy were founded just after the establishment of the Republic of Korea in August 1948 and played integral roles in the establishment of anticommunist hegemony on the mainland and on Jeju. Concerning the latter, the marines were particularly crucial. The navy sought to organize amphibious military operations in order to conduct landing maneuvers and defend against invasions by sea.[44] As such, the Korean Marine Corps (KMC) was created in April 1949. The first two groups of recruits were selected from the navy, and their maiden mission was to quash communist invaders, in accord with the second line of "Our Pledge." This effectively meant killing the surviving rebels of the Yeosu-Suncheon incident, who had taken refuge around the area of Mt. Jiri, seventy kilometers (43.5 miles) from

Suncheon. After the marines vanquished the rebels by the end of 1949, they came to Jeju to suppress the remaining insurgents of Jeju 4.3. However, with the outbreak of the Korean War, the relationship between the marines and the island's population began to change as recruitment for the KMC on Jeju began. Examining the complex motivations for recruitment will shed light on how this relationship changed.

"Country First"

In their memoirs, Jeju marines emphasized their fervent patriotism as their reason for enlisting in the KMC, parroting the government's slogan "The country first." Most Jeju native veterans I met confirmed this sentiment. One former teacher told me, "I will never forget when I discussed [it] with other teachers in my school at the time of volunteering. We discussed that 'no people can exist without country,' 'no school can exist without people,' 'no teacher can exist without school,' and 'no student can exist without a teacher.'"[45] Another veteran heard exactly the same lecture from his teacher and said that it was the viewpoint of the entire country.[46] All middle school principals lectured to their students: "The country is now at the critical moment because of the invasion by North Korea, and, so, you must save it by joining the military."[47] Rightists were even more stalwart in their patriotism. At the beginning of the war, the National Student Corps on Jeju trumpeted slogans such as "Let's annihilate the puppet army of North Korea," "Let's attack communists by students' forces," and "Let's take a gun instead of a pen."[48] One former leader of the National Student Corps in Hallim Middle School told me that he first voluntarily applied to the marines with a blood petition when his principal gave a lecture on patriotism.[49] One female veteran, a former student, also said that she first volunteered among the students in her school out of patriotism and anticommunism. According to her, her brother was falsely accused as a communist and executed by the South Korean government right after the outbreak of the war. She blamed the government for this, but she decided to volunteer "for the country" because "the country would have been occupied by North Korean communists if nobody saved it."[50]

This patriotic impulse for enlisting in the KMC was nourished by the cultural remnants of Japanese militarism during Japan's colonial reign in Korea. During the war, Korean young people were widely encouraged by pro-Japanese Korean social leaders to show their desire to join the Japanese army through a blood application, following Japanese military custom. These applicants usually bit their third finger till it bled, and then wrote a brief application letter, often expressing their loyalty and patriotism (盡忠報國), on a white sheet or cloth. To show their commitment, some Jeju residents did the same when applying to join the KMC, especially when they failed to pass the physical examination. Shin Hyeon-jun, the first commander of the Korean marines, acknowledged the cultural meaning of a blood petition, and ordered the recruiters to accept applicants who petitioned in blood.[51] Undoubtedly, the Japanese militarist legacy and patriotism contributed to the patriotic narrative expressed by the recruits. However, while local newspapers praised the recruits for their "eruption of patriotism,"[52] the slogan of "country first" masked less visible but more formidable motivations for enlisting.

Personal Safety

A more influential reason why Jeju people enlisted in the KMC was to keep themselves and their families safe. The recruits believed that the civil war on Jeju was more dangerous to them than fighting in battles on the mainland. The government's jailing of suspected communists after the outbreak of the Korean War was a strong impetus for enlistment. One marine veteran from Bukchon village, which was stigmatized as the worst "Red" village and the location of a horrendous massacre, said he joined the marines because he could not find any other means to survive.[53] He was terrified of being detained as a leftist and thought only of escaping Jeju. Previously detained prisoners likewise saw recruitment as an avenue for safety and the rehabilitation of their reputations. For example, one former political prisoner that I interviewed joined to escape preventive detention.[54] Members of the National Guidance League, a mass organization created by the government who were suspected of being leftists, also found no other options after they were released from detention than to join the army. One enlisted even with a serious wrist injury,[55] while another joined at the unusually old age of thirty-five, in turn indicating the desperation that many of these "volunteers" felt.[56] Meanwhile, another applied for the army three times until he was accepted.[57] Some veterans later attributed their volunteering to the tense political atmosphere on Jeju. One said, "At the time, the war was extremely unfavorable for us. We had no choice but to join. Otherwise, we would have been considered traitors and in danger of losing our lives."[58] Many veterans said that they preferred participating in combat to being suspected of being leftists, or to enduring attacks by rebels at night and counterinsurgency forces during the day.[59] As the above testimonies all indicate, concerns over personal safety were powerful motivating factors.

The concern over safety was not only individual but also included families. A veteran whose father had been executed in late 1949 on the grounds of being a communist informed me, "I volunteered because my family needed social identification as the family of a solider for safety."[60] Another female interviewee told me that she decided to protect her parents and eight siblings by volunteering.[61] She herself had been tortured for allegedly being a sympathizer of rebels by the military police, about seven months before the outbreak of the war. She had been released without charge, but the military police reexamined her immediately following the North Korean invasion. She finally decided to "sacrifice myself for the country" to clear suspicion and protect her family, indicating how clearly the lines between overt patriotism and familial preservation had been blurred. Volunteers knew that family members of soldiers were safe from mass executions, while simple cooperation with the police and rightest organizations or participation in the anticommunist activities of the National Student Corps would not necessarily keep them out of harm's way.

Removing the Stigma of Being Reds

Related to, but nevertheless distinct from, concerns over safety was the desire to escape stigmatization at the personal, familial, or village level. One individual editor who collected a memoir of Jeju marines said that they enlisted primarily due to the false communist charges.[62] Enlistment could clear individuals, their family members, or their villagers of false communist charges. One veteran joined the marines with a blood application because his brother was falsely accused of being a communist by the NWYA and he wanted to clear the allegation.[63] Similarly, another veteran joined to clear their village of false communist charges by the NWYA and rehabilitate their honor.[64] One army veteran said that the enlistment was the best chance to remove his stigma of being a supporter of the rebels and lead a blameless life. He narrowly enlisted in the army after failing to enlist in the marines.[65]

Finally, in a minority of cases, revenge was another motivation for enlisting. People who suffered from cruel beatings by the police or members of the NWYA sometimes said they joined the military not only to avoid such beatings but to exact revenge by achieving the superior status of a soldier.[66] This was due to the fact that a soldier was able to beat or shoot villagers and police officers in wartime due to their superior rank. Some recruits who emphasized patriotism as their primary motivation admitted that they also resolved to retaliate when given the opportunity.[67] In certain cases, this resolution was fulfilled. During a leave from service, some Jeju recruits took revenge against notoriously violent police officers by severely beating or shooting them.[68]

NATIONAL ORGANIZATIONS

Recruitment was more easily facilitated by the presence of existing national organizations. From its inauguration, the Rhee government formed and reformed mass organizations to propagate the One People Principle, build public support, and regulate the population. By constructing a hierarchical system of mass organizations, the government hoped to reeducate leftists and potential leftists so that they would become good citizens, while getting ordinary people to obey its rule. The main mass organizations were the National Guidance League, Daehan Youth Association, National Association, Daehan Women's Association, and National Student Corps.[69] On Jeju, the branches of these organizations accelerated their efforts during Jeju 4.3, forcing residents to become members while trying to indoctrinate them in the cause of anticommunism. These groups also played a key role in enlisting people in the KMC at the administrative and coercive levels.

National Guidance League

The National Guidance League engaged in surveillance and the retraining of ex-leftists, including former members of the SKLP. The league was formed in April 1949 to turn these into "One People," or loyal citizens under the supervision of the Ministry of Home Affairs.[70] The ideological basis for the league was the One People Principle; accordingly, because the ex-leftists also belonged to the same Korean bloodline, if they converted into anticommunists, they could be part of the "One People" of South Korea. The central headquarters of the league expanded its organizational structure, forming branches in every region throughout the country, with the support of the police and the offices of the prosecution. By the start of the Korean War, the number of league members nationwide was estimated to be three hundred thousand, though many of them had not ever been engaged in the leftist organizations.[71] To convert the members into good citizens, the league utilized a variety of activities to instill discipline, such as rallies, cultural events, forced education, and confessions.[72] If the members passed the strict examination of conversion, they were released from the league. Just after the war broke out, however, as many as two hundred thousand members were executed as potentially treacherous elements by the police and the Counterintelligence Corps of the Korean army headquarters.[73]

On Jeju, the police already had a blacklist of leftists with a detailed description of each suspect's activities, ideological orientation, and family relations. However, the local police organized a branch of the National Guidance League on the island according to the mainland national police's plan. Although many suspected leftists had already been killed on Jeju, the total number on the island stood at twenty-seven thousand when the war began.[74] The numbers were high in part because the police sometimes enlisted people who had not participated in any leftist activities in the past. In Jongdal village, for example, the police enlisted all the young people regardless of their past.[75] The office of the National Guidance League on Jeju was established in each of the four police districts, Jeju-eup, Seoguipo, Moseulpo, and Seongsanpo, by November 1949, and its members were placed under strict surveillance by the police. A villager testified that in Seongsanpo in eastern Jeju, the National Guidance League hosted public lectures on anticommunism and performed a play, but it was the police in Seongsanpo who arranged the events.[76]

National Guidance League members suspected of being leftists became the first targets of preventive detention in South Korea. Shortly after the Korean War began, the police on Jeju started to detain members of the league as well as "other rebellious elements" on the blacklist according to the order of "preventive detention" from the central government.[77] The police authorities on Jeju classified the detainees into four groups on the basis of their police records or the seriousness of their past communist activities.[78] The detainees who had participated in the insurgency were placed into the two groups that were considered the most serious offenders. The detainees who had recently joined any organizations that were deemed "leftist" were classified into the two other groups. Although the police's list of suspected communists was created with limited hard evidence, the Jeju Martial Law Command (in headquarters of the Marine Corps on Jeju) executed between 1,150 and 1,300 members in the first two groups from the end of July to the end of August.[79] Meanwhile, the detainees from the other two groups were confined to detention sites until the police authorities decided to release them in the middle of September 1950 following pressure from the public.[80] However, provisions were not sufficient in the overcrowded detention cells, and as a result some detainees died of disease or starvation.[81] Given this situation, many young members of the National Guidance League rushed to enlist in the military to avoid being put in custody, while the surviving members who were detained eagerly tried to enter the military to save their lives as soon as they were released.[82]

Daehan Youth Association

The members of the Jeju branch of the rightist Daehan Youth Association first volunteered to join the marines in July 1950. The marines accorded them priority because they had been vetted and trained by the police or the marines. The group was fully integrated into the state at both the administrative and ideological levels. The president of the Daehan Youth Association was President Rhee himself, while its doctrine was the One People Principle. The reach of the group was considerable as the association had provincial branches, seventeen district branches, and 180 city branches. By the end of 1948, its membership had swelled to over three million.[83]

With the founding of the Daehan Youth Association, the organizational system uniting rightist youth was strengthened. Every young villager, including females under forty years old, was forced to join the group, and a member's schedule and duties was tightly monitored by the police. The members usually stood guard at police stations or around villages and helped policemen search for insurgents. One marine veteran recalled that he made the rounds of his assigned block with a baton during the daytime and then stood guard with a bamboo spear at night.[84]

Despite belonging to a rightist group, members of the Daehan Youth Association from Jeju were often harassed and abused for trivial reasons by the police and members of the NWYA. Given the stigma of being labeled as from an "Island of Reds," Jeju Islanders, regardless of organizational membership, were still often treated as potential leftists. Indeed, even those who attained relatively high positions in the group's organizational structure were not necessarily safe. The president of the Daehan Youth Association in Seongsan-myeon, who had been regarded as a model rightist on Jeju, was almost killed by a member of the NWYA.[85] Another active member of the Daehan Youth Association in Kosan village was even shot without verification of his status by a policeman after someone reported that he was suspected of being a leftist.[86] Loyalty and trust were often predicated on the willingness of islanders to engage in savage violence against rebels. For example, according to an ex-member of the Daehan Youth Association, the police did not consider the Jeju natives to be on their side until they "cut off a rebel's head."[87]

Despite this culture of stigmatization and mistreatment, when the marines began to recruit on Jeju in the middle of July 1950, Daehan Youth Association members took the initiative.[88] In Yeongnak village, a recruiting soldier asked the chairman of the Daehan Youth Association in the village to make a list of applicants.[89] Successful enlistment usually depended on an examination of physical strength, which included a test for height, weight, chest size, arm movement, eyesight, and hearing. When several hopeful recruits failed the examination, they petitioned to be accepted with a blood application, writing, "Long live the Republic of Korea" or "Unification of the South and the North."[90] Some 1,500 people, mostly members of the Jeju branch of the Daehan Youth Association, enlisted by the end of July.

National Student Corps

Another group whose members joined in large numbers in the early stages of recruitment was the Jeju branch of the National Student Corps. The National Student Corps was organized nationwide on the order of the Ministry of Education in January 1949 to instill progovernment sympathies among teachers and students after the Yeosu-Suncheon incident. An Ho-sang was the national commander of the corps, which was established in every secondary school and college. The corps, modeled after the military, engaged in anticommunist education and military training exercises for students while establishing an internal mutual surveillance system.[91] Like other mass organizations, the National Student Corps on Jeju stepped up its efforts during the Jeju massacre and continued into the Korean War.

The middle school student leaders of the corps were the most committed to achieving the goals of the KMC and propagating the cause of anticommunism. Even before the National Student Corps was established, many of the student leaders had taken part in military exercises. A marine veteran testified that a total of 138 students from the middle schools in Jeju-eup had received military training and education for a month on the recommendation of the military authorities on Jeju.[92] After the National Student Corps was established, every student did military drills for three to four hours a week, while the student leaders of the corps voluntarily joined a special military program to be military officers. According to one student leader in Jeju Agriculture Middle School, he was commissioned as a reserve officer as early as the fifth grade.[93]

When the Korean War broke out, members of the corps fervently demonstrated their loyalty to the state. At the end of July 1950, the corps organized a big rally under the slogans "Let's annihilate the puppet army of North Korea" and "Let's attack communists by students' forces."[94] Teachers and leaders of the corps asked their principal, their immediate superior in the corps (both teachers and principals were involved in it), to allow a blood application to the KMC. According to one leader of the corps in Hallim Middle School, he wrote with his bloodied third finger, "Please let me go to the 38th parallel" and *"pilsajeuksaeng"* [if you fight prepared for death, then you win] in Chinese characters (必死卽生)—a quotation from Admiral Yi Sun-shin, the heroic admiral from the Hideyoshi invasions of 1592–1598.[95] About 125 students in Hallim Middle School immediately followed their leader's example.

The corps' leaders also organized their own student troops, the Student Shock Force. The force operated under the slogan "Let's achieve the unification of South and North with our own hands" and began training on August 2, 1950.[96] The local newspaper, the *Jeju Sinbo*, encouraged the force's 145 members to "demonstrate a sense of loyalty of Jeju Islanders by contributing to the unification of the motherland."[97] They all voluntarily joined the KMC on August 17. From the onset of the Korean War, Jeju students formed a core reservoir for the marines.

Beyond these core youth groups, there were various other student recruits. The backgrounds and motivations of these groups were heterogeneous and worthy of a brief discussion. Similar to military-aged islanders, youth with suspicious backgrounds often joined. For example, students under surveillance as potential communists organized a training camp to join the KMC. Predictably, their motive was not patriotism but saving their own or their families' lives. One KMC veteran said he thought that military training by a teacher and an officer of the National Guard would prove the trainees' ideological standing as anticommunists.[98] His team, which was composed of about thirty students, volunteered for a month of intensive training. Many other students decided to join the KMC after being advised to do so by their teachers or school principals. In early August, Chief of Staff of the Marines Kim Seong-eun called all influential people on Jeju and informed them of the national emergency facing South Korea. Kim urged Jeju Islanders to enlist in the marines, warning that they might face a disaster like the fighting on Jeju or even worse if the Northern enemy was not defeated.[99] After a meeting with Kim, school principals on Jeju appealed to their students "to follow the patriotic students who already joined," "to save the country," and "to rise up against the communist invasion."[100] After the principals' speeches, almost all students stood up within minutes to volunteer for the marines,[101] though, again, some did for their own safety. Authorities then selected recruits according to their height and finger dexterity for shooting.[102] In other middle schools, the authorities forcibly recruited. At Seogui and Daejeong Middle Schools, marines gathered the upper-grade students in the school playground and selected the tallest students.[103] In sum, survival, guidance by authorities, or coercion were motivating factors in deciding to join.

Young females also voluntarily joined or were targeted for recruitment. A total of 126 female members of the National Student Corps, both unmarried teachers and middle school students, enlisted with the KMC in August. Some of them did so voluntarily, but fear clearly played a role. According to my interviews and other sources, in late August, teachers who were single were asked to visit an educational affairs section in the administrative office of the schools on Jeju with their name seals, which were registered at the local government office.[104] A school inspector then asked them to stamp their seals on an application form for the KMC to complete the application. The teachers hesitated but decided to join for their safety. Similar to the male students, some female students followed their teachers' persistent urgings to join the KMC. According to one, she could not resist the repeated entreaties from her teacher when students who were even smaller than her were taking the physical examination.[105] Finally, deception was also sometimes utilized. For example, one of my interviewees said she was ordered to stand in a line with other students according to their height but failed to realize that this was part of her enlistment until after she had completed the physical examination.[106]

Female recruitment therefore followed similar patterns to male recruitment, with a few exceptions. As the above summary of youth recruitment suggests, a mixture of patriotism, fear, coercion, and the influence of social superiors motivated young Koreans to join the marines throughout the summer of 1950, regardless of gender. As the nation faced a desperate situation, this environment made Jeju into fertile ground for potential recruitment. Indeed, by August 1950, about 1,500 members of the National Student Corps had already enlisted with the KMC, thus complicating the island's relationship to the early state-building process.

RITUALS FOR BOOSTING MORALE

Military recruitment in the early stages of the Korean War was undoubtedly crucial in the process of assimilating the island's population into the emerging anticommunist state. Upon entrance into the military, the process was further entrenched by the military culture of the South Korean state, which was imbued with patriotism and boosted the morale of the marine recruits. Like Japanese soldiers during the Second World War, the recruits received a big national flag emblazoned with words of encouragement from family members, friends, neighbors, and villagers. The most common were "congratulations on your enlistment," "盡忠報國" (loyalty and patriotism), and "武運長久" (good fortune in war).[107] Veterans vividly remembered their receipt of the flag and words of encouragement with pride.

Another customary enlistment ritual was wearing a cloth belt (*chuninchim* in Korean, *sennimbari* in Japanese) made through "a thousand's needlework," which was a mythic guarantee of returning alive. The veterans said they believed the belt to be an amulet to prevent any unfortunate accidents during the war. The words of encouragement were stitched by hundreds of villagers onto the belts, in turn forging bonds between the individual, the family, and the nation. The veterans recalled the thrill of receiving the villagers' best wishes through the belt, a gift from the heart. Following custom, the recruits wore it proudly when they left for the war.[108] A big farewell party typically hosted by a village or county was also implemented to boost morale. The recruits were elated that all of the villagers, including the head of the village or county, held these parties for them. The head of the village or county would wrap a big national flag around them from their left shoulder to their right one, following another Japanese military custom. The events of 4.3 often cast a sobering shadow over these celebrations. In Daejeong-myeon, for example, the village head encouraged the recruits "to remove the stigma of a Red island by winning battles."[109]

When three thousand Jeju recruits left for Jinhae in South Gyeongsang Province from the port of Jeju-eup on September 1, they saluted their parents while wearing their marine uniforms and carrying a good-luck charm and a national flag. Regardless of their differing motivations for enlistment, the Jeju recruits were becoming loyal, anticommunist nationals; they had moved beyond advocating anticommunism (*bangong*) to internalizing the importance of actually obliterating communism (*myeolgong*). The reintegration of Jeju people within the national boundary through mobilization for the Korean War was an important process of strengthening national identity under the One People Principle in the early state-building process. The experience of war itself would solidify these emerging bonds.

NOTES

1. Sang-ho Lee and Young-sil Park, *6.25 jeonjaeng: Sonyeonbyeong yeongu* [The Korean War: A Study of Child Soldiers] (Seoul: Institute for Military History Compilation, Ministry of National Defense (MND), 2011), 94–96. The 1949 Military Service Law stipulated drafting twenty-year-old men every year. In March 1950, however, the enforcement of this law was suspended and the district recruiting command was dissolved because the South Korean army had already reached its goal of retaining one hundred thousand regular soldiers.

2. Ibid., 69.

3. Ibid., 67–86. After the Incheon Landing, the South Korean government began to establish district recruiting command in every province for efficient drafting and issued the Act on the Establishment of National Defense Army on December 21, 1950, to mobilize a reserve force. This act, however, was abolished in May 1951 because some high-ranking officers embezzled war supplies, which resulted in 120,000 among a total 500,000 recruits dying of starvation, disease, or exposure between December 1950 and February 1951. Instead, in May 1951, the revision of Military Service Law was established to draft people in the most effective way by adopting a prior notification system. In August 1951, the Ministry of Defense set up the administration of military affairs for the systematic recruitment of all males between nineteen and twenty-eight years of age, pending a physical examination.

4. Ibid., 72–77.

5. Gap-saeng Jeon, "Hangukjeonjaeng jeonhu daehancheongnyeondanui jibang-jojikgwa hwaldong" [The Daehan Youth Association's Local Branches and Their Activities in Pre– and Post–Korean War Periods], *Jenosaideu Yeongu* [Genocide Studies] 4 (2008): 55.

6. Korea Institute for Military Affairs, *Hangukjeonjaeng jiwonsa: Insa, gunsu, minsa jiwon* [The History of Defense Support for the Korean War: Personnel, Military, and Civil Support] (Seoul: Korea Institute for Military Affairs, 1997), 153–55.

7. Institute for Military History Compilation, Ministry of National Defense (MND), *6.25 jeonjaeng: Yeogun chamjeonsa* [The Korean War: The History of Female Soldiers Engaging in the War] (Seoul: Ministry of Defense, 2012), 102–3.

8. Ibid., 106–7. The qualifications for recruits in the female army were to be unmarried, at least a middle school graduate, and between eighteen and twenty-five. According to a 2012 investigation by the Ministry of Defense, about two thousand women in the region volunteered after the army authorities appealed to their patriotism through an extensive recruitment campaign, including posting public notices,

broadcasting in the streets, and giving lectures during the middle of August. The authorities selected five hundred among these volunteers by physical examination, written test, and oral interview. Im-ha Lee, who studied the Korean War and women, noted that the application for the female army was almost semicompulsory on the level of local administrations or schools. See Im Ha Lee, "The Korean War and the Role of Women," *Review of Korean Studies* 9, no. 2 (2006): 91–98.

9. Institute for Military History Compilation, Ministry of National Defense (MND), *Yeogun chamjeonsa*, 105–11.

10. Ibid., 437.

11. At the time of their enlistment, the middle school used a four-year system except for Jeju Agriculture Middle School, which adopted the new six-year system. Most of the student recruits were sixteen and seventeen years old, and some were even fifteen.

12. *Jejusori*, July 3, 2020; interview with Jeong Su-hyeon on January 11, 2010, on Jeju. Jeong is a specialist on the Korean War and also the editor of a collection of Jeju veterans' memoirs. He collected memoirs of 354 Jeju veterans, including 174 marines, and published them in eleven volumes between 2006 and 2019.

13. Diane B. Kraft, "South Korea's National Security Law: A Tool of Oppression in an Insecure World," *Wisconsin International Law Journal* 24, no. 2 (2006): 627–30.

14. Ibid., 629.

15. Deuk-jung Kim, *'Ppalgaengi'ui tansaeng* [The Birth of the "Reds"] (Seoul: Seonin, 2009), 528–30.

16. Syng-man Rhee, *Ilminjuui gaesul* [Outline of One People Principle] (Seoul: Committee for Promotion of Ilminjuui, 1949), 4–10.

17. Ho-sang An, *Ilminjuui-ui bonbatang* [The Basis of One People Principle] (Seoul: Ilminjuui Research Institute, 1950), 27–29

18. Rhee, *Ilminjuui gaesul*, 17–21; An, *Ilminjuui-ui bonbatang*, 38–40, 49–52.

19. An, *Ilminjuui-ui bonbatang*, 24–26.

20. Jun-man Kang, *Hanguk hyeondaesa sanchaek: 1950nyeondae pyeon 1* [A trip through Modern Korean History: The Period of the 1950s, vol. 1] (Seoul: Inmulgwa Sasangsa, 2004), 27.

21. An, *Ilminjuui-ui bonbatang*, 30.

22. Ibid., 30.

23. Chong-Myung Im, "The Making of the Republic of Korea as a Modern Nation-State, August 1948–May 1950" (PhD diss., University of Chicago, 2004), 71.

24. Ibid., 70.

25. An, *Ilminjuui-ui bonbatang*, 32–33.

26. Ibid., 25.

27. Im, "Making of the Republic of Korea," 60.

28. Ibid.

29. *Chosun Ilbo* and *Donga Ilbo*, December 20, 1949.

30. Soo-ja Kim, "Rhee Syng-man-ui ilminjuui-ui jechanggwa nolli" [The Advocacy and Logic of Rhee Syng-man's One People Principle], *Hanguk Sasangsahak* [Korean History of Thoughts] 22 (2004): 464.

31. Eun-hee Kim, "Jeju 4.3sigi 'jeollyakchon'ui hyeongseonggwa jumin saeng-hwal" [The Formation of the "Strategic Village" and the Life of the Villagers during Jeju 4.3], *Yeoksa Minsokhak* [Journal of Korean Historical Folklife] 23 (2006): 185–86.

32. Jeju 4.3 Research Institute, ed., *Manbengdui-ui nunmul* [Tears of Manbengdui Cemetery] (Seoul: Hanul Academy, 2015a), 51, 139, 148, 188; interview with Kang Il-hwa on April 18, 2012, on Jeju.

33. Jeju 4.3 National Committee, *Jeju April Third Incident Investigation Report*, 393.

34. Jeju 4.3 Peace Foundation and Jeju 4.3 Research Institute, *Saneseodo museopgo areseodo museopgo*, 75–78.

35. Kim, "Jeju 4.3sigi 'jeollyakchon'ui hyeongseonggwa jumin saenghwal," 193–95.

36. Ibid., 193.

37. Ibid., 195–96.

38. Michel Foucault, *Discipline and Punish: The Birth of the Prison*, trans. Alan Sheridan (New York: Vintage Books, 1995), 200–228.

39. Jeju 4.3 Research Institute, *Manbengdui-ui nunmul*, 189–90.

40. Kim, "Jeju 4.3sigi 'jeollyakchon'ui hyeongseonggwa jumin saenghwal," 197.

41. Jemin Ilbo 4.3 Reporting Team, *4.3eun malhanda 5*, 217.

42. Jeju 4.3 Research Institute, ed., *Gudeong-i pare bihaengjang-e gatda wan* [We Went to the Airport to Dig a Hole] (Jeju: Jeju 4.3 Peace Foundation, 2015), 195.

43. Interview with Lee Yeong-hui on May 4, 2012, on Jeju.

44. Jeju Defense Command, *Jejuwa haebyeongdae* [Jeju and the Korean Marine Corps] (Jeju: Jeju Defense Command, 1997), 45–49.

45. Interview with Kim Yeong-hwan, a former teacher in Jeju City, on April 20, 2012, on Jeju.

46. Interview with Ko Ji-seon, a former student of Hallim Middle School, on September 20, 2012, on Jeju.

47. Interview with Kim Hyeong-geun on April 5, 2012, on Jeju; interview with Moon Chang-hae on April 26, 2012, on Jeju; Third and Fourth Groups of the Korean Marines Corps (KMC), ed., *Chamjeonsillok* [A True Record concerning Those Who Fought in the Korean War] (Seoul: Munchang Yeongusa, 2002), 640–50. This history book included personal memoirs of 134 veterans and brief descriptions of the battles of the Korean War in which they participated. It was primarily distributed to schools but also colleges, public offices, and public libraries on Jeju.

48. Su-hyeon Jeong, ed., *Jageun yeongungdeurui iyagi* [The Story of Little Heroes] (Jeju: Cultural Center of Southern Jeju, 2006), 21–22; Third and Fourth Groups of the KMC, *Chamjeonsillok*, 130. The term "puppet army" here refers to the fact that the North Korean army was allegedly controlled by the Soviet Union. This term was widely circulated during and after the Korean War in South Korea.

49. Interview with Ko Ji-seon on September 20, 2012, on Jeju.

50. Interview with Lee Su-haeng on September 17, 2012, in Incheon.

51. Interview with Kim Hyeong-geun on April 5, 2012, on Jeju.

52. *Jeju Sinbo*, August 1, 1950.

53. Jeju 4.3 Research Institute, *Ijesa malhamsuda 1*, 149.

54. Interview with Go Tae-myeong on January 4, 2020, on Jeju.

55. Jeju 4.3 Research Institute, *Dasi hagui junghakwoneul gieokhamyeo*, 50.

56. Committee for Promotion of Academic and Cultural Projects in Commemoration of the Fiftieth Anniversary of Jeju 4.3, ed., *Ireobeorin maeureul chajaseo* [Searching the Lost Villages] (Seoul: Hakminsa, 1998), 229.

57. Jeju 4.3 Research Institute, *Billemotgul*, 33–34.

58. Interview with Bu Chang-ok on April 12, 2012, on Jeju.

59. Third and Fourth Groups of the KMC, *Chamjeonsillok*, 242; Jeju 4.3 Research Institute, *Manbengdui-ui nunmul*, 31; Jeju 4.3 Research Institute, *Garibangeuro gieokhaneun yeoldu sal sonyeonui 4.3*, 65.

60. Interview with Moon Chang-hae on April 26, 2012, on Jeju. His father was a political prisoner in the early phase of the Jeju 4.3 events but released following the president's decree of amnesty in September 1948. However, his father was executed on the grounds of being a former prisoner by government troops two months later.

61. Interview with Lee Sun-seon on April 16, 2012, on Jeju.

62. Interview with Jeong Su-hyeon on January 11, 2020, on Jeju.

63. Third and Fourth Groups of the KMC, *Chamjeonsillok*, 248.

64. Ibid., 445.

65. Jeju 4.3 Research Institute, ed., *Jeo saram pokdo aniudage geunyang bonaejupseo* [That Person Is Not a Rioter. Please Let Him Go] (Jeju: Jeju 4.3 Peace Foundation, 2015), 223–24.

66. Jeju 4.3 Peace Foundation and Jeju 4.3 Research Institute, *Sanaeseodo museopgo araeseodo museopgo*, 22–26, 162–64; Jeju 4.3 Research Institute, *Billemotgul*, 62.

67. Interview with Kim Yeong-hwan on April 20, 2012; interview with Kang Dae-hyeon on January 18, 2020.

68. Jeju 4.3 Research Institute, *Gudeong-i pare bihaengjang-e gatda wan*, 159. One of my interviewees told me that he also shot a policeman during his leave from service but did not receive any punishment. He was called to the front lines immediately, however. One notorious policeman named Noh in Gimnyeong village was killed by the Jeju army. Jeju 4.3 Peace Foundation and Jeju 4.3 Research Institute, *Sanaeseodo museopgo araeseodo museopgo*, 24–25.

69. The Daehan Dongnip Chokseong Gungminhoe or Great Korean Independent National Association, a right-wing political group, was founded in December 1946 and renamed the Gungminhoe (National Association) two years later. The National Association aimed to build an anticommunist South Korean society. The Daehan Women's Association, a right-wing women's organization, was organized in September 1946 to promote anticommunism and a spirit of service to the country and to improve women's social standing.

70. Hwang, *Korea's Grievous War*, 93. For more details on the National Guidance League, see chapter 3 of Hwang, *Korea's Grievous War*, and Wright, "Civil War, Politicide, and the Politics of Memory," 91–122.

71. *Kyunghyang Sinmun*, November 26, 2009; Hwang, *Korea's Grievous War*, 99–102.

72. Hwang, *Korea's Grievous War*, 95–98.

73. *Kyunghyang Sinmun*, November 26, 2009; *Hankyoreh*, December 6, 2009.

74. Jeju 4.3 National Committee, *Jeju April Third Incident Investigation Report*, 516.

75. Ibid., 517–18.

76. Ibid.

77. Ibid., 520–21.

78. Ibid., 522–23.

79. The Truth and Reconciliation Commission in South Korea established in 2005 announced the results of its investigation about preventive detention on Jeju in *Hankyoreh*, July 21, 2010.

80. Jeju 4.3 National Committee, *Jeju April Third Incident Investigation Report*, 531–32; *Jeju Sinbo*, September 17 and September 23, 1950.

81. Jeong-hee Cho, "Hangukjeonjeang balbal jikhu Jeju jiyeok yebigeomsokgwa jipdanhaksarui seonggyeok" [The Characteristics of the Preventive Detention and Massacre in Jeju Island Right after the Outbreak of the Korean War] (MA thesis, Jeju National University, 2013), 25–26; Jeju 4.3 Peace Foundation, *Jeju 4.3 sageon*, 447–49.

82. Committee for Promotion of Academic and Cultural Projects in Commemoration of the Fiftieth Anniversary of Jeju 4.3, *Ireobeorin maeureul chajaseo*, 104; Jeju 4.3 Research Institute, *Geuneul sogui 4.3*, 162.

A unique incident of preventive detention happened in early August 1950 on Jeju. Referred to as *Youji sageun*, or the Incident of Local Dignitaries, sixteen local dignitaries were arrested, including the head of the Jeju District Court, the director of prosecution, the head of Jeju-eup, and other prominent leaders on Jeju. They were accused of forming a reception committee for North Korean soldiers. The incident demonstrated that any Jeju Islander could be suspected of being a communist or a communist sympathizer. This horror influenced the young Jeju people's choice to enlist. See Jeju 4.3 National Committee, *Jeju April Third Incident Investigation Report*, 425.

83. Jun-man Kang, *Hanguk hyeondaesa sanchaek: 1940nyeondae pyeon 2* [A Trip through Modern Korean History: The Period of the 1940s, vol. 2] (Seoul: Inmulgwa Sasangsa, 2006), 168.

84. Third and Fourth Groups of the KMC, *Chamjeonsillok*, 153.

85. Jemin Ilbo 4.3 Reporting Team, *4.3eun malhanda 5*, 68–69.

86. *Jemin Ilbo*, April 25, 1998.

87. Jeju 4.3 Research Institute, *Dasi hagui junghakwoneul gieokhamyeo*, 244.

88. The Daehan Youth Association was incorporated into the Youth Defense Corps in March 1950, in accordance with a presidential decree. Su-hyeon Jeong, ed., *6.25 jeonjaenggwa Jeju yeongungdeul 3* [The Korean War and the Heroes from Jeju, vol. 3] (Jeju: Yeollimmunhwa, 2011), 17.

89. Ibid., 340; interview with Kim Su-jin, a former member of the association in this village, on January 22, 2020, on Jeju.

90. Interview with Kim Seok-jin on April 5, 2012, on Jeju.

91. Cumings, *Roaring of the Cataract*, 211–13.

92. Third and Fourth Groups of the KMC, *Chamjeonsillok*, 14.

93. Jeong, *Jageun yeongungdeului iyagi*, 14–20.

94. Ibid., 21–22; interview with Kang Sang-jin, June 16, 2012, in Yanggu, Gangwon Province.

95. Interview with Ko Ji-seon on September 20, 2012, on Jeju.

96. Su-hyeon Jeong, ed., *6.25 jeonjaenggwa Jeju yongsadeul 7* [The Korean War and the Heroes from Jeju, vol. 7] (Jeju: Jeju Veterans Association, 2015), 37–38.

97. *Jeju Sinbo*, August 4, 1950.

98. Interview with Moon Chang-hae on April 26, 2012, on Jeju.

99. Jung-hee Kim, "Ugukgangyeon" [A Lecture of Patriotism], in *Hanbeon haebyeongeun yeongwonhan haebyeong* [Once a Marine, Always a Marine], ed. Seon-ho Lee (Seoul: Jungudang, 1997), 389–91.

100. Third and Fourth Groups of the KMC, *Chamjeonsillok*, 642–44.

101. Interview with Kim Hyeong-geun on April 5, 2012, on Jeju; interview with Bu Chang-ok on April 12, 2012, on Jeju.

102. According to the veterans I interviewed, the standard height needed for acceptance was 160 centimeters (5.2 feet).

103. Third and Fourth Groups of the KMC, *Chamjeonsillok*, 550; Su-hyeon Jeong, ed., *6.25 jeonjaenggwa Jeju yeongungdeul* [The Korean War and the Heroes from Jeju] (Jeju: Yeollimmunhwa, 2009), 330.

104. Jeong, *6.25 jeonjaenggwa Jeju yeongungdeul*, 297–99; interview with Kang Il-hwa, a former elementary school teacher, on April 18, 2012, on Jeju.

105. Interview with Hyun Ae-soon on June 15–16, 2012, in Yanggu.

106. Interview with Ko Sun-deok on June 15–16, 2012, in Yanggu.

107. Third and Fourth Groups of the KMC, *Chamjeonsillok*, 44–45; interview with Kim Seok-jin on April 5, 2012, on Jeju; interview with Kim Dong-hak on January 23, 2020, on Jeju.

108. Interview with Kim Seok-jin on April 5, 2012, on Jeju; interview with Ko Ji-seon on October 4, 2012, on Jeju; interview with Kang Dae-hyeon on January 18, 2020.

109. *Jeju Sinbo*, September 2, 1950.

Chapter 4

Reintegration 2: Jeju Marines as Ghost Busters

By the end of the Korean War in 1953, the Jeju marines were widely regarded as true anticommunists. In fact, by many accounts, they were considered to be the most anticommunist, pro-American battalion of all the South Korean military units. They were the most loudly sung heroes of the Korean War by President Rhee Syng-man, who bestowed on them titles such as the "Invincible Marine Corps." This was not merely a construction of the state, as many marines returned home ultraconservative in their ideological orientation. Given the events of the previous years, this is a remarkable inversion and one that provides valuable insight into the process of South Korean state building and the uniqueness of Jeju Islanders in this historical arc. In this chapter, I argue that three related processes were critical to this transformation: the obedience training in the military that the recruits received, the formation of their group identity and solidarity, and the construction of an imagined national community that was forged in the context of Korea's fratricidal conflict. Each of these processes, I argue, were integral to the cultivation of the marines' loyalty to the South Korean state.

OBEDIENCE TRAINING

Obedience training was critical to developing loyalty among the Jeju marines, and they underwent more intense training than other recruits before they participated in battles on the mainland. Given the stigma outlined in previous chapters, this is hardly surprising: because the Jeju recruits were still regarded as potential rebels by their superiors, their military training focused as much on instilling obedience and discipline as on increasing their physical strength and abilities. It began immediately with their enlistment. The first group of Jeju recruits to the KMC received training for a month at Jeju-eup or Moseulpo in southwestern Jeju before their departure for Jinhae on the mainland on September 1, 1950. At that time, all other recruits on the mainland were trained for only one week, or fifteen days at the most, before participating in combat because of the immediate need for new recruits on the front line.[1] The longer training period is indicative of a more rigorous screening process, and testimonies from veterans portray a harsh and austere regimen. According to veterans' memories and my own personal interviews, from six in the morning until night, they received military training on the use of firearms and bayonets, individual combat techniques, and marching, as well as basic training. Part of their training in Moseulpo required climbing Mosel Hill, which was 181 meters (594 feet) high, every day. The last ones to summit the hill had to repeat the grueling climb. In the Jeju-eup training center, the recruits had to crawl on their bellies for about 500 meters (1,640 feet) on an unpaved road and had to run with a gun to Sara Hill, which was 9.5 kilometers (5.9 miles) apart, every day. Those who did not properly follow instructions were beaten with sticks by the trainers, who were their superiors from the mainland. One veteran who had been trained in Moseulpo said, "We had only one training uniform, a hat, a pair of shoes, and one pair of underwear. It was very warm weather in August. We all got soaked in sweat and blood. We had a chance to take a bath and to do laundry with spring water near the seaside once a week, but we continued training even while our uniform was still wet."[2] Another veteran who had been trained in Moseulpo remembered, "The training on the sandy beach during the warm summer was so horrible that I wished to commit suicide by shooting myself. We could not sleep because of the stench of the sweaty clothes and the hungry mosquitos at night."[3] Others who had been trained in Jeju-eup said, "We had to continue crawling on our belly while our elbows and knees were bleeding. Women who passed by us burst into tears. We all got bruises all over our body."[4] As these accounts universally indicate, the early training regimen was brutal and without pity.

In addition to the remorseless of the regimen, the recruits in both training centers were subjected to physical and verbal abuse. The primary form of corporal punishment was called *ppatda*, which was derived from the Japanese pronunciation of the English word "bat." According to veterans, they got beaten on their hips with sticks by trainers five to ten times a day for trivial reasons, or simply on the grounds of being suspected communist rebels. The level of cruelty was in part dictated by the temperaments of their superiors as they were beaten ten to thirty times a day if the trainers were in a bad mood.[5] One veteran recalled that his squad was beaten with the wooden legs of a bed fifty times a day for no reason at all.[6] Collective punishment was also carried out. For example, if a member of a platoon made a mistake, such as misplacing his gun, then all the members of the platoon were beaten.[7] Other punishments included being kicked, having their heads forced into the ground with their hands clasped behind their backs, and being beaten with the butt of a rifle.

These dehumanizing beatings were coupled with a culture of verbal and psychological abuse. As already intimated, Korean mainlanders were heavily biased against Jeju Islanders, and these attitudes spread into the early military culture. Jeju marines were seen as the "sons of rebels" by the trainers, who often called the Jeju recruits "son of a Red," "son of a Jeju Islander," or simply "son of a bitch." Because Jeju villages were based on a kinship community that closely shared and cooperated in family affairs and work activities, these derogatory names had not been used toward relatives or neighbors and therefore were quite shocking. Mistrust and stigma justified this treatment. At a welcoming party just after South Korea's recapture of Seoul, for example, one marine overheard a mainlander say, "How can Jeju Islanders, communists all of them, be South Korean soldiers?"[8] The recruits felt as though they were not human beings when they were called these names. One veteran said, "We were indeed treated like a dog or a pig."[9] The dehumanization of the Jeju recruits was complimented by emasculation. One soldier from the mainland derided Jeju men as "impotent and helpless in the kingdom of women."[10]

Female Jeju marines had similar experiences during their military training, which lasted for forty days at the Jinhae Training Center. A female veteran later recounted, "We were pushed from morning till night. We marched every morning around the whole city of Jinhae while carrying a heavy gun. We were also forced to learn how to swim and fire guns."[11] Another veteran said, "We were often beaten on our hips with sticks. Sometimes we were beaten half to death, and some needed medical care."[12] Like the male recruits, the females were known as members of the "Red Island," albeit there were specifically gendered slurs such as "bitch of Red Jeju." Class bigotry also persisted, with many Jeju women being denigrated as "sweet potato eaters on Jeju."[13] (Sweet potatoes had long been considered a rice substitute for the poor on the mainland, but on Jeju they were a staple because they were a primary crop.) In short, the trainers used a variety of methods to break the women down psychologically.

The female marines escaped the relentless verbal and physical abuse after forty days of military training. Fifty-one of the 126 female marines, those who were young students or were needed to help their family's economy, returned home after the September 1950 liberation of Seoul. The seventy-five others performed military duties in Jinhae for a year, which included work in communications, management, distribution, and nursing in support of the war.[14]

For the male Jeju marines, however, the hard training and *ppatda* punishment continued on the front lines—even in battle. The Jeju marines' officers sometimes beat them in the snowy winter after stripping them almost naked.[15] Others beat them in front of prisoners of war, which was an affront to the

marines' honor in the Korean culture of face-saving.[16] The punishment was
so harsh and arbitrary that some Jeju marines, not surprisingly, wanted to kill
their trainers.[17] Additional training was one of the few reprieves from this
onslaught. Between battles, Jeju marines received military training on skills
such as shooting rifles and using flamethrowers alongside the U.S. marine
advisory groups who were assigned to each Korean marine battalion.[18] Jeju
marines called the training "opportunity education" because they received it
at every opportunity, even if it meant forfeiting rest.[19]

In the long run, however, the harsh culture of the South Korean military
did not alienate the Jeju marines. According to Jeju veterans, they internalized
the lessons of obedience and self-control that they were taught and became
humble and compliant toward their immediate superiors. One said, "A soldier
lives and dies to follow orders. I had no other choices but to follow the orders
of superiors in order to survive the combat."[20] Another veteran recalled, "We
called the *ppatda* punishment the spirit of *ppatda*, because the persistent
training cultivated the marines' endurance and mental strength to overcome
difficulties."[21] Under the military training and the mental abuse, they resolved
to rid themselves of the stigma of their "Red" origins by "fighting for the state
till the last."[22]

The United States' support to the South Korean military further contributed
to developing the Jeju marines' sense of duty. In the wake of North Korea's
invasion, the United States exerted an extensive effort to rapidly strengthen
the South Korean military force. It expanded the number of the military
advisers in South Korea to train and educate South Korean forces from a
few hundred to almost two thousand by the fall of 1950.[23] The military training and education, according to U.S. Army Commander General Matthew
Ridgway, was geared toward developing "a will to fight, an aggressive leadership ability, a professional pride, and a sense of duty" in addition to their
combat capabilities.[24] The U.S. military advisers in South Korea focused on
implementing "American ideals of military efficiency, duty, and patriotism"
to South Korean officers.[25] They closely trained and monitored activities of
the South Korean soldiers, and the battlefield was often an educational site.[26]
In December 1951, the KMC established its own military educational system,
including a replacement training center, an officers school, and a noncommissioned officers school in Jinhae with the support of the U.S. Marine Corps.
There the Jeju marines underwent intensive military training for amphibious
warfare, street combat, and other forms of combat for about a month.[27] Some
Jeju marines assigned to the U.S. Marine Corps attended a course of instruction at a noncommissioned officers school, while others were dispatched
to learn about the operation of new weapons from the U.S. military.[28] Jeju
marines developed a sense of loyalty to the military partially through joint

operations with U.S. marines, and they were impressed that the U.S. marines followed their superiors' orders unquestioningly.[29]

GROUP IDENTITY AND SOLIDARITY AMONG RED ISLANDERS

The experience of war was profound in shaping group identity of the Jeju marines and their complex relationship to the state. The social theorist Michel Foucault argues that the army functions like a machine that controls every movement to create a docile body.[30] Each disciplined soldier is part of the army machine, and group identity and solidarity increase the spirit of sacrifice of the individual for the group. Pauline Kaurin, an American specialist in military ethics, argues that "the group identity has a powerful effect on the ethical frameworks of the group members, which in turn can affect things like unit cohesion and combat effectiveness."[31] According to Kaurin, a military group is "not simply defined by what they were or believe, how they are trained, but by how these effect [*sic*] what they do, how they do it, and why they do it."[32] Such was the case for the Jeju marines.

Unlike other soldiers in the army or the navy, the first three thousand KMC recruits from Jeju largely participated in the battles together. They composed the majority in all four of the battalions of the KMC because the total number of the KMC was only 4,200 at the time of their first battle and 5,610 by the end of 1950.[33] Sociologically, these units were quite cohesive as they were composed of recruits who were roughly the same age; were often school friends, hometown neighbors, or relatives; and shared a common culture with the same dialect. In comparison, the number of soldiers in the army reached over 214,000 by the end of 1950, and its soldiers had diverse backgrounds.[34] The veterans said that the Jeju marines' common background and participation in the same battles fostered comradeship. Their first battle was the Incheon Landing, a decisive victory and strategic reversal in favor of the United Nations led by United Nations Commander Douglas MacArthur in mid-September 1950. The veterans stressed that only the KMC and the Seventeenth Regiment of the army among the South Korean soldiers participated in this historical battle. Their second battle was the Seoul Recovery, which liberated the capital from the Korean People's Army at the end of September and constituted a major military and symbolic victory for the United Nations. These victories in major battles instilled a sense of pride among the Jeju marines, as they had proved their worth as soldiers and refuted their hometown's history as the "Island of Reds." According to one veteran I interviewed, "We Jeju marines felt pride over our contribution to the victories. We also cleared our homeland of the false image and further improved Jeju Island's standing nationwide."[35]

These battles also created a new sense of identity among the Jeju marines as members of the KMC rather than simply as Jeju Islanders. One veteran recalled that "I can't tell you how we were deeply moved when citizens of Seoul enthusiastically cheered and waved *Taegeukgi* (the national flag of South Korea) in the streets after the recapture of Seoul."[36] Another veteran said, "Every citizen in Seoul held the *Taegeukgi* in their hands and shouted, 'Hooray for the Korean Forces.' It was my first time that I felt like a solider of the Republic of Korea."[37] One veteran, who introduced himself as a surviving victim of Jeju 4.3 to me, said that he got a thrill from winning battles as a soldier in the end though it took some time given his recent past. He vividly remembered:

> When we entered the Yongsan and Mapo area of Seoul, a former member of the South Korean navy who had hidden underground during the three-month occupation by the North Korean army rushed out with a long beard. On the following day, he submitted a list of collaborators with the North Korean army to my company commander. On that day, I followed my company commander to the nearby railroad bridge in Noryangjin where American soldiers were already pointing a gun at the collaborators on the list. I thought that some might be falsely charged just like Jeju Islanders. I had to shoot them in obedience to orders, but I slightly raised my gun and fired it into the air. . . . [However], later I felt a thrill as a soldier when my platoon killed fifteen enemies without any damages to my side.[38]

After the Tongyeong Battle of August 17–19, 1950, when a small number of Korean marines from the mainland recaptured the area of Tongyeong in South Gyeongsang Province, Marguerite Higgins, a correspondent for the *New York Herald Tribune*, praised the KMC in an article titled "Ghost-Catching Marines." Higgins wrote in biblical language and said that the KMC "might capture even the Devil." Henceforth, the Korean marines were called "Ghost-Catching Marines" or "Ghost Busters" by most of the South Korean population as well as American soldiers.[39] Most of the veterans I interviewed eagerly explained how they acquired the nickname. This flattering identification strengthened the Jeju marines' identity as South Korean marines, which in turn increased their resolve to endure hardship and commit themselves fully to battles. According to one Jeju marine's memoir, they charged toward Kim Il-sung Hill in order to uphold the honor of the marines at the risk of their own lives.[40] They at first had hesitated to attack the hill due to countless land mines laid by the enemy; however, they rushed into a fortress on the hill when a U.S. Army officer spoke to them sardonically, "Are you truly Korean marine soldiers, the so-called Ghost-Catching Marines?"[41]

After they won the ferocious Dosol Battle in Yanggu in June 1951, a strategically important battle for readvancing on North Korea, President Rhee gave the Jeju marines the title "Invincible Marine Corps." This further solidified their sense of duty to the state and the KMC. The veterans repeatedly boasted about their achievements in this battle and expressed their pride. According to many veterans, there were twenty-four impregnable forts on the mountain of Dosol. Initially, the Fifth Regiment of the U.S. marines attempted to attack the enemy there but withdrew without capturing a hill. Then the Korean marines took over with supporting fire from the U.S. marines and captured all the forts in seventeen days. Despite suffering many casualties, they felt great pride in this accomplishment as they not only received handwritten calligraphy of "Invincible Marines" (無敵海兵) from President Rhee but did what even the U.S. marines could not do. They again demonstrated their bravery in their next battles on Kim Il-sung Hill and Mao Zedong Hill in late August and early September 1951 and earned additional commendation for "admirable service by superhumans" from President Rhee. Following their victory, the Jeju marines cheered for *Daehanminguk* (the Republic of Korea) and *Haebyeongdae* (KMC).[42] Once maligned as "Reds," the Jeju recruits were now enmeshed in a process of cultivating reciprocal bonds with the state, forged through life-and-death struggles on the battlefield.

Jeju marine group solidarity was furthered by the fact that they had the highest educational levels among the Korean troops.[43] As discussed in the first chapter, Jeju's youth received a higher level of education compared to most other South Koreans because of their experiences during the colonial period. As such, the Jeju marines consisted mainly of middle school students and teachers, whereas in the Korean army, there were so many illiterate recruits that Korean language teachers were arranged in each troop unit.[44] The higher levels of education instilled a sense of pride. For example, one veteran, a student at the time of enlistment, boasted that they learned how to disassemble an M1 rifle after only one lesson.[45] This self-perception was mirrored by many superiors. Kim Seong-eun, chief of staff of the marines, wrote in his autobiography that he selected Jeju marines as artillerymen and members of tank crews because they quickly learned the technique of using artillery and tanks by applying their mathematical knowledge.[46] Moreover, their knowledge of both Japanese and English enabled them to read the American strategic map, which was charted by Japanese. (The English was written in a way that was consistent with the way that Japanese normally pronounced the Korean language.) Until college students were recruited and assigned to each troop unit at the end of December 1950, Jeju marines also undertook translation duties.[47] They often heard U.S. marines say "KMC, Number One" when they managed to communicate with them in English.[48] This stood in stark contrast to how mainlanders were often viewed by the U.S. soldiers, who often used the racist slur "gook" to refer Korean soldiers—North and South.[49] According to the Jeju veterans, the U.S. soldiers did not denigrate the KMC soldiers to the same degree. Rather, they said that the U.S. soldiers lauded the KMC soldiers' esprit de corps.[50] How much of this was myth is an open question. However, such perceptions of the Jeju marines suggests that they had a strong sense of pride as educated and self-disciplined soldiers—one that was furthered by the perceived approval from the American military.

The Jeju dialect, previously a marker of difference during the 4.3 killings, was used as a secret code in battles. Jeju troops were often called *molekuda*, which means "I do not know" in the Jeju dialect but alluded to their thick accent that made them appear stupid to some mainlanders. However, in the context of the war, the dialect proved advantageous in numerous ways. For example, Jeju marines used words like *dosegi*, or "pig," in the Jeju dialect, or *Aewol*, a county on Jeju, to speak surreptitiously to each other after they found that their radio receivers were being tapped by the North Korean army.[51] These creative uses of the dialect furthered the bonds of group solidarity.

It was on the battlefield, however, where group solidarity was most strongly nurtured. In recalling their heroic stories, the veterans often stressed how they overcame their hardships together, which in turn formed intense interpersonal bonds. They spent a whole winter fighting side by side without once finding time to take off their shoes, marched while dozing off from lack of sleep, and even starved together. They believed that their mutual support saved their lives, especially when it came to overcoming injuries. One veteran said, "How could I survive all the perils in the battles without the help of my comrades?"[52] According to the veterans, a marine never left when another marine was in trouble, even for his assigned leave from service.[53] Another veteran told me that selfless sacrifice for his comrades was his duty.[54] Due to an injury he suffered, he decided to explode a hand grenade to kill both the enemy and himself (he survived). Remarkably, he was a veteran who had enlisted to keep himself and his family safe.

Veterans recalled that their comradeship was stronger than the bond between blood brothers. One veteran said, "I was changed after my comrade died in front of me. Before that, I had not the remotest idea of what a battle was."[55] Another remembered, "In the battlefield, a comrade was more valuable than the state [at that one moment]."[56] The comradeship of the Jeju marines made them more inclined to follow orders, given their spirit of sacrifice for their brothers and the state. The Jeju marines, in fact, became known as the most obedient of all Korean soldiers.[57] Kim Seong-cun pointed out in his memoir that Jeju natives rarely ran from battles, keeping the military line, as ordered.[58] On the other hand, some veterans told me that many armies and some marines from the mainland ran from the battle, especially when they had to retreat.[59] High-ranking American officers also found that South Korean soldiers "just broke and ran" during the first two years of the war,[60] and the Morse code "HA" was used across the front line to signal that South Korean forces were "hauling ass."[61] Comparatively, one company commander in the KMC recounted, "The Jeju marines' bravery was admirable. They eagerly volunteered to be human shields on battlefields. . . . I had never met such courageous soldiers while I participated in three big wars, the Second World War, the Korean War, and Vietnam War, in my career."[62] As the above testimonies indicate, a number of related features provided the Jeju marines with a latent capacity for solidarity that was fortified through the experiences of training and fighting together. These, I argue, provided the building blocks for a larger integration into the emerging nation-state.

CREATION OF AN IMAGINED NATIONAL COMMUNITY

Benedict Anderson, a prominent scholar of Indonesia and the history of nationalism, argues in his 1983 book *Imagined Communities* that the spirit of patriotism is based on the fraternity of an imagined community or nation. For Anderson, a nation is a socially constructed community, imagined by the people who perceive themselves as part of that group. In addition, "the nation is always conceived as a deep, horizontal comradeship. Ultimately, it is this fraternity that makes it possible, over the past two centuries, for so many millions of people, not so much to kill, as willingly to die for such limited imaginings."[63]

As discussed earlier, from the establishment of South Korea in August 1948, the Rhee government pursued the state ideology of the One People Principle and a more general anticommunist policy, called *bangong*, to create an anticommunist community based on the same blood lineage (*minjok*). This notion of a Korean nation rooted in the same blood lineage actually predated Rhee and originated during the thirty-five years of Japanese colonialism. Leaders of the Korean independence movement evoked feelings of a Korean national identity by promoting the myth of a single nation with a five-thousand-year history in which everyone descended from one progenitor, Dangun. For example, Sin Chae-ho, a leader of the movement and the founder of Korean nationalist historiography, argued that modern Korea inherited blood, history, and culture from Dangun and his kingdom, the first Korean *minjok*-state, and thereby Korea had its own inherent sovereignty.[64] This idea that "all Koreans are descendants of Dangun, related by blood" had an important effect on mobilizing people in the 1919 March First Independence Movement and came to prominence in the 1920s.[65]

As such, in the early days of the Korean War, South Korean people did not automatically regard North Korea as the enemy, a different *minjok*, or a different state. Nor did they necessarily identify with the South Korean state. In fact, according to Kim Dong Choon, a Korean sociologist who studies the Korean War, while the elites of South Korea supported the South Korean government, many laborers supported the North Korean regime.[66] Meanwhile, when the North Korean army first entered the South, South Korean peasants simply kept farming and ordinary young people often just observed the situation.[67] Historian Steven Lee further notes that many Seoul-based politicians, students, and leaders of the labor movement voluntarily collaborated with the new northern government during its three-month occupation on account of their antipathy or ambivalence toward Rhee's government.[68] In part, this was a reflection of the brittle nature of the emergent state's ideology. As Choong Nam Kim, a specialist of Korean politics, illustrated, most South Korean people were ideologically confused at the time.[69] According to Kim, South Korean people did not fully understand the meanings of "democracy" or "communism" and were more dedicated to national unification, or "full independence."[70] Even as late in 1951, lack of patriotism toward the South Korean state was considered a significant national threat. As an editorial of *Donga Ilbo* noted, even South Korean soldiers on the front line lacked a sense of purpose and patriotism to the state of the Republic of Korea.[71]

Confronted with a massive military invasion and weak ideological support from the population, the new Rhee government therefore needed a stronger state-building policy. Rhee opted for one that advocated not just being anti-communist (*bangong*) but actually obliterating communism (*myeolgong*).[72] This maneuver enabled Rhee to elevate the state (*gukga*) above the ethnic nation (*minjok*) to better foster patriotism for South Korea. The government defined the "we" as South Korean people who would fight for freedom and independence, whereas it regarded "the national enemy" as uncivilized communist invaders and their puppets.[73] This framing advocated a sense of nation that was more clearly tied to the beleaguered state. From this, the government encouraged the citizens, or *gungmin*, of South Korea to aggressively fight against communists, regardless of their shared blood. President Rhee emphasized in media interviews that the *gungmin*, like soldiers, should be willing to fight to the death against communists; otherwise, the state would not protect them and their property.[74] In some cases, Rhee went beyond simply prioritizing the state and argued that communists were not part of the ethnic nation. In his Liberation Day address in 1951, Rhee declared that communists should be treated as a different nation or ethnicity "even if they are younger brothers and sisters."[75] The government used media and literature written by supporters to promote its concepts of *gungmin* and *minjok*. During the war, reporters and writers in South Korea portrayed North Korean soldiers as "inherent ruthless barbarians of a different ethnicity."⁷⁶ In these depictions, North Koreans' place in the *minjok* could be quite fluid. For instance, they also portrayed many North Korean people as victims of the North Korean regime who could still be part of the Korean ethnic nation. The South Korean government hoped its fight against communism would forge a new national identity, an imagined national community. And, in fact, according to Kim Dong Choon, the loyal *gungmin* perceived the Republic of Korea as a new *minjok*.⁷⁷

The Jeju marines were perhaps the first South Korean soldiers to elevate the state above the nation. From the war's inception, the South Korean military authorities had sold the spirit of sacrifice to the state. The official slogan of the chief of the Naval General Staff read: "I will respectfully put my life on the line for my state and my nation." The Jeju marines were introduced to this message on the way to the Incheon Landing by Shin Hyeon-jun, the first commander of the marines. The commander addressed the marines through loudspeakers: "The destiny of our motherland [the Republic of Korea] depends on the battle of the marines. Be loyal to our motherland at the risk of your own lives."⁷⁸ The Jeju female marines repeated the slogan before every meal in the Jinhae Training Center. This indoctrination was integrated during battles. The male veterans often repeated the slogan and heard it from their commanders during battles.⁷⁹ One veteran suffers from nightmares today over the following instruction that marines were given: "It is time to offer our body and soul as sacrifices for the motherland. You are like pigs that are fed and groomed as sacrifices for an ancestor ceremony."⁸⁰ Despite the dehumanizing tone in some of these slogans, the indoctrination made it possible for the Jeju marines to more easily justify their sacrifice as saving the motherland.⁸¹

U.S. psychological warfare during the Korean War further encouraged loyalty to the South Korean state by shaping soldiers' attitudes toward the communist enemy. The U.S. Army engaged in intensive psychological warfare through leafleting, radio broadcasting, use of loudspeakers, and other methods of propaganda.⁸² During the Korean War, the U.S. Army distributed more than two and a half billion leaflets over the Korean Peninsula by aircraft and artillery shells, a third of the amount distributed in all of the Second World War.⁸³ From the early days of the war, the primary targets of the psychological warfare were South Korean soldiers and civilians. The propaganda condemned the many atrocities that were allegedly being committed by the communists. The U.S. Army also used leaflets to strengthen the United Nations' support for South Korea.⁸⁴ For example, the U.S. Army produced newsreels and documentaries about the Korean War to justify the participation of the United Nations on the U.S. side and to denounce the Soviet Union for manipulating North Korea from behind.⁸⁵ According to one veteran, while receiving military training, Jeju marines watched these newsreels and documentaries in Incheon just after their participation in the Seoul Recovery.[86] Beginning in November 1950, the U.S. Army began to heavily leaflet North Korean and Chinese soldiers to lower their morale and induce them to surrender.[87] The leaflets, written in Korean, usually portrayed the North Korean regime as a puppet of the Soviet Union and China, revealing appeals to patriotism in the their anticommunist psychological warfare.[88]

In addition to such propaganda, the marines' first battles in Incheon and Seoul had a galvanizing influence on viewing the North Korean army as their enemy. It was in these brutal life-and-death struggles that they first realized the misery of war and began to distinguish friend from enemy. One veteran vividly recalled the carnage: "Incheon was burnt to the ground. We saw the enemy's tanks destroyed on the Incheon–Seoul highway. The bodies of dead North Korean army were on the top of their tanks. When we passed by the Han River, the bridge was destroyed and the bodies of dead people were floating on the water."[89] Another veteran said:

> Seoul was miserable beyond description. The houses were burned down. An old man was in a state of great dejection just after losing his grandson, and another woman was crying with her dead baby in her arms. . . . When we moved to Miari of Seoul we saw numerous bodies of dead American soldiers who first fought with the North Korean army. The South Korean prisoners of war looked like they were just killed by the North Korean army. We also witnessed that North Korean soldiers had killed civilians on the truck they had kidnapped as they were about to retreat.[90]

The marines were also surprised when they found the portrait of not only Kim Il-sung, the founder of North Korea, but also Joseph Stalin, secretary-general of the Communist Party of the Soviet Union and premier of the Soviet state, on the wall in most buildings in Seoul.[91] One veteran said that this convinced them that the North Korean regime was a puppet of Communist Soviet Union.[92]

Through this process, the Jeju marines soon came to believe that South Korean communists were likewise their enemy, in turn expelling them from the imagined nation. During the street battles in Seoul, they searched for collaborators with the North Koreans who had hidden underground while they also received information about them from Seoul citizens. According to one veteran, they transferred the collaborators to the South Korean police if the police were available, but otherwise they executed them.[93] Another veteran said, "When a citizen informed us that someone was a collaborator or a communist, we immediately shot the guy on the spot. He had a gun."[94] He added that "I never thought the collaborators were the same Koreans with me. They were just like the rebels at Mt. Halla."[95] Although some hesitated to execute them, the Jeju marines excluded the South Korean collaborators and North Koreans from the South Korean *minjok*. As President Rhee had urged, they began to treat communists as a different nation even if the communists shared the same blood.

Punctuating this animosity was the routine phenomenon of watching their fellow soldiers get injured or killed. One veteran said, "My comrades were killed in a string of bombings. Their bodies looked like pigs singed by fire that I had seen in the countryside on Jeju. We could not identify who they were."[96] Their anger over the death or injury of a comrade was directed at communists or the North Korean leaders. One veteran said, "My comrade's body was split in two. Who started this miserable war? It was the North Korean communist leaders!"[97] The female Jeju marines had similar feelings. One female veteran who served in the Jinhae Training Center said, "The recruits had been trained in the center for only two weeks. The notice of their death came to the center shortly after they went to the front line. We burst into a rage at the time. How come these people died? If the communist North Koreans had not invaded, they would not have died. I swore I myself would defend my state."[98]

Complex and often contradictory psychological legacies from 4.3 were also channeled into fervent anticommunism. Some veterans said that they took revenge on their enemies to compensate for the dishonor of being from the "Island of Reds."[99] One veteran from Bukchon village said that he took the initiative in every battle to remove the stigma toward his village.[100] Another veteran, a political prisoner of Jeju 4.3 who was released, also said that he had wanted to fight with the enemy as soon as possible since his enlistment.[101] One war correspondent noted that "the Jeju marines defended the state from the attack of communists because they wanted to disprove that Jeju was a den of Reds."[102] A more complex sentiment is reflected in the realistic novel *Suni Samchon* by Hyun Gi-yeong, the first writer on the Jeju massacre. In one moment, the narrator reflects: "Where did their [the Jeju marines'] valor come from? Was it overcompensation? Having narrowly escaped death several times after being unfairly labeled communists, they must have been eager to disprove that stigma by demonstrating their anti-communist ferocity. But that wasn't all. Underlying that valor may have been a deep-seated desire for retribution, a desire to visit upon the communist northerners the atrocities of the Northwest Youth Association northerners."[103]

The Jeju marines nevertheless maintained their humanity toward North Korean civilians when they retreated from North Korea due to the Chinese intervention in late October 1950. According to the veterans I interviewed, they felt sorry when they could not help all the North Korean refugees who gathered in the port of Wonsan or in Hamheung. According to the veterans, a rumor was spread that the U.S. military would drop a nuclear bomb to defend against the Chinese invasion. The veterans vividly remembered that the refugees were "wailing and weeping," "roaring," "swimming and trying to go on the ship," or "carrying a sack on their back" in Wonsan or Hamheung.[104] For the marines, the North Korean refugees were the people of North Korea, but the refugees shared the same Korean blood like themselves. Therefore, the refugees also could be part of the South Korean *gungmin* if they were not communists. In the end, some of the marines personally helped a few refugees by first putting them on the ship to leave for South Korea in Wonsan or by disguising them as soldiers and getting them on military airplanes in Hamheung.[105] In this sense, their loyalty to the emergent anticommunist state did not preclude solidarity with other potential members of the Korean *minjok*.

SOUTH KOREAN PATRIOTISM
AND PRO-AMERICANISM

The distinction between friend and enemy that was predicated on anticommunist ideology also led to strong pro-Americanism among the Jeju marines. When the Jeju marines and the U.S. marines fought together, America was regarded as the savior of South Korea and the guardian against "global anticommunism."[106] Displays of technological prowess and plentitude helped forge these bonds as American firepower was a major factor in the large battles, and the Jeju marines appreciated America's support. Marines recall that on the first day of the Incheon Landing, they paused to take in the sea, which was brilliantly illuminated by rays of light from the numerous American fleets, and heard the thunderous guns on the U.S. warships. It was the first time they really saw America's enormous military power.[107] They observed the combat planes, tanks, amphibious trucks, and other American weapons. "The entire Han River turned pure, bright, and snowy white when the amphibious trucks sailed to Seoul," one veteran said.[108] Afterward, they saw that the U.S. soldiers participated in all major battles with them in face of danger by providing them with covering fire.[109] Meanwhile, their unlimited military supplies from America, such as C-rations (individual prepared meals on the front line) and medical equipment, helped save their lives.[110]

Jeju marines were also impressed by the character of U.S. soldiers. The veterans said that U.S. soldiers were "brave," "gentle," and "kind."[111] The Jeju marines noted the rapid reactions of the U.S. marine advisory groups during joint operations. Although the U.S. marines appeared uncommitted at first blush, the Jeju marines found them conscientious about their duties and obedient to orders from their superiors.[112] They were also appreciative of the U.S. soldiers' sacrifice for them and South Korea. One veteran said, "We were hemmed in by enemies in Wonsan. The U.S. soldiers who had tried to save us were all killed. We were indebted to them."[113] Another veteran recollected that, "When our marines and the U.S. soldiers retreated from North Korea together, it was extremely cold. Some U.S. soldiers suffered from frostbite and could not put on their boots. They walked barefoot, the boots in hand and eventually had their leg amputated. We all shed tears. Why did these young men suffer from such a horrible thing here? We felt that we had no choice but to fight for the state till the last."[114] Whenever Jeju marines saw the bodies of dead American soldiers, they felt sorry for them and blamed the communist invaders. Cumulatively, these experiences fed their pro-Americanism, anticommunism, and support for the South Korean state—an entity that had previously authored a mass slaughter in their homeland.

By the time the Korean War ended in a bitter stalemate, a profound shift had occurred in the status of many Jeju Islanders, most notably the Jeju marines. If at the beginning of the war they were maligned as potential subversives, by 1953 they returned home as anticommunist, loyal *gungmin* of the Republic of Korea.[115] As this chapter has traced, this conversion occurred through an intense process of state engineering and group identity formation that was intensified by the raw experiences of the battlefield that worked toward strengthening the bonds between the marines and the emergent anticommunist state. As the brutality of conflict receded into the cold peace of an armistice, the marines had overcome the "Red" stigma, though it came at a heavy price: some 346 among three thousand Jeju marines were killed and over one thousand were seriously wounded during the war.[116] Motivations for joining the campaign were complex and multifaceted, but the result was durable. Marines returned home with intense feelings of patriotism and anticommunism that were congruent with the broader project of anticommunist state building in South Korea.

NOTES

1. Lee and Park, *6.25 jeonjaeng*, 74–75.
2. Interview with Kim Yeong-hwan on April 20, 2012, on Jeju.
3. Interview with Kim Seok-jin on April 5, 2012, on Jeju.
4. Interview with Kim Su-jin on January 22, 2020, on Jeju.
5. Interview with Kim Jeong-su on April 17, 2012, on Jeju.
6. Interview with Lee Yeong-hee on May 4, 2012, on Jeju.
7. Interview with Kim Seok-jin on April 5, 2012, on Jeju.
8. Interview with Moon Chang-hae on April 26, 2012, on Jeju.
9. Interview with Kim Su-jin on January 22, 2020, on Jeju.
10. Jung-hee Kim, ed., *Jeonmol haebyeongui sugi* [Memoirs of Korean Marines Killed in Action] (Seoul: Office of Information and Education of Headquarters,

Korean Marine Corps (KMC), 1965), 43. The editor was a correspondent during the Korean War who accompanied the KMC.

11. Interview with Lee Sun-seon on April 16, 2012, on Jeju.

12. Interview with Yoon Yeon-suk on April 7, 2012, on Jeju.

13. All of my female veteran interviewees said that the verbal abuse was the most memorable experience during their training in Jinhae.

14. Institute for Military History Compilation, Ministry of National Defense (MND), *Yeogun chamjeonsa*, 212–15; interview with Moon Jeong-yeol, September 5, 2013.

15. Interview with Kim Seok-jin on April 5, 2012, on Jeju.

16. Third and Fourth Groups of the KMC, *Chamjeonsilrok*, 177.

17. Interview with Moon Chang-hae on April 30, 2012, on Jeju.

18. Seong-eun Kim (chief of staff of the Korean Marine Corps), *Naeui jani neomchinaida* [My Cup Runneth Over] (Seoul: Itemple Korea, 2008), 306, 326, 328–29.

19. Interview with Moon Chang-hae on April 26, 2012, on Jeju.

20. Interview with Kim Hyeong-geun on April 5, 2012, on Jeju.

21. Interview with Kim Yeong-hwan on April 20, 2012, on Jeju

22. Interview with Kim Jeong-su on April 17, 2012.

23. Brazinsky, *Nation Building in South Korea*, 78–79.

24. Robert Ramsey III, *Advising Indigenous Forces: American Advisors in Korea, Vietnam, and El Salvador* (Fort Leavenworth, KS: Combat Studies Institute Press, 2006), 9.

25. Brazinsky, *Nation Building in South Korea*, 79.

26. Ibid., 80.

27. Kim, *Naeui jani neomchinaida*, 362–63; Chang-ok Bu, *Hangukjeonjaeng sucheop: Eoneu hakdobyeongui chamjeon ilgi* [A Note of the Korean War: A Diary of a Student Soldier] 3rd ed. (Goyang: Dongmunchaekbang, 2014), 71–73. This memoir is based on the author's personal diary, where he wrote about his everyday activities during the war.

28. Kang Sang-jin, a Jeju marine, completed a course of instruction in the First Marine Division Noncommissioned Officers School from March 25 to June 20, 1953. Moon Chang-hae, a Jeju marine veteran, showed me a copy of Kang Sang-jin's certificate of completion of the course. Interview with Kang Sang-jin on June 16, 2012, in Yanggu; interview with Moon Chang-hae on April 30, 2012, on Jeju; interview with Kim Dong-hak on January 23, 2020, on Jeju.

29. Interview with Kang Sang-jin on June 16, 2012, in Yanggu; interview with Moon Chang-hae on April 26, 2012, on Jeju; interview with Bu Chang-ok on April 12, 2012, on Jeju; interview with Kim Dong-hak on January 23, 2020, on Jeju.

30. Foucault, *Discipline and Punishment*, 13–69.

31. Pauline Kaurin, "Identity, Loyalty and Combat Effectiveness: A Cautionary Tale," 2006 Conference of the International Society for Military Ethics (ISME), http://isme.tamu.edu/JSCOPE06/Kaurin06.html.

32. Ibid.

33. Lee and Park, *6.25 jeonjaeng*, 80.

34. Ibid. According to Jeong Su-hyeon, an individual editor of collected memoirs of Jeju veterans, the Eleventh Infantry Division of the Korean Army retained about 80 percent of Jeju native soldiers and platoon leaders, and the infantry demonstrated their bravery in the battles. Interview with Jeong Su-hyeon on January 11, 2020, on Jeju.

35. Interview with Kim Hyeong-geun on April 5, 2012, on Jeju.

36. Interview with Kim Dong-hak on January 23, 2020, on Jeju.

37. Interview with Kang Dae-hyeon on January 18, 2020, on Jeju,

38. Interview with Kim Seok-gyu on April 28, 2012, on Jeju.

39. Kim, *Naui jani neomchinaida*, 280–81.

40. Kim, *Jeonmol haebyeongui sugi*, 66.

41. Ibid.

42. Third and Fourth Groups of the KMC, *Chamjeonsilrok*, 362.

43. The Student Volunteer Army, who consisted of mostly middle school students and some college students, was organized in July 4, 1950, and the number reached 275,200, including the three thousand Jeju marines, by April 1951. (The army authorities classified the Jeju marines as the Student Volunteer Army.) However, the members of this student volunteer army from the mainland were dispersed into the army, the navy, the air force, or the UN forces. Ja-kyung Kwon, "Hangukjeonjaeng, jeonhu bokguwa jawon dongwon" [The Korean War, Postwar Rehabilitation, and Resource Mobilization], *Hanguk Geobeoneonseu Hoebo* [Korean Governance Review] 18, no. 2 (2011): 283–84.

44. Interview of Kim Dong-hak on January 23, 2020, on Jeju. A Jeju army veteran recalled that there was the Korean Language Education Corps within the army recruit training center on Jeju that took charge of teaching Korean language to illiterate recruits from the mainland for up to two weeks. *Jeju News*, June 24, 2020.

45. Interview with Moon Chang-hae on April 26 and April 30, 2012, on Jeju.

46. Kim, *Naui jani neomchinaida*, 421.

47. Interview with Moon Chang-hae on May 3, 2012, on Jeju.

48. Interview with Kim Seok-gyu on April 28, 2012, on Jeju.

49. Bruce Cumings, *The Korean War: A History* (New York: Random House, 2010), 80. This derogatory term developed first in the Philippines and was frequently used by the U.S. military during the Korean War and the Vietnam War.

50. Interview with Bu Chang-ok on April 12, 2012, on Jeju; interview with Kim Hyeong-geun on April 5, 2012, on Jeju; interview with Kang Sang-jin on June 16, 2012, in Yanggu; interview with Ko Tae-myeong on January 4, 2020, on Jeju.

51. Interview with Kim Seok-jin on April 5, 2012, on Jeju; interview with Moon Chang-hae on April 26, 2012, on Jeju.

52. Interview with Kim Seok-jin on April 5, 2012, on Jeju.

53. Interview with Bu Chang-ok on April 12, 2012, on Jeju; interview with Kim Su-jin on January 22, 2020, on Jeju.

54. Interview with Moon Chang-hae on April 26, 2012, on Jeju.

55. Interview with Bu Chang-ok on April 12, 2012, on Jeju.

56. Interview with Kim Seok-jin on April 5, 2012, on Jeju.

57. Interview with Moon Chang-hae on April 30, 2012, on Jeju.

58. Kim, *Naui jani neomchinaida*, 150.

59. Interview with Bu Chang-ok on April 12, 2012, on Jeju.

60. Cumings, *Korean War*, 14.

61. Ibid.

62. Mun Kim, *Janggunui bimangnok 2* [Memorandum of Korean Generals, vol. 2] (Seoul: Byeolmang, 1998), 323.

63. Benedict Anderson, *Imagined Communities: Reflections on the Origin and Spread of Nationalism* (London: Verso, 1983), 16.

64. Myeong-gu Kim, "Hanmal iljegangjeom chogi Sin Chae-ho-ui minjokjuui sasang" [Sin Chae-ho's Nationalism in the Late Jeoseon Period and the Early Period of Japanese Colonial Rule], *Baeksanhakpo* [The Baek-San Hakpo] 62 (2002): 238.

65. Yeong-hun Jeong, "Hanminjogui jeongcheseonggwa Dangun minjokjuui" [Korean National Identity and Dangun Nationalism], *Minjokmunhwa Nonchong* [Korean Cultural Studies] 55 (2013): 120.

66. Kim, *Jeonjaenggwa sahoe*, 78.

67. Ibid., 79.

68. Steven Lee, *The Korean War* (New York: Routledge, 2001), 61–62.

69. Choong Nam Kim, "The Impact of the Korean War on the Korean Military," *International Journal of Korean Studies* 5, no. 1 (2001): 175–76.

70. Ibid.

71. *Donga Ilbo*, January 30, 1951.

72. Kim, *Massacres at Mt. Halla*, 42.

73. Dong-ro Kim, "Hangukjeonjaenggwa jibae ideollogi" [The Korean War and the Ruling Ideology], *Asia Munhwa* [Asian Culture] 16 (2000): 292–96.

74. *Chosun Ilbo* and *Donga Ilbo*, December 6, 1950.

75. Syng-man Rhee, *Daetongnyeong Rhee Syng-man baksa damhwajip* [A Collection President Rhee Syng-man's Speeches] (Seoul: Public Information Agency, 1953), 59.

76. *Donga Ilbo*, October 5, 1950, and October 11, 1950; *Chosun Ilbo*, October 28, 1950, and November 7, 1950; Jerôme De Wit, "The Representation of the Enemy in North and South Korean Literature from the Korean War," *Memory Studies* 6, no. 2 (2013): 150–51.

77. Kim, *Jeonjanggwa sahoe*, 8.

78. Bu, *Hangukjeonjaeng sucheop*, 17.

79. Interview with Kim Dong-hak on January 23, 2020, on Jeju; interview with Ko Tae-hyo on January 24, 2020, on Jeju.

80. Bu, *Hangukjeonjaeng sucheop*, 167.

81. Ibid., 105–6.

82. John Riley and Leonard Cottrell, "Psychological Warfare in Korea," *Public Opinion Quarterly* 15, no. 1 (1951): 65; Yong Wook Chung, "6.25 jeonjaenggi migunui simnijeon jojikgwa jeongae yangsang" [How the U.S. Military Organized and Carried Out Psychological Warfare during the Korean War], *Hanguksaron* [Korean History Studies] 50 (2004): 372–78.

83. Yong Wook Chung, "Leaflets, and the Nature of the Korean War as Psychological Warfare," *Review of Korean Studies* 7, no. 3 (2004): 95–96.

84. Seong Choul Hong, "Propaganda Leaflets and Cold War Frames during the Korean War," *Media, War, and Conflict* 11, no. 2 (2018): 251.

85. Ryeo-sil Kim, "Nyuseuril jeonjaeng: Hangukjeonjaeng chogi migukui nyuseurilgwa <ribeoti nyuseu>ui tansaeng" [Newsreel War: U.S. War Newsreels and the Birth of *Liberty News* during the Early Days of the Korean War], *Hyundai Yeonghwa Yeongu* [Modern Film Studies] 25 (2016): 79–81.

86. Bu, *Hangukjeonjaeng sucheop*, 49–50.

87. Chung, "6.25 jeonjaenggi migunui simnijeon," 380.

88. Chung, "Leaflets, and the Nature of the Korean War," 96–98; Hong, "Propaganda Leaflets and Cold War Frames," 259.

89. Interview with Kim Dong-hak on January 23, 2020, on Jeju.

90. Interview with Kim Seok-gyu on April 28, 2012, on Jeju.

91. Interview with Bu Chang-ok on April 12, 2012, on Jeju; interview with Kim Dong-hak on January 23, 2020, on Jeju.

92. Interview with Ko Tae-hyo on January 24, 2020, on Jeju.

93. This interviewee requested anonymity.

94. Interview with Kang Dae-hyeon on January 18, 2020, on Jeju.

95. Ibid.

96. Interview with Kim Seok-gyu on April 28, 2012, on Jeju.

97. Third and Fourth Groups of the KMC, *Chamjeonsilrok*, 109, 361.

98. Interview with Moon Jeong-yeol on September 5, 2013, on Jeju.

99. Kim, *Jeonmol haebyeongui sugi*, 45; Jeong, *Jageun yeongungdeului iyagi*, 21–22.

100. Interview with Lee Yong-bae on January 3, 2013, on Jeju.

101. Interview with Ko Tae-myeong on January 4, 2020, on Jeju.

102. Third and Fourth Groups of the KMC, *Chamjeonsilrok*, 700.

103. Gi-yeong Hyun, *Suni Samchon*. This novel was translated into English by Jung-hi Lee (Seoul: Asia Publishers, 2012), 133–35.

104. Interview with Kim Yeong-hwan on April 20, 2012 on Jeju; interview with Kang Dae-hyeon on January 18, 2020, on Jeju; interview with Kim Seok-gyu on April 28, 2012, on Jeju; interview with Ko Tae-hyo on January 24, 2020, on Jeju.

105. Interview with Kim Yeong-hwan on April 20, 2012, on Jeju; interview with Moon Chang-hae on April 26 and May 3, 2012, on Jeju.

106. Kim, "Social Grounds of Anticommunism in South Korea," 19.

107. Interview with Yang Jin-hyun on September 17, 2012, in Incheon; interview with Ko Ji-seon on October 4, 2012, on Jeju.

108. Interview with Kim Seok-kyu on April 28, 2012, on Jeju.

109. Interview with Bu Chang-ok on April 12, 2012, on Jeju.

110. According to the veterans, a C-ration box contained cans of beef, chicken, and corn, a biscuit, chocolate, cocoa, coffee, sugar, milk, and a pack of Lucky Strike cigarettes.

111. Interview with Bu Chang-ok on April 12, 2012, on Jeju; interview with Kang Sang-jin on June 16, 2012, in Yanggu; interview with Ko Tae-hyo on January 24, 2020, on Jeju; interview with Ko Tae-myeong on January 4, 2020, on Jeju.

112. Interview with Moon Chang-hae on April 26, 2012, on Jeju; interview with Kang Sang-jin on June 16, 2012, in Yanggu.

113. Interview with Bu Chang-ok on April 12, 2012, on Jeju.

114. Interview with Kim Dong-hak on January 23, 2020, on Jeju.

115. Most of the Jeju marines served in the Korean Marine Corps for several years after the July 1953 armistice because the KMC still needed them to maintain its strength.

116. Interview with Kim Hyeong-geun on April 5, 2012, on Jeju. Kim was the vice president of their veteran association at the time of the interview.

Chapter 5

Reconstruction: Jeju Wise Mother, Good Wife on the Island of Working Women

After the Korean War, the Rhee Syng-man government accelerated the process of incorporating its subjects into the Cold War nation state. However, rather than merely relying on coercion, it sought a more voluntary form of hegemony that was based in part on the consent of the population. The logic of national security and economic recovery were foundational to this agenda, and women would play a prominent role. The material and cultural conditions of postwar South Korea lent themselves to this fusion of gender and statecraft. The Korean War not only destroyed about 42 percent of the 1949 manufacturing industry[1] but also left at least three hundred thousand war widows in the South.[2] Moreover, the South Korean society was rapidly changing under the United States' military and cultural influence. American products and food entered the Korean market largely through American aid and welfare works, and South Korea began to be regarded by some as "small America."[3] Due to this influx, many women were adopting American values and lifestyles as they began to wear American clothes, copy American hairstyles, and even enjoy American dance parties. For South Korea's patriarchal leaders, this presented a dilemma as they worried that the adoption of American culture and values promoted sexual deviation, divorce, and child abandonment, which would ultimately hinder reconstruction efforts. By emphasizing "tradition" as a national moral principle in this radically changed society, the Rhee government and aligned intellectuals hoped to solidify the South Korean national identity and inspire a sense of citizen responsibility and duty to the state. Although controversial among many progovernment intellectuals, women were given the responsibility for restoring "traditional" family values and gender roles.[4]

In this context, progovernment intellectuals and the Ministry of Education propagated a female ideal known as *hyeonmoyangcheo*, or "Wise Mother, Good Wife," as a fundamental moral principle. The idea itself was hardly original. The idea of Wise Mother, Good Wife first appeared in Korea in the 1890s to advocate the importance of women's education for the modern nation-state through the medium of the family among Korean enlightenment intellectuals.[5] As will be discussed later, the specific notions of the female ideal varied over the period of Japanese colonialism, but they all tended to uphold the idea that the Wise Mother, Good Wife should raise good children and support her husband's work while performing her household duties with streamlined efficiency.[6] In postwar Korea, progovernment intellectuals often emphasized this notion of the ideal woman but focused on creating the image of a sacrificial mother to control women's sexuality, especially that of war widows, and to put the responsibility of child rearing on them. The postwar Wise Mother, Good Wife was expected to nurture future generations by sacrificing herself to care for the injured, orphans, and her children, while also having the primary responsibility for her family's economic well-being when there were no men available to do so. Motherhood was glorified as an act of sacrifice, and mothers were portrayed as saviours of society through the media, schools, and women's organizations.[7]

The Wise Mother, Good Wife ideal continued into the Park Chung-hee regime (1961–1979), which seized power in May 1961 through a military coup a year after Rhee's resignation in the wake of the fraudulent presidential election of 1960. Compared to the Rhee regime, the Park regime was more devoted to transforming its citizens, including women, into active participants in its economic development projects.[8] The Wise Mother, Good Wife was now expected to keep a balance between work and child rearing in support of the nation. Contrary to the 1950s, the idea of woman working beyond their domestic duties emerged as a key aspect of the ideal woman. The working mother was praised as a patriot or an industrial warrior, while at the same time she was expected to manage her home with a rational and scientific mind as a modern housewife. In this sense, the ideal women represented both a continuation and subversion of long-held patriarchal tropes.

This chapter explores the multifaced process of making and becoming the Wise Mother, Good Wife on Jeju during the 1950s through to the 1970s. It considers how the Rhee and Park governments attempted to implement their own ideas of the feminine ideal in Jeju society and the dynamics ways Jeju women responded to them. In the postwar period, Jeju received the moniker "Island of Women," as it had the lowest male–female ratio in South Korea following the Korean War[9]—seventy-nine males for every one hundred females—which was largely the result of the massacre of men during Jeju 4.3.[10] Relatedly, Jeju also had a lower birthrate than the national average due to many young men's deaths.[11] It was not until the early 1980s that the ratio of men to women among Jeju Islanders in their forties reached parity.[12] Thus, from the Rhee and Park governments' perspective, Jeju was a community urgently requiring regulation of women's labor and sexuality. This regulation of women bodies enmeshed women in broader processes of state building, such as economic development and capitalist modernization. However, within these patriarchal boundaries, Jeju women exercised considerable agency over the specific nature of their integration.

JEJU WISE MOTHER AND GOOD WIFE
IN THE POSTWAR YEARS

The Emergence of Wise Mother and Good Wife in the Postwar Years

The postwar motherhood ideal of Wise Mother and Good Wife emphasized "traditional" family values and women's roles, but it was not the result of Korean tradition. Rather, as gender historian Hyaeweol Choi has argued, it was a modern, global construct. According to Choi, the idea of Wise Mother, Good Wife in Korea was shaped through a convergence of Joseon's Confucian notion of womanly virtue, Japan's Meiji gender ideology, and the importation of Western domesticity and modernity.[13] In the latter part of the nineteenth century, the late Joseon Dynasty was confronted with an influx of new and modern ideas from foreign countries. In this milieu, Korean enlightenment intellectuals emphasized women's modern education for the advancement of modernity and national sovereignty but still placed a high value on the Confucian notion that women should engage in the domestic sphere.[14] In particular, Meiji Japan's ideology of *ryousaikenbo*, or "Good Wife, Wise Mother," had an influential role in the discourse of new womanhood in Korea during the enlightenment and colonial periods. Amid the rise of the nuclear family in the 1890s, the Meiji government constructed the feminine ideal of Good Wife and Wise Mother as part of women's modern education. The ideal women in Japan were expected to be educated and cultivated housewives while still being subordinate to their husbands by taking responsibility for household duties including chores and nurturing their children for the modern nation-state.[15] American Protestant missionaries who arrived in Korea's enlightenment period, according to Choi, also provided new perspectives on both "the role of educated women in the advancement of Korea to the status of a civilized country and the new ethics of gender relations in the Christian family."[16] The Christian schools and organizations, which took the lead in

Korean women's education since the late nineteenth century, introduced the idea of "women's work for woman," or "domesticity," to Korean women.[17]

While influenced by Japanese Good Wife and Wise Mother (*ryousaikenbo*) ideology and missionary ethos, Korean intellectuals stressed the aspect of the Wise Mother over that of the Good Wife.[18] In the initial period of colonization, they further emphasized the role of strong-willed mothers to raise children who could transform Korea into a nation that was capable of having a glorious future.[19] These intellectuals became advocates of "scientific" homemaking, which included the prevention of diseases, the maintenance of good hygiene, and nutrition, which were seen as necessities for raising heathy children and advancing civilization in Korea.[20] Child rearing was consequently integrated into gendered concepts of what it meant to be a modern national subject.[21]

This concept of a new, modern woman continued throughout the 1920s and 1930s under Japanese "cultural rule," which allowed a certain degree of cultural expression for elite Koreans. Korean women's magazines and newspapers promoted the role of women as mother-educators and scientific homemakers within the family. For example, in January 1929, the *Chosun Ilbo* emphasized that the education of women to successfully fulfill the duty of mother-educators would eventually promote "national prosperity and human welfare."[22] To buttress this ideal, Korean intellectuals introduced historical women of talent to the public to inspire national pride in a colonial context. Until the end of the 1930s, Shin Saimdang (1504–1551), the mother of Yi Yul-gok, the most respected Confucian scholar during the Joseon Dynasty, appeared as "the great model and representative for Joseon women" as she cultivated her talents and academic knowledge while serving as a wise mother-educator and good wife.[23]

However, during the early 1940s, the Japanese government reconstructed the image of ideal women as "mothers and wives of a militant nation" for wartime mobilization.[24] The new ideal women were expected to willingly send their men to the battles while exercising frugality to support the war.[25] Meanwhile, pro-Japanese Korean intellectuals projected the image of the mother of the militant nation in Korea who would raise a loyal subject for Japanese imperialism and take charge of protecting the home front.[26] Unsurprisingly, when the Korean War first began, this same idea appealed to Korean political leaders.[27] Women were encouraged to support the military with everything they could offer in the background, such as nursing, laundry, cooking, donations, and relief for refugees.[28]

In the early postwar years, political and social leaders reshaped the concept of Wise Mother, Good Wife by emphasizing "traditional" family values and gender roles to promote national identity and reconstruction. The postwar Wise Mother, Good Wife was expected to sacrifice herself for her family, and

Shin Saimdang was again offered as a shining example. Shin was reinvented in 1950s media as a national symbol of *only* a Wise Mother, Good Wife who infinitely sacrificed herself to raise her son to be a great scholar while helping her husband develop a rational mind.[29] She was no longer described as a learned or artistically talented woman in her own right. According to this configuration, the Wise Mother, Good Wife worked outside the home only when necessary. Therefore, while the South Korean government glorified female family providers as guardians of tradition, it limited the scope of their activities to earn a livelihood by emphasizing that these outside activities should be temporary and were undesirable. Although working women were often praised in women's journals, negative perceptions of outside work, such as the notion that employment infringed on the family's happiness and their husbands' dignity, were widespread among ordinary people of the day.[30]

Political and social leaders were also concerned that Korean women's sexual relations with Americans threatened the establishment of a national South Korean identity.[31] The ideal woman was expected to follow "traditional" sexual morals, such as faithfully serving a single husband. The ruling elite tried to control women's sexuality through the promotion of patriarchal ideology, while characterizing the perceived free love, romance, and consumerism of Western culture as threats not only to the health of families but also to economic development and anticommunist ideology.

Thought leaders in the cultural and artistic spheres bifurcated women as "normal" and "abnormal" according to the standards of "good" and "bad."[32] Bad women took pleasure from consuming and dancing or having love affairs with men, while good women made a commitment to uphold traditional family values by staying at home. Images of bad women were highlighted in novels, films, magazines, and newspapers. *Madam Freedom*, a novel about a woman's extramarital affair,[33] and the idea of the "apres-girl"—a liberal, calculating woman who attempted to gain wealth through love and sex—were subjects of incessant discussion during the period of reconstruction.[34] The character in "Madam Freedom" became a metaphor for egoistic freedom, vanity, overconsumption, or sexual dissolution, and the dance hall emerged as an example of the loss of Korean morality and the dangerous acceptance of Western materialism.

The Rhee government tried to implement the model of Wise Mother, Good Wife nationwide through school textbooks, media of virtually every type, national women's organizations, and official ceremonies and commemorations. For example, a national cabinet meeting in August 1955 declared the eighth of May as Mother's Day in order to praise a mother's spirit of sacrifice.[35] The government recommended that Koreans wear a carnation, as was customary in the United States at the time.[36] However, the government went beyond this and encouraged a whole week dedicated to the celebration of the same spirit of motherly sacrifice.[37] To help advance this gendered patriotic spirit, it promoted a piece called "Song for Mother," which was produced by the Ministry of Health and Social Affairs and distributed to school students and citizens.[38] On May 8, 1956, Seoul City invited one thousand mothers of fallen soldiers and policemen to celebrate the first anniversary of Mother's Day in the Changdeok Palace, a royal palace from the Joseon Dynasty. At this ceremony, they presented awards to thirty-seven mothers who delivered more than ten children or sent three or more sons to the war.[39] These awards highlighted a mother's importance in rebuilding the state through her child-bearing capacity, therefore upholding the patriarchal family system. Motherhood was further glorified in the following years through media, which spread the mantra that "Women are weak, but mothers are strong."[40] At times, the gap between the state's rhetoric and its actual treatment of women was glaring. For example, the Rhee government deprived remarried war widows of their pensions.[41]

Similar to subjects covered in the previous chapters, organizations played a key role in this aspect of the state-building process. Backed by the national government, the Daehan Women's Association (DWA) took the lead in implementing the feminine ideal. The DWA was created by the Ministry of Health and Social Affairs in September 1946 to promote anticommunism and improve women's social standing. The executives of the DWA consisted of female members of the power elite, and its honorary president was Francesca Donner, the inaugural First Lady of South Korea. It supported the establishment of orphanages, nursing homes, and correctional facilities for street children. The DWA encouraged women to be foster mothers of the orphans or street children they supported. The leaders of the DWA often visited military forces to cheer up and aid disabled ex-servicemen and held a special campaign for fostering young soldiers or sons of soldiers.[42] It had branches throughout the country, including on Jeju. Its Jeju branch sought to implement the female ideal by following the activities of the national DWA. The local media played a major role in coordinating this program.

The Role of the Local Media

While refugees from the mainland revitalized art and literature on Jeju temporarily during the Korean War,[43] Jeju residents in general had less opportunity than people in Seoul to avail themselves of other means of communication such as novels, magazines, and films.[44] Newspapers, therefore, were the primary medium for cultural expression and consequently were at the forefront of disseminating the Wise Mother, Good Wife ideology throughout the island. The *Jeju Sinbo*, the only local newspaper until 1956,[45] glorified the patriotic mother and the virtuous wife as heroines during the war. Stories of sacrificial female heroism were coupled with propagandistic headlines. For example, one story about a nineteen-year-old wife's loyalty to her deceased husband was titled "With Devotion for the Nation, Mrs. Yang Killed Herself While Holding Her Husband's Belongings in Her Arms."[46] Another, titled "Bless Mrs. Oh! Her Four Sons Were Sacrificed for the Nation!,"[47] told the story of a widow's patriotism expressed through nurturing four sons all by herself before sending them to the battlefield. Both of these stories revealed highly gendered narratives of female sacrifice.

Newspapers also were the crucial vehicle for promoting patriotic charity campaigns that reenforced gendered ideals. Following the end of the Korean War, the *Jeju Sinbo* held a campaign urging families to adopt an orphan, with the goal of supporting a thousand orphans (a relief fund for this purpose had been shut down after the war).[48] It praised members of the Pyoseon Bunyeohoe (Pyoseon Women's Society) as "*maeumssi joeun anakdeul*," or "warmhearted women," after they presented food to the area military command near Mt. Halla.[49] It encouraged citizens and school students to wear red or white carnations to "repay mother's love" on Mother's Day, or display the words "*Eomeoni Gamsajugan*," meaning "Thank You, Mother!," on their shirts and jackets during Mother's Week.[50]

The *Jeju Sinbo* contrasted these "good" woman with "bad" woman by highlighting the latter's sexual immorality. It published stories of prostitutes, hostess bars, and the prominence of sexual diseases among them. The *Jeju Sinbo* often reported news about prostitutes, pointing out "problems of the comfort women camp" while running pieces about their residency in private houses and the high possibility that these houses would transition into brothels.[51] Stories of perceived social contagions such as mixed-raced children, disease, and abuse proliferated. Thus, headlines such as "Cursed Mixed Negro Boy Died from His Stepfather's Kicking,"[52] "The Cannibalistic Market: Hostess Bars Are Booming,"[53] and "Divorced Women or Widows with Babies Were Wandering in the Streets; Over 60 Percent Infected"[54] were all circulated to reinforce the adverse effects of women's deviation from the Good Wife.

Jeju Wise Mother, Good Wife 1: The Elite Women

The question then arises as to what extent women on the island absorbed or actively participated in this process of subjectivity formation. This process was quite complex and distinct between classes. In general, women of elite social status who were primarily composed of the Jeju branch of the DWA readily accepted the female ideal. This was in part due to the modern education that they received, and they perceived themselves as being the vanguard for instilling among other women the proper role of the mother. The Jeju branch of the DWA was established in September 1948 by reorganizing the Jeju Women's Association, the first women's organization on Jeju in the wake Korea's liberation.[55] Some of these elite women were professionals, such as teachers and doctors, while others were full-time housewives who were married to influential men. According to former leaders of the DWA's Jeju branch, the branch was extensively organized, and almost every adult woman was signed up with the DWA by the end of 1950s although only the leaders were active.[56] Charitable work was a principal activity of the early postwar DWA. The leaders constructed orphanages, such as the Songjuk Nursery School and Jeju Nursery School, for war orphans from the mainland and the Jenam Nursery School for Jeju orphans, while supporting economic independence for war widows. One former leader of the DWA remembered that the Jeju branch raised funds for these works, and the leaders often voluntarily looked after war orphans.[57] Another former leader of the branch, who founded the Jenam Nursery School, said that she tried to nurture orphans as if they were her own children, stressing her motto, "Sacrifice was about love."[58] Underwriting this devotion was a strong sense of moral judgement and duty. For example, Ko Su-seon, the chairperson of the DWA's Jeju branch, promised "to become a true mother" to the outcast "western princesses" who prostituted themselves with U.S. soldiers.[59]

The elite women's embrace of this ideal was nurtured during the years of Japanese colonial rule.[60] Ko Su-seon notes in her memoir that she gave up her desire to have her own children when she married a man with children. She decided to follow a Japanese high school teacher's lesson that a good woman should give up pregnancy in such a situation.[61] Meanwhile, a former DWA chairwoman in southern Jeju who had received her high school education in Japan said that "I had learned that mothers should sacrifice for children through thick and thin."[62] The founder of the Jenam Nursery School also reported that "the most important lesson I had learned in schools in Japan was sacrifice."[63]

The Jeju branch of the DWA also promoted *Sinsaenghwal Undong*, or the New Life Movement, a governmental campaign to improve living conditions through the instillation of rational thinking. The movement on Jeju endeavored to simplify household duties, manage the necessities of life in a sanitary way, rid people of superstitions, and persuade them to use lavatories. (Conventional lavatories on Jeju, where human waste was fed to pigs, were seen as unsanitary.) The movement further regarded the indigenous religion of shamanism, which was widespread on the island, as an irrational belief. The leaders of the Jeju branch visited every village and educated the members about the New Life Movement, while chairperson Ko Su-seon petitioned Choi Seung-man, the governor of Jeju, to make the movement more active throughout the island.[64] A newspaper reported that some of the campaign's achievements were the "simplification of formal ceremonies," such as wedding and funeral rites, and the "enlightenment of prostitutes."[65] However, the movement on the whole appears to have had limited success as the majority of women on Jeju did not accept its ideals and retained their beliefs in shamanism and traditional lavatory practices.[66]

While patriarchal to its core, the Wise Mother, Good Wife ideology and its associated campaigns provided some space for Jeju women to challenge the male-dominated political landscape. Kim Myeong-suk, who promoted reconstruction projects such as women's enlightenment, assisting neighbors, and the New Life Movement, became a town representative in Daejeong in western Jeju in 1952.[67] Ko Su-seon chanted, "Let women go to the national assembly," during the 1954 national election, emphasizing the importance of women's political activity on an island where women outnumbered men. She also delivered a famous speech on gender equality during the 1954 election campaign, titled "After the Hen Cackles, Morning Comes and an Enlightened Society Arrives." The male candidates who opposed her slandered her political activity by quoting the proverb, "It goes ill with the house where the hen crows louder than the cock."[68] Finally, Kim Jung-kyo joined the police in 1947 and contributed to the New Life Movement in the early postwar period.[69] Though these challenges to gender roles did not change the government's policy, these elite women expanded their roles in the political and public sectors through their support for the government's Wise Mother, Good Wife campaign. In this sense, the ideology had certain progressive, if heavily circumscribed, manifestations.

Jeju Wise Mother, Good Wife 2: The Working Mother

While the South Korean government and local elites attempted to institutionalize the image of the female ideal, ordinary Jeju women often assumed the primary responsibility for ensuring their family's survival. The postwar years were highly perilous, and many islanders were destitute. In 1953, the *Jeju Sinbo* reported that almost ninety thousand Jeju 4.3 refugees were barely surviving in subhuman conditions, without any assistance.[70] Furthermore, droughts and typhoons during the 1950s made family survival nearly impossible. Famines swept the island following severe droughts in 1952, 1953, 1955, and 1957. The drought of 1957 was particularly devastating, as it was the worst in forty years and left almost 60 percent of the rural population without food. Typhoon Sara in 1959, meanwhile, was the deadliest in modern Korean history. After the typhoon, there were 63,406 refugees on Jeju (comprising 17,588 households), and over sixty thousand square meters (14.8 acres) of farmland and public facilities were severely damaged.[71] Through all of these hardships, Jeju mothers provided support and hope throughout the island. According to survivors, Jeju mothers never neglected their children, and they also took care of children of even remote relatives when the children were orphaned.[72]

Even under these conditions, Jeju women's participation in the workforce was considerable—particularly in comparison to the mainland. Throughout mainland South Korea, working women returned to their domestic duties once the war ended in 1953, largely reverting to prewar patterns. In 1949, before the war started, the percentage of women who participated in the workforce was below 30 percent, and most women worked in agriculture. While the rate more than doubled to 60 percent during the war in 1951 and 1952, it rapidly decreased to about 35 percent after the war.[73] This pattern reflects women's view on the mainland that their participation in the workforce was temporary and undesirable, perhaps partially accepting the patriarchal logic that underpinned the Wise Mother and Good Wife ideology.[74]

Comparatively, Jeju women's participation in the workforce did not decrease after the Korean War ended. Rather, they continued to believe that they should take responsibility for securing their family's livelihood. This had a strong historical precedent. During the 1930s, Jeju women's participation in agricultural labor on the island was almost equivalent to that of men.[75] While men plowed a field using cattle, women sowed seeds, weeded out, and harvested. The staple crops on Jeju were sweet potato, millet, and barley, which women had to relentlessly cultivate throughout the year. Beyond the fieldwork, women were also responsible for housework such as hauling spring water and firewood from the mountains for cooking. Certain vocations were dominated by females. When it came to shell fishing, for example, Jeju was dominated by female divers, or *haenyeo*, who harvested marine algae and shellfish under the sea without the aid of scuba equipment. This work was not isolated to Jeju as from the end of the nineteenth century female divers spread out to the mainland, Japan, or even Russia to increase family income. It is estimated that the number of female divers who moved to new areas was about four thousand by 1910 and over five thousand in 1932.[76] Industrial work also proliferated during the colonial period as other young women worked in Japanese factories. In sum, Jeju women were already economically active, internalizing a sense of labor cooperation and familial duty among women.

As such, in the early postwar years, Jeju women embraced the traditional idea of women as family providers and often took the lead in the national reconstruction project even if it was often under grueling and exploitive conditions. In 1953, about 90 percent of Jeju's people were engaged in agriculture or fishing, both of which entailed hard and physical work.[77] Many of my interviewees remembered that they worked days and nights to provide for their families. In some cases, even only three or four days after giving birth, women carried spring water for cooking and worked the field so that they would not miss the harvest period.[78] The female divers became an important symbol on the island when they resumed working off the coast of the mainland to earn cash income after the Jeju massacre. The leaseholders of the sea fields, especially in North Gyeongsang Province, took advantage of the islanders' desperate economic conditions. They overcharged them diving fees and sales commissions and consistently undervalued their harvest. Local newspapers on Jeju continually raised the problem of the "exploitation of female divers" and other human rights violations.[79] However, rather than give up the opportunity to early badly needed income, the female divers continued to dive until a boycott campaign in the early 1970s. In turn, the government's campaigns glorified Jeju women's hardship and labor as an expression of a mother's love. As a result, the reputations and images of Jeju women as *ganghan yeoseong*, or "Strong Woman, Working Mother," became more entrenched.

However, ordinary women did not blindly follow the idea of motherhood as sacrifice to the nation. Rather, they developed and expanded their own communal networks through solidarity and cooperation. Woman survivors said that they went through these perilous times by supporting each other through ties of kinship or village community.[80] Much of this solidarity was a function of women being discriminated against by men in terms of the traditional division of physical labor. While men generally did the work of plowing of fields, women were responsible for weeding and fertilization. It was often the case that women's work was more time consuming, and it was said by locals that for every day a man worked in the field a women had to work four or five days.[81] To reduce the burden, women tried to join together by reorganizing a labor network called the *sunureum*, or "labor cooperative."[82] Moreover, similar to the elite women discussed above, some women challenged the traditional gendered division of labor. In one unnamed mountainous village, where many men were killed and houses were burned down during the massacre, the widows constructed houses one by one by using a women's labor cooperative.[83] Prior to this, these women had never had any experiences of building houses, but out of necessity they challenged the traditional concept of gendered work. In addition, those widows established a new network among themselves to recover from the aftermath of Jeju 4.3.[84] In the case of female divers, for example, they pooled some of their income to build elementary schools and repair roads in their villages, which enhanced their position in the village.[85] Through such actions, many Jeju women organically forged subjectivities that were adjacent to, but independent of, those instilled by the patriarchal anticommunist state.

The Kinship Community and the Good Wife on Jeju

While promotion of the ideal of a Wise Mother by the government and its allies was successful to varying degrees among the divergent classes of Jeju women, the promotion of the Good Wife ideal was considerably less successful outside of elite circles. At their core, Jeju's traditional gender roles, particularly the issue of polygamy, did not mesh well with the concept of the Good Wife. The acceptance of polygamy in Jeju society conflicted with the monogamous sexual norms attributed to the Good Wife, and the shortage of men and the poor economic conditions reinforced the custom in the postwar period. Concubinage raised a specific ideological and cultural conflict. For South Korean mainlanders and the power elite of Jeju, being a Good Wife did not include being a concubine as concubines were blamed for making a living off the sexual temptations of men. However, for many common Jeju women, it was a way of protecting themselves against sexual abuse and maintaining a functional family life. Polygamy had long been socially acceptable on Jeju as a result of an imbalanced male–female ratio since the middle of fifteenth century during the Joseon Dynasty. Many men had migrated into the mainland to escape heavy taxes, tributes, and labor imposed by the local and national government between the fifteenth and the seventeenth centuries.[86] Though on the mainland concubines were generally limited to men of elite status, keeping concubines had been much more widespread on the island. According to a mainland official dispatched from the central government of Joseon in the early seventeenth century, "Jeju women outnumbered men by three to one, and even beggars had concubines. . . . Even the sick men had eight or nine concubines."[87] This official's observation is likely an exaggeration, but it indicates that polygamy had been acceptable among ordinary people on Jeju. It is likely that concubinage was neither admirable nor a taboo in Jeju society. Rather, concubines were treated as second wives, which meant they were legitimate family kin.

The family system on Jeju was based on a *gwendang* (*gwondang* in the Jeju dialect), or "kinship community," rather than an extended family line based on blood. The kinship community was a network of sharing and cooperation in family affairs and a means of providing for close kin. A second wife became a member of *gwendang* by having sons and fulfilling family duties such as serving at ancestor ceremonies, which was the most significant ceremony for maintaining a sense of solidarity.[88] By belonging to a *gwendang*, a woman could benefit from cooperative labor in farming and housework and ensure a proper memorial rite performance after her death.

On the mainland, concubines became the targets of public morality campaigns in the postwar period. Problems involving concubines were frequently raised in newspapers and magazines after the war. They were called "blood-sucking leeches," "subhumans with servility," "gluttons," or "parasitic insects."[89] There were also reports of violent conflicts between wives and concubines, suicides by wives and concubines, murders of each other, and even murders of each other's children.[90] However, no such articles appeared in Jeju's newspapers. Rather, the practice was widely integrated into society. For example, concubines on Jeju were expected to participate in important family affairs, such as weddings and funeral ceremonies.[91] They had the right to receive the all-important memorial rite upon their deaths, conducted by descendants of the family line. The concubine usually lived in the same village as the man's first wife but in a separate house, where she took full responsibility of her own children. Family property, however, went to the first wife's sons, indicating a subordinate status. This tradition continued into the period of reconstruction after the war.

According to my interviewees, keeping two or three concubines was very popular in postwar Jeju. "The economically competent man had even five or six concubines," one person told me.[92] The concubines were almost always widows who had no sons or means to make a living.[93] In some cases, married couples without a son asked a widow to become a second wife in order to pass on their family line by bearing a son instead of adopting sons.[94] An anthropological study of one village found an increase of second wives after a mass killing by counterinsurgency forces.[95] The killing left many widowed households, and quite a few of the widows, who had no farmland or kinship community to provide economic support, became second wives. Almost every surviving man had at least one concubine, thereby increasing his family's labor power.

Similarly, many ordinary Jeju women resisted the New Life Movement's attempt to break up the indigenous religion of shamanism. Shamanic worship of shrine gods and goddesses occupied an important place in the island's culture, in particular women's religious life.[96] The places where shrines dwell are called "the original villages," or *bonhyang*, and are named as sacred shrines, or *dang*.[97] The shamanic shrine, *dang*, had been the central society in every village, and villagers regularly worshiped for their well-being and prosperity in there. Women had often visited *dang* to make a wish to the shrine goddess, *halmang* ("grandmother" in the Jeju dialect), and female divers had their own goddess, *yeongdeung halmang*, who provided their safety and prosperity. In spite of the New Life Movement campaign, Jeju women were persistent in upholding their religious rituals. However, between the end of 1960s and the early 1970s, the local government forcibly demolished most of *hamang-dang* as part of the Park regime's modernization programs.[98] Even after the destruction of village shrines, Jeju women continued lamenting the spirits of the dead, particularly victims of Jeju 4.3, through shamans. In Jeju shamanistic practice, the spirit of a person who died an unnatural or wrongful death wanders around in this world as a spiteful soul. Shamans, who have an ability to possess the spirit, convey the soul's story about the death and may therefore provide a release from this purgatorial condition.[99] According to anthropologist Seong-nae Kim, this shamanic practice was one of the few ways to preserve memories of Jeju 4.3 during the authoritarian decades. Therefore, it provided an essential communal function as well as a potentially subversive critique of the state.[100] Similar to the cultural practice of polygamy, these shamanistic practices exposed the clear limits on how far the state-mandated ideology of the Wise Mother, Good Wife could be embraced by Jeju's women. Even under the weight of a highly gendered and authoritarian modernization campaign, Jeju's women selectively adapted themselves to the process of state building.

JEJU WISE MOTHER AND GOOD WIFE IN THE 1960S AND THE 1970S

Working Woman as a New Model of Wise Mother, Good Wife

The Park regime, which seized power through a military coup in 1961, sought to legitimize itself through economic development. The regime, according to Jung-han Kim and Jeong-mi Park, utilized "the desires of the majority of the people living in absolute poverty by promising economic prosperity" while transforming them into active participants in various economic development projects.[101] In the realm of gender, the ideology of Wise Mother and Good Wife was continued but refashioned to serve the interests of the nascent capitalist economy. A key pivot was that the traditional domestic obligations were dwarfed by the need for labor to fuel industrialization. Now the ideal woman was expected to participate in the capitalist modernization as a patriotic obligation. This is turn represented a broader cultural shift as the ideal women transitioned from one who supported her family to one who supported the state. This shift was apparent early in Park's rule. In April 1963, President Park delivered a speech in the groundbreaking ceremony of the Women's Center in Seoul, emphasizing the importance of women's role in promoting a healthy family, democracy, and modernization.[102] He said, "All our people must keep it mind that a healthy democracy comes from a healthy family and a healthy family comes from a good mother."[103] Again, in a message titled "Dear Housewives" that was published in a women's magazine in 1966, President Park asked women to be a "Wise Mother and Good Wife" who would inherit traditional women's virtues and participate in national modernization for the future of the state.[104] Yuk Young-soo, the wife of President

Park, also stated on Mother's Day in 1967 that an ideal mother should perform a variety of roles, including that of "an educator, a home manager, and a citizen of democracy," simultaneously.[105]

The change in the idea of what constituted the ideal woman was also signaled by the recipients of the exemplary mother prize by the Ministry of Health and Social Welfare, Seoul City, the Korean Women's Association (KWA), and other associations. (The national KWA was established in 1963 by restructuring the DWA.)[106] In these cases, the recipients were mostly working women who gave their children a decent education *and* contributed to serving the state through economic and social activities. The recipients were teachers, doctors, common laborers, or local leaders of women's associations who contributed to capitalist modernization through their occupational attainment and voluntary help for the poor, orphans, and the sick.[107] Ko Su-seon, the chairperson of the KWA's Jeju branch, and other Jeju women received the prize from the KWA or Ministry of Health and Social Welfare, indicating the importance of women's participation in the various national development projects.[108] As a dramatic illustration of the decline of the importance of traditional domesticity and motherhood, the Ministry of Health and Social Welfare announced in 1966 that a mother who delivered too many children was no longer eligible for its prize of Wise Mother, Good Wife.[109] Meanwhile, Seoul City set a priority for a socially active woman in awarding its exemplary mother prize at the end of 1960s.[110]

Shin Saimdang was again reshaped as the role model of Wise Mother, Good Wife—this time as a creator of a healthy family and an agent of modernization.[111] The Park regime highlighted her new image to mobilize its people for national restoration or modernization under the slogan "Modernization of the Fatherland."[112] With the active support of the government, the Korean Housewife Club, a club that was established in 1966 by elite Korean women, legislated that July 1 would be Shin Saimdang Day and created the Shin Saimdang Prize. The recipients of the prize were primarily elite women who successfully reconciled working and family life while cultivating their artistic talents.[113] In 1976, President Park ordered the building of the Saimdang Academy in Gangneung in Gangwon Province, Shin's hometown, to promote Shin's new images, a sense of loyalty, and national development for schoolgirls, schoolteachers, and woman leaders.[114] Though the government changed Mother's Day to Parents' Day in 1973 in order to enhance filial piety, respect for elders, and loyalty to the state, the government, the KWA, or other civic organizations continuously awarded the exemplary mother prizes to promote the Wise Mother and Good Wife ideology during the regime.[115]

In a substantial reversal from the dominant patriarchal values of the 1950s, women working outside the home was now encouraged and praised. Statistics reflect this pivot: women's labor force participation rate increased from 28.4

percent in 1960 to 38.4 percent in 1980.[116] In accordance with the government's export-oriented industrialization strategy, many women worked in light industries such as textiles and clothes during the 1960s and the 1970s. While they received low pay, excessive work hours, and poor working conditions, progovernment leaders and media praised these women workers as industrial warriors or patriots who helped obtain foreign currencies for economic development.[117] Jeju's local media and intellectuals parroted this ideology as they praised working women on Jeju, in particular female divers, as industrial warriors and "goddesses of work."[118]

Moreover, the Park government encouraged women's voluntary participation in various national movements. Immediately in the wake of Park's seizure of power in May 1961, the regime launched the National Reconstruction Movement. The goal of the movement was to boost public support for the regime by establishing a self-supporting economy and breaking down corrupt practices. The government adopted a sense of cooperation and self-help as mantras for the movement.[119] The national branches of the KWA were again mobilized to promote aspects of this national movement, such as encouraging savings and efficient home management. However, this movement officially ended in 1975 without fruitful results. More substantial was the New Village Movement, which was launched in 1970 and aimed to raise the standard of living in every village across the country. As part of this movement, the regime organized the New Village Women Association to mobilize women in villages across the country. This time the slogan of the movement was a sense of diligence, self-help, and cooperation. To boost morale and compliance, the national and local media consistently reported successful stories of woman farmers,[120] while leaders of the women's association emerged as exemplary models of the Wise Mother, Good Wife and often received the exemplary mother prize from the national government or the KWA[121] or the exemplary woman prize from the Yuk Young-soo Memorial Committee.[122] In sum, the ideal woman was expected to be diligent, cooperative, and economically active. In a sense, the ideal of self-sacrificing motherhood for the family was converted into that of the self-sacrificing female laborer for the state.

Jeju Woman Emerge as a Symbol of Strong Working Women

The women of Jeju were hardly isolated from these campaigns and once again responded in an adaptive fashion. In the early years of Park's rule, the local media began to report on a new ideal woman who voluntarily participated in state campaigns for economic development. In 1963, the headline "Miracle on the Plateau Achieved by a Housewife. Balance of Family and Working Life" told the story of a woman who developed wasteland in a mountainous area by herself while also managing a happy family.[123] Indeed, throughout the 1960s and 1970s, the local media continued reporting about "hardworking tough women" as a model of the Wise Mother, Good Wife.[124] For example, a local newspaper reported at length about "a tough woman" in a fishing village who contributed to increases in household income of the villagers and the village fund by effectively managing a fishing ground and establishing a conch cultivation business.[125] The local government and its aligned social leaders celebrated Jeju women's diligence and promoted their voluntary participation in the various economic development projects. Evidence of this appeared in *Jejudo* (Jeju Province), a periodical publication published by the local government from 1961 that promoted the feminine ideal as a diligent working woman who participated in the life improvement programs that began in the 1960s.[126]

Given Jeju's cultural conditions, female divers once again became symbols of this ideal. In 1966, the local government hosted a hundred female divers' mass performance in the water to demonstrate their sense of diligence to the public.[127] Historical female figures from Jeju's past were likewise utilized as symbols. For example, it offered Kim Man-deok (1739–1812), a merchant and businesswoman of the island who donated all her assets to save the starving islanders at the time of a deadly famine, as a "symbol of the diligent Jeju woman."[128] Further, the government opened the Kim Man-deok Memorial Hall in 1978 and created the Kim Man-deok Prize in 1980 to spread its message. The first recipient of the prize was Ko Su-seon, who took on a leadership role in the New Life Movement on Jeju during the Rhee and Park regimes. Jeju City and the Jeju branch of the KWA also tried to implement the ideal woman by creating an exemplary mother prize independent from government directives. The recipients of this prize were mostly women who actively participated in the National Reconstruction Movement and the New Village Movement and brought up children who pursued higher education.[129] This well-regarded prize contributed to the construction of the ideal woman image throughout the small rural villages of Jeju.

Beginning in the 1970s, the local media increased its reporting on female divers, thus elevating their symbolic value. The process was complex as the tribulations and sacrifices of the divers were recast into the narrative script of state development. The media reported on their wretched working conditions, human rights problems, occupational diseases, and export achievement while calling them "the symbol of Jeju women" and "industrial warriors."[130] The Jeju government likewise praised the female diver's sense of diligence as an "exceptional case in the whole world."[131] The symbolic currency of the divers was not isolated to Jeju, however. The national media also often reported Jeju female divers due to their distinct characteristics and reputations. Jeju female divers were already known to mainlanders as primary economic actors and anticolonial activists. The *Donga Ilbo*, an influential newspaper, introduced female divers as "women who work the most in South Korea,"[132] "the symbol of diligence and frugality,"[133] and "the symbol of Korean working women and the great mother."[134] Other influential newspapers, such as the *Chosun Ilbo* and the *Kyunghyang Sinmun*, also reported on Jeju female divers' hard work and strong volition for the development of the local and national economy.[135] Through this process, the reputation and image of Jeju female divers became enhanced and has persisted until today. Indeed, in 2016, the culture of Jeju female divers was inscribed on the UNESCO List of Intangible Cultural Heritage.

Compared to the 1950s, Jeju women readily accepted the idea of women's participation in the economic recovery and development, which drove them into voluntarily committing themselves to the modernization projects. Jeju's women were already culturally disposed toward such a campaign as they had already internalized the ideas of diligence, self-help, and cooperation due to their traditions and postwar experiences. Jeju women were still the primary economic actors in the agricultural and fishery industries. Much of this had to do with the aforementioned gender imbalance. It was not until the early 1980s that the male–female ratio of Jeju Islanders in their forties was at the level of 100. Meanwhile, the male–female ratio for those in their fifties was 60.7, and that in their sixties was 50.3.[136] Agriculture and fisheries were the main industries throughout the Park years, as the percentage of islanders who were engaged in either of these industries was 88.1 percent in 1960, 72.2 percent in 1970, and 68.6 percent in 1980.[137] Based on these statistics, we can conclude that from the 1960s to the 1980s, Jeju's women were a key component of the state's modernization drive.

By most indicators, Jeju women cooperated with the national government's regional plan of economic development. However, economic opportunities, rather than blind patriotism, appear to have been the central motivating factors. An illustrative example was the island's development of the tangerine industry. In 1964, President Park directed the local government to encourage the tangerine industry on Jeju. Under the plan, many Jeju farmers switched their major crop to tangerines between the end of 1960s and the early 1970s, in turn completely altering the island's agricultural industry. The tangerine area sharply increased from 413 hectares in 1964 to 11,200 hectares in 1974, and 91 percent of farmers were engaged in tangerine farming by 1973.[138] The profits from tangerines were very high, which further drove farmers to commit themselves to the national economic projects. Islanders referred to the tangerine tree as a "college tree" because the sale of tangerines could be used to pay for their children's college tuition. According to female farmers whom I interviewed, while they worked hard by weeding, giving water, spraying agricultural pesticide, and fertilizing dry fields or tangerine farms, they felt rewarded for their work.[139]

Concurrently, many women also participated in the New Village Movement. Following the government initiative, the Jeju New Village Women's Association was organized and its branches established in every village from the New Village Movement's inception. Jeju women were already frugal due to traditional practices and poor economic conditions after Jeju 4.3. However, they participated in programs of the association, such as opening a bank account and the simplification of living. They also cooperated with village men through projects such as village cleaning, road expansion, and the creation of village funds as well as other communal projects.[140] In 1979, a local newspaper reported on the "remarkable achievements of the New Village Movement" during the first half of the year, such as the establishment of fifteen village funds and the creation of a flowery path to develop the tourist industry.[141] I heard from my fellow villagers during my research that woman farmers and divers indeed worked hard during those years. I myself have observed elderly women's industriousness and economic independence regardless of their family income and property. It is still common today that elderly women do the housework and work on the farm as long as they can walk.

The female islander's embrace of the state-led capitalist modernization project, however, was not uncritical. Women may have felt pride with their diligence and ability to raise and educate their children, but they did not want to pass down their extreme labor burden to their daughters.[142] Once again, the diving industry became representative of this shift. Female divers participated in numerous boycott campaigns to protest their labor exploitation on the mainland.[143] Others left the industry by transforming themselves into full-time farmers on tangerine farms to earn more income or work in a more comfortable workplace.[144] This resulted in a profound irony as the number of female divers was reduced by one-third between 1965 and 1975 even while they became widely known as the national symbol of working women. Indeed, while in 1965 some 23,081 female divers worked in the industry, the number of divers decreased to 14,143 in 1970 and to 8,402 in 1975.[145]

Younger women likewise sought a more comfortable and decent lifestyle that was less exploitative and burdensome than that of their elders. In particular, young women who received a higher education and consumed the lifestyles of middle-class Seoul women through television did not readily accept a hardworking, sacrificing woman as the female ideal. For example, when she revisited the fishing village in 1986 after her 1976 fieldwork, anthropologist Cho Hae-jeong found that young women favored more comfortable and decent jobs such as teachers and nurses, while the number of female divers in the village remarkably decreased.[146]

If on the whole Jeju women embraced the economic opportunities presented by the state-building process, albeit in a selective and adaptive fashion, more resistance was found in the cultural sphere. On the one hand, it is true that more ordinary women began to support the new life improvement programs through the New Village Movement and women's associations.[147] A former leader of the KWA said that the association actively promoted the new life improvement programs such as cleaning villages and encouraging savings with the support of the local government.[148] However, many ordinary women selectively participated in these programs. They willingly participated in cleaning villages, saving their income, and kitchen and roof improvements, but they resisted the idea of eliminating their shamanic worship of shrine gods and goddesses.[149] Jeju women as well as Jeju men also resisted the move away from the use of traditional lavatories, even though the local government financially supported their abolition. Indeed, according to a report from the Jeju government in the middle of the 1980s, roughly three thousand traditional lavatories still remained in Jeju households.[150] Jeju people believed that a disaster would strike their family if they improved their lavatories. In the intimate domains, Jeju women's own traditional beliefs could still supersede the national movement.

As this final example indicates, Jeju women's relationship to the postwar state-building project was an ambiguous and highly adaptive one. In the aftermath of the twin cataclysms of 4.3 and the Korean War, the state sought to mobilize women for development projects through a long-held patriarchal ideology that nevertheless proved malleable under certain conditions. In the Rhee years, Jeju women were subjected to the domestic pressures of the Wise Mother, Good Wife ideology, whereas in the Park years, this ideology was reconfigured to integrate women into the state-led project of capitalist modernity. In cases where these ideological pressures conformed with existing traditions on the island or provided Jeju women with economic opportunities, Jeju women embraced their role. However, Jeju women, especially from agrarian or working-class backgrounds, selectively resisted aspects of the Good Wife, Wise Mother ideology, particularly when it conflicted with long-held indigenous traditions. This ambivalent relationship to the state would continue into the transition to democracy.

NOTES

1. Jong Won Lee, "The Impact of the Korean War on the Korean Economy," *International Journal of Korean Studies* 5 (2001): 98.

2. Im Ha Lee, *Yeoseong jeonjaengeul neomeo ireoseoda* [Women Rise beyond the War] (Seoul: Seohaemunjip, 2004), 28–34.

3. Eun-kyung Kim, "Hangukjeonjaeng hu jaegeon yulliroseoui 'jeontongnon'gwa yeoseong" ["Tradition" and Women in the Process of Reconstruction after the Korean War], *Asia Yeoseong Yeongu* [Journal of Asian Women] 45, no. 2 (2006): 36.

4. Ibid., 12–17.

5. Hyaeweol Choi, "Wise Mother, Good Wife: A Transcultural Discursive Construct in Modern Korea," *Journal of Korean Studies* 14, no. 1 (2009): 5–6; Soojin Kim, "Vacillating Images of Shin Saimdang: The Invention of a Historical Heroine in Colonial Korea," *Inter-Asia Cultural Studies* 15, no. 2 (2014): 277–78.

6. Choi, "Wise Mother, Good Wife."

7. Eun-kyung Kim, "1950nyondae moseong damnongwa hyeonsil" [Motherhood Discourse and the Reality in the 1950s], *Yeoseonghak Yeongu* [Journal of Women's Studies] 21, no. 1 (2011): 127–29.

8. Jung Han Kim and Jeong-Mi Park, "Subjectivation and Social Movements in Post-colonial Korea," in *The History of Social Movements in Global Perspective: A Survey*, ed. Stefan Berger and Holger Nehring (London: Palgrave Macmillan, 2017), 303.

9. According to national statistics, the average sex ratio nationwide was 100.03 in 1955 (National Archives of Korea, http://theme.archives.go.kr/next/populationPolicy /statisticsPopup_02.do), while the ratio was 79 on Jeju in 1953. Bu, *Gwangbok Jeju 30nyeon*, 116.

10. Jeju 4.3 Peace Foundation, *Jeju 4.3 sageon*, 88.

11. Jeju had a birthrate of 2.33 per one thousand people in 1958, whereas the national average was 3.27. *Jeju Sinbo*, September 14, 1960.

12. See Chang-ki Lee, *Jejudoui inguwa gajok* [Population and Families of Jeju Island] (Daegu: Youngnam University Press, 1999), 76, for the male–female ratio between 1925 and 1995 on Jeju.

13. Choi, "Wise Mother, Good Wife," 3.

14. Ibid., 5–6.

15. Ana Micaela Araújo Nocedo, "The 'Good Wife and Wise Mother' Pattern: Gender Differences in Today's Japanese Society," *Critica Contemporanea: Revista de Teoria Politica* 2 (2012): 159–60; Kim, "Vacillating Images of Shin Saimdang," 278.

16. Choi, "Wise Mother, Good Wife," 5.

17. Ibid., 10–11.

18. Ibid., 5–6, 13–14; Kim, "Vacillating Images of Shin Saimdang," 278; So-young Yoon, "Geundae gukga hyeongseonggi hanirui 'hyeonmoyangcheo'-ron" [A Study of an Image of the "Wise Mother and Good Wife" of Korea and Japan in the Formative Period of Modern Nations], *Hangukminjok Undongsa Yeongu* [Journal of Studies of Korean National Movement] 44 (2005): 108–11.

19. Choi, "Wise Mother, Good Wife," 14.

20. Ibid.

21. Ibid.

22. *Chosun Ilbo*, January 1, 1929.

23. Kim, "Vacillating Images of Shin Saimdang," 280.

24. Ibid., 281.

25. Ibid.

26. Ibid., 282–83; Yang-hee Hong, "Hyeonmoyangcheoui sangjing, Shin Saim-dang: Singminjisigi Shin Saimdang-ui jaehyeongwa jendeo jeongchihak" [Shin Saim-dang, the Symbol of the "Wise Mother and Good Wife": Shin Saimdang's Images and Gender Politics during the Japanese Colonial Period], *Sahak Yeongu* [Review of Korean History] 122 (2016): 176–79; *Donga Ilbo*, March 13 and March 18, 1940. Song Yeong, a pro-Japanese intellectual, wrote a script of the play *Shin Saimdang* and performed it in January 1945. In this play, Shin Saimdang projected the image of a militant mother who successfully educated her son, Yul-gok, during her husband's absence. However, this new image of Shin did not widely spread among Korean people. For more details, see Kim, "Vacillating Images of Shin Saimdang," 282–83; Hong, "Shin Saimdang," 181–84.

27. In-hee Hahm, "Hangukjeonjaeng, gajok, geurigo yeoseongui dajungjeok geundaeseong" [The Korean War, Families, and Women's Multilayered Modernity], *Sahoewa Iron* [Society and Theory] 9 (2006): 161–62.

28. Ibid., 161–62.

29. *Chosun Ilbo*, December 12, 1955; *Kyunghyang Sinmun*, December 14, 1955; Kim, "Hangukjeonjaeng hu jaegeon yulliroseoui 'jeontongnon'gwa yeoseong," 24.

30. Hyun Sun Kim, "Life and Work of Korean War Widows during the 1950s," *Review of Korean Studies* 12, no. 4 (2009): 90–96.

31. Kim, "Hangukjeonjaeng hu jaegeon yulliroseoui 'jeontongnon'gwa yeoseong."

32. Yoon Heo, "Hangukjeonjaenggwa hiseuteriui jeonyu: Jeonjaeng mimanginui seksyueollitiwa jeonhu gajokjilseoreul jungsimeuro" [The Korean War and the Appropriation of Hysteria: With a Focus on War Widows' Sexuality and Postwar Family Order], *Yeoseongmunhak Yeongu* [Feminism and Korean Literature] 21 (2009): 93–124.

33. *Madam Freedom*, written in 1954 by Jeong Bi-seok, dealt with an extramarital affair of a professor's wife. The subject matter brought tremendous attention to the book. At the time, wives of professors were perceived as models of the Wise Mother, Good Wife, so their extramarital affairs were unimaginable. The novel was made into a film in 1956 by Han Hyeong-mo, and women's sexuality once again became a very hot topic.

34. Eun-ha Kim, "Jeonhu gukga geundaehwawa wiheomhan mimanginui munhwa jeongchihak" [A Study on Cultural Politics of Postwar Modernization and Danger-ous Widows], *Hangukmunhwa Irongwa Bipyeong* [Korean Literature Theory and Criticism] 14, no. 4 (2010): 211–29; Kim, "Hangukjeonjaeng hu jaegeon yulliro-seoui 'jeontongnon'gwa yeoseong"; Mi-hyang Kim, "1950nyeondae jeonhu soseore natanan gajok hyeongsanghwawa geu uimi" [Family Configuration and Its Meaning Contained in Postwar Novels in the 1950s], *Hyeondaesoseol Yeongu* [Modern Fiction Studies] 43 (2010): 227–53.

35. *Kyunghyang Sinmun*, September 6, 1955. Mostly Christian churches and orga-nizations had informally celebrated "International Mother's Day" on the second Sun-day in May in Korea since 1928 (*Donga Ilbo*, May 8, 1956). Korean newspapers had annually reported on the origin and convention of Mother's Day in America (*Donga Ilbo*, May 14, 1933; *Donga Ilbo*, May 13, 1935). According to *Donga Ilbo*, Seoul City began to celebrate Mothers' Day on a large scale in 1950, awarding mothers who

raised more than ten children and senior women aged seventy-five and over. *Donga Ilbo*, May 18, 1950.

36. Korean newspapers introduced the American custom of Mother's Day. Those people whose mothers were still living wore a red carnation, while those whose mothers were dead wore a white carnation. *Kyunghyang Sinmun*, May 8, 1955; *Donga Ilbo*, May 9, 1956.

37. *Kyunghyang Sinmun*, April 22, 1956.

38. *Kyunghyang Sinmun*, April 27, 1957; *Jeju Sinbo*, May 7, 1959.

39. *Donga Ilbo*, May 8, 1956; *Kyunghyang Sinmun*, May 9, 1956.

40. *Kyunghyang Sinmun*, May 9, 1958.

41. Ministry of Patriots and Veterans Affairs, *Bohun 50nyeonsa: 1961–2011* [The Fifty-Year History of Patriots and Veterans Affairs: 1961–2011] (Seoul: Ministry of Patriots and Veterans Affairs, 2011), 70.

42. Kim, "1950nyondae moseong damnongwa hyeonsil," 134–35; *Donga Ilbo*, November 27, 1950; *Donga Ilbo*, February 3, 1952; *Chosun Ilbo*, November 25, 1952.

43. Byeng-tak Kim, *Jeju yesurui sahoesa* [Social History of Art and Literature in Jeju] (Jeju: Research Institute for Tamla Culture, 2010), 133–252.

44. Interview with Moon Jeong-yeol, a college graduate, on September 5, 2013, on Jeju. Moon remembered that she read novels and magazines published in Seoul and watched the film version of *Madam Freedom* on Jeju. However, according to her, neither the novel nor the film became the talk of town. Other interviewees hadn't heard of the film, although the *Jeju Sinbo* inserted an ad for it on November 29, 1956. Radio broadcasts probably contributed to the transmission of the government's policy on Wise Mother, Good Wife. With the opening of Jeju KBS on September 10, 1950, the number of radios gradually increased.

45. The *Jeju Sinbo* was founded in January 1946 by liberal intellectuals. It was occupied by the Northwest Youth Association, the rightist paramilitary group, for a year from October 1948. Digital Jejusi Grand Culture, "Jeju Sinbo," http://jeju .grandculture.net/jeju/toc/GC00702072.

46. *Jeju Sinbo*, February 8, 1952.

47. *Jeju Sinbo*, June 1, 1952.

48. *Jeju Sinbo*, March 27, 1955.

49. *Jeju Sinbo*, February 28, 1956.

50. *Jeju Sinbo*, May 7, 1959.

51. *Jeju Sinbo*, September 1 and September 5, 1952.

52. *Jeju Sinbo*, July 17, 1955.

53. *Jeju Sinbo*, April 2, 1957.

54. *Jeju Sinbo*, June 18, 1957.

55. The Jeju Women's Association had been established by Choi Jeong-suk, a teacher, and Ko Su-seon, a doctor. It created and executed a women's enlightenment campaign, including a crusade against illiteracy, until the outbreak of Jeju 4.3. Si-hong Ko, "Ko Su-seon," in *Jeju yeoinsang* [An Image of Jeju Women], ed. Jeju Cultural Center (Jeju: Hwasinmungo, 1998), 405.

56. Interview with Ko San-seok, a chairperson in the southern district of Jeju, on February 7, 2013, on Jeju; interview with Kim Jin-hyeon, a vice chairperson of the Jeju branch, on March 30, 2013, on Jeju.

57. Interview with Ko San-seok on February 7, 2013, on Jeju.

58. Interview with Kim Jin-hyeon on March 30, 2013, on Jeju.

59. *Jeju Sinbo*, January 31, 1953.

60. Jeju Business and Professional Women's Club, "Jeju-ui jeonmunjik yeoseong seongakja-ege baeunda" [Lessons to Learn Jeju Professional Women, Pioneers], *Women's Network* 10 (2006): 35.

61. Su-seon Ko, "Naega saraon gil" [The Way I Lived], *Jeju Sinmum*, June 19, 1978.

62. Interview with Ko San-seok on February 7, 2013, on Jeju.

63. Interview with Kim Jin-hyeon on March 30, 2013, on Jeju.

64. Jeju Business and Professional Women's Club, "Jeju-ui jeonmunjik yeoseong," 38.

65. *Jemin Ilbo*, December 22, 1961.

66. Interview with residents of Bomok village in southern Jeju. The movement was centered around Jeju City, the biggest city on Jeju. According to the police's inspection of the lavatories, the number of converted lavatories was fifty out of 2,364 in Jeju City in the summer of 1957 (*Jeju Sinbo*, July 11, 1957). Jeju-eup (town) was upgraded to a city in September 1955. Digital Jeju Grand Culture, "Byeonso gaeryang undong" [Toilet Improvement Movement], http://jeju.grandculture.net/jeju/toc/GC00700882.

67. Jeju Government and Jeju Special Committee for Women, eds., *Sidaereul apseo gan Jeju yeoseong* [Jeju Women Who Were Way ahead of Their Time] (Jeju: Gak, 2005), 86–91.

68. Jeju Business and Professional Women's Club, "Jeju-ui jeonmunjik yeoseong," 31, 37.

69. *Jeju Sinbo*, June 18, 1957; Jeju Government and Jeju Special Committee for Women, *Sidaereul apseo gan Jeju yeoseong*, 76–84.

70. *Jeju Sinbo*, November 6, 1953.

71. *Jeju Sinbo*, September 22, 1959.

72. Jeju 4.3 Peace Foundation and Jeju 4.3 Research Institute, eds., *Amuri eoryeowodo saljago hamyeon saneunbeop* [Those Willing Can Survive However Hard the Situation Is] (Jeju: Hangeuru, 2010), 157–58: Jeju Government and Jeju Special Committee for Women, *Gusullo mannaneun Jeju yeoseongui sam geurigo yeoksa* [An Oral Story of the Life and History of Jeju Women] (Jeju: Jeju Government, 2004), 173–74.

73. Kim, "Life and Work of Korean War Widows," 88.

74. Kim Hyun Sun pointed out that the increasing labor participation of women did not improve women's rights or change the idea of gender roles on the mainland. Lee Im Ha agreed, but she suggested that the participation created momentum for the expansion of women's roles. See Kim, "Life and Work of Korean War Widows"; Im Ha Lee, "Hangukjeonjaenggwa yeoseong nodongui hwakdae" [The Korean War and the Expansion of Women's Labor], *Hanguksa Hakbo* [Journal for the Studies of Korean History] 14 (2003): 251–78.

75. Takahashi Nobu, *Joseonbandoui nongbeobgwa nongmin: Jejudo* [Farming Techniques and Peasantry in Joseon: Jeju Island] (Jeju: Woodang Library, 2000). This book was first published in Japan in 1939.

76. Gwan-hun Jin, "Iljeha Jeju gyeongjewa haenyeo nodong-e gwanhan yeongu" [A Study on Female Divers' Labor and the Local Economy System of Jeju Island during Japanese Colonial Control], *Jeongsin Munhwa Yeongu* [Korean Studies Quarterly] 27, no. 1 (2004): 159.

77. Bu, *Gwangbok Jeju 30nyeon*, 208.

78. Jeju Government and Jeju Special Committee for Women, *Gusullo mannaneun Jeju yeoseongui sam*, 209–10; Jeju Government and Jeju Special Committee for Women, eds., *Jeju yeoseongui saengae: Saramsinan saratju* [Life Stories of Jeju Women: We've Barely Survived] (Jeju: Jeju Government, 2006), 293.

79. *Jeju Sinbo*, February 14, 1955; April 24, 1955; March 14, 1956; and April 17, 1959.

80. Jeju Government and Jeju Special Committee for Women, *Gusullo mannaneun Jeju yeoseongui sam*, 174, 188; Jeju Government and Jeju Special Committee for Women, *Jeju yeoseongui saengae*, 457.

81. Seong-nae Kim et al., "Jeju 4.3ui gyeongheomgwa maeul gongdongcheui byeonhwa" [The Experience of Jeju 4.3 and Changes in a Village Community], *Hangukmunhwa Illyuhak* [Journal of Korean Cultural Anthropology] 34, no. 1 (2001): 103.

82. The Jeju Government and Jeju Special Committee for Women, *Gusullo mannaneun Jeju yeoseongui sam*, 174, 188. The *sunureum* was a traditional network of cooperation in farming and household matters. Kim, "Jeju 4.3ui gyeongheomgwa maeul gongdongcheui byeonhwa," 95–97; Seong-nae Kim, "Memory Politics and the Emergence of a Women's Sphere to Counter Historical Violence in Korea," in *Gender, Transitional Justice and Memorial Arts*, ed. Jelke Boesten and Helen Scanlon (New York: Routledge, 2021), 88–91.

83. Kim, "Jeju 4.3ui gyeongheomgwa maeul gongdongcheui byeonhwa," 96.

84. Ibid., 127–28.

85. Jeju Government and Jeju Special Committee for Women, *Gusullo mannaneun Jeju yeoseongui sam*, 75–76; Rimhwa Han and Soonhee Kim, "Jeju Women's Lives in the Context of the Jeju April Third Uprising," *Asian Women* 17 (2003): 33; *Jemin Ilbo*, June 4, 2004.

86. Yeong-gwon Lee, "15–17segi Jeju yuminui sahoesajeok yeongu" [A Social History Study of Drifting People in Jeju between the Fifteenth and the Seventeenth Centuries] (PhD diss., Jeju National University, 2013), 35–41.

87. Kim Sang-heon was dispatched as a royal emissary who traveled incognito to check on local governments on Jeju in 1601. He wrote *Namsarok* [Travel Diary of Namsa] in Chinese characters, which included details of Jeju's weather, customs, economics, and geography. Hui-dong Kim translated this document into the Korean language (Seoul: Yeonggamunhwasa, 1992), 59.

88. For more details, see Gui-young Hong, "Becoming a 'Legitimate' Ancestor: A Sociocultural Understanding of a Sonless Jamnyeo's Life Story," *Forum: Qualitative Social Research* 5, no. 3 (2004). http://dx.doi.org/10.17169/fqs-5.3.565.

89. Lee, *Yeoseong jeonjaengeul neomeo ireoseoda*, 186–88.

90. Ibid., 175–81; *Kyunghyang Sinmun*, July 31, 1954; *Chosun Ilbo*, December 29, 1954; May 1, 1955; August 30, 1956; *Kyunghyang Sinmun*, February 1, 1957; May 15, 1957; *Donga Ilbo*, November 10, 1958.

91. Lee, *Jejudoui inguwa gajok*, 262–67; Young-ja Yang, "Sesi pungsokgwa jeonseung minnyo" [Seasonal Customs and Folk Songs Handed down for Generations], in *Jeju yeoseong jeonseung munhha* [Traditional Culture Handed down among Local Women in Jeju], ed. Jeju Culture, Art, and History Compilation Committee (Jeju: Jeju Government, 2004), 32–35.

92. Interview with Ko Ji-seon, a marine veteran and former public official, on October 4, 2012, on Jeju.

93. Interview with Ko Sun-deok on April 29, 2013, on Jeju. According to a war widow who had only daughters, the preference for male offspring was so strong that she was forced by her sister-in-law to work like a slave to make up for her lack of male sons. The Baekjoilson Bereaved Family Association, *Baekjoilson yeongnyeong 60nyeonsa* [The Sixty-Year History of Baekjoilson Victims] (Jeju: Baekjoilson Bereaved Family Association, 2011), 453.

94. Shin-ji Jeong, "Georeumeong bomeong deureumeong" [Walking, Looking, and Listening], *Jejusori*, August 11, 2012.

95. Kim, "Jeju 4.3ui gyeongheomgwa maeul gongdongcheui byeonhwa," 102.

96. Seong-nae Kim, "Shamanic Epics and Narrative Construction of Identity on Cheju Island," *Asian Folklore Studies* 63 (2004): 59.

97. Ibid., 60.

98. *Jeju Sinmun*, February 21, 1969, and February 22, 1972.

99. Seong-nae Kim, "Placing the Dead in the Postmemory of the Cheju Massacre in Korea," *Journal of Religion* 99, no. 1 (2019): 83–84.

100. Ibid., 84.

101. Kim and Park, "Subjectivation and Social Movements in Post-colonial Korea," 302–3.

102. Soojin Kim, "Jeontongui changangwa yeoseongui gungminhwa: Shin Saimdang-eul jungsimeuro" [The Invention of Tradition and the Nationalization of Women in Postcolonial Korea: Making Shin Saimdang an Image of the "Wise Mother and Good Wife"], *Sahoewa Yeoksa* [Society and History] 80 (2008): 236.

103. Ibid.

104. Ibid., 257.

105. *Maeil Gyeongje*, May 8, 1967.

106. The Jeju branch of the KWA was established in November 1964, and the number of its members reached over sixty-five thousand. *Jeju Sinmun*, June 10, 1975.

107. *Chosun Ilbo*, May 9, 1964; May 2, 1965; *Donga Ilbo*, May 7, 1965; *Chosun Ilbo*, May 4, 1969; April 29, 1970; *Kyunghyang Sinmun*, May 1, 1970; *Chosun Ilbo*, April 30, 1972; *Maeil Gyeongje*, May 8, 1972.

108. *Maeil Gyeongje*, May 3, 1967; *Jeju Sinmun*, April 17, 1970; May 8, 1973; May 8, 1974.

109. *Chosun Ilbo*, April 13, 1966.

110. *Chosun Ilbo*, May 3, 1970.

111. Kim, "Jeontongui changangwa yeoseongui gungminhwa," 236–40.

112. O-heon Gwon, "Yushin chejeui Shin Saimdang ginyeomgwa hyeonmoyang-cheo mandeulgi" [The Yushin Regime's Attempt to Set Shin Saimdang as a Role Model and Encourage Women to Be a "Wise Mother and Good Wife" after Her], *Journal of Korean Culture* 35 (2016): 68–69.

113. Kim, "Jeontongui changangwa yeoseongui gungminhwa," 241–43.

114. Gwon, "Yushin chejeui Shin Saimdang," 72, 78.

115. *Donga Ilbo*, May 8, 1973; *Kyunghyang Sinmun*, May 3, 1974; *Chosun Ilbo*, May 8, 1977; *Donga Ilbo*, December 22, 1978.

116. National Bureau of Statistics of Economic Planning Board, *1960 ingu jutaek guksejosa bogo* [1960 Population and Housing Census Report] (Seoul: Economic Planning Board, 1963); National Bureau of Statistics of Economic Planning Board, *1980 ingu mit jutaek census bogoseo* [1980 Population and Housing Census Report] (Seoul: Economic Planning Board, 1982).

117. Kim and Park, "Subjectivation and Social Movements in Post-colonial Korea," 307.

118. *Jeju Sinmun*, June 11 and November 3, 1975; Dae-won Kang, *Haenyeo yeongu* [A Study of Female Divers] (Seoul: Hanjin Munhwasa, 1973), 70.

119. Eun Heo, "'5.16 gunjeonggi' jaegeongungminundongui seonggyeok" [The Characteristics of the National Reconstruction Movement under the Military Government That Seized Power through a Coup in May 1961], *Yeoksamunje Yeongu* [Critical Studies of Modern Korean History] 11 (2004): 21.

120. *Kyunghyang Sinmun*, February 8, 1975; *Chosun Ilbo*, December 11, 1975; *Kyunghyang Sinmun*, June 26, 1976.

121. *Chosun Ilbo*, April 30, 1972; *Donga Ilbo*, May 7, 1977; *Kyunghyang Sinmun*, August 5, 1977.

122. *Kyunghyang Sinmun*, November 13, 1976. Yuk Young-soo was killed in 1974 during an attempted assassination of her husband, President Park.

123. *Jeju Sinmun*, August 20, 1963.

124. E.g., *Jeju Sinmun*, May 22–June 9, 1964; April 20, 1970; January 10, 1974; April 3, 1978.

125. *Jenam Sinmun*, April 3, 1978.

126. Dong-gyu Kim, "Jaegeon cheong/buinhoe-e baraneun geot" [What I Would Like the National Reconstruction Youth Association and the Women's Association to Do], *Jejudo* [Jeju Province] 5 (1962): 32–36; Du-hui Ko, "Yeoseonggwa sinang" [Women and Belief], *Jejudo* [Jeju Province] 13 (1964): 147; Gyeong-hwan Kim, "Jeju yeoseongui jiyeokjeok gwaeop" [The Role of Jeju Women in the Community Development], *Jejudo* [Jeju Province] 13 (1964): 149–54.

127. The Public Information Office of the Jeju Government introduced the photo of female diver's mass performance in its edited magazine, *Jejudo* [Jeju Province] 26 (1966).

128. *Jeju Sinmun*, September 18, 1973, and July 14, 1978.

129. *Jenam Sinmun*, May 9, 1968; April 28, 1969; May 8, 1969; May 8, 1972; May 8, 1973; May 8, 1974.

130. E.g., *Jeju Sinmun*, May 2, 1970; August 27, 1970; October 22, 1973; June 11, 1975; November 3, 1975; June 27, 1977.

131. Yeong-don Kim, "Jejudominui geunmyeonseong" [Diligence of Jeju Residents], *Jejudo* [Jeju Province] 43 (1970): 193–94.

132. *Donga Ilbo*, July 1, 1970.

133. *Donga Ilbo*, July 29, 1970.

134. *Donga Ilbo*, August 6, 1970.

135. *Kyunghyang Sinmun*, March 19, 1973; *Chosun Ilbo*, September 20, 1975.

136. Lee, *Jejudoui inguwa gajok*, 76.

137. Eun-ju Lee and Ok-hwa Oh, "Yeoseongui sahoechamyeo hwakdae bangan" [Ways of Expanding Women's Social Participation], in *21segi modureul wihan jejudo* [Jeju Island for All in the Twenty-First Century], ed. Jeju Development Research Institute (Jeju: Jeju Development Research Institute, 1998), 215.

138. Digital Jeju Grand Culture, "Gamgyul" [Tangerine], 2011, http://jeju.grandculture.net/jeju/toc/GC00700046.

139. Interviews with tangerine farmers in Bomok village in southern Jeju; Jeju Government and Jeju Special Committee for Women, *Gusullo mannaneun Jeju yeoseongui sam*, 118, 201.

140. Jeju Government and Jeju Special Committee for Women, *Jeju yeoseongui saengae*, 64–65, 67–68, 490–91; *Jeju Sinmun*, May 29, 1978, and June 30, 1978.

141. *Jenam Sinmun*, July 23, 1979.

142. Jeju Government and Jeju Special Committee for Women, *Jeju yeoseongui saengae*, 133–34, 329.

143. *Jeju Sinmun*, May 21, 1970, and July 8, 1976.

144. *Jenam Sinmum*, October 22, 1973.

145. Department of Fisheries in Jeju Provincial Government, unpublished, 2003.

146. Hae-jeong Cho, *Hangukui yeoseonggwa namseong* [Korean Women and Men] (Seoul: Munji Publishing, 1988), 317–18.

147. *Jeju Sinmun*, December 9, 1975.

148. Interview with Ko San-seok on February 7, 2013, on Jeju.

149. Jeju Government and Jeju Special Committee for Women, *Jeju yeoseongui saengae*, 69, 487.

150. Digital Jeju Grand Culture, "Byeonso gaeryang undong."

Chapter 6

Reconciliation: The Jeju 4.3 Peace Park

The year 2003 represented a watershed in Jeju 4.3's place in South Korean national history. The Jeju 4.3 National Committee first authored a history of the mass killings in which the state was portrayed as the principal architect and the official victims mainly consisted of those who were accused of being communists. Moreover, President Roh Moo-hyun officially apologized for the state violence and promised to reconcile the conflict before the victims and the bereaved families. Both of these events were the result of decades of work by activists that culminated in the passage the Jeju 4.3 Special Act in 2000, which sought to investigate the truth of Jeju 4.3 and honor the victims and their families. Given the nature of the atrocity and South Korea's historical identity as an anticommunist state, it is dramatic that it acknowledged its own past wrongdoings. Indeed, roughly a decade and a half prior to this, survivors could not publicly share their memories unless they fit the authoritarian regimes' official narrative. Tellingly, the title of the first collection of testimony about the events published in 1989 was *Ijesa malhaemsuda*, or "Now We Speak Out"—indicating a cathartic release to decades of repression and enforced silencing.[1]

Throughout the decade, the momentum continued. Two years after the apology, Roh declared Jeju an Island of World Peace to sublimate the tragedy of Jeju 4.3 into a story of reconciliation and coexistence that contributed to world peace. Given that it was once labeled an "Island of Reds," this inversion is remarkable. Perhaps most importantly, the Jeju 4.3 National Committee began to construct the Jeju 4.3 Peace Park, the only national memorial museum and park dedicated to Jeju 4.3.[2] Opened in 2008, the park covers 395,380 square meters (88.8 acres) and includes the Memorial Tablets Enshrinement Room, the Memorial Service Altar, the Headstone Monument Engraved with the Names of the Deceased, the Tombstone Park for the Missing, the Jeju 4.3 Peace Memorial Hall, and the Ashes Enshrinement

119

Hall.[3] The park has remained a potent expression of the reconciliation efforts for Jeju 4.3, and an official annual memorial ceremony for Jeju 4.3 has taken place on April 3 at the site of the park since 2000. In addition to visiting the park on this day, students, tour groups, families, and individuals make pilgrimages throughout the year. For example, about four hundred thousand people visited the park yearly before the arrival of the coronavirus pandemic in 2020.[4] According to a survey of South Korean visitors to the park in 2008 conducted by scholars, the visitors found the site "emotional, powerful and memorable."[5] The park has also attracted visitors from around the world through the emerging global phenomenon of "dark tourism," which involves travel to historic sites associated with mass suffering.[6] In short, the park is becoming more important in the creation of a new public memory of Jeju 4.3, both locally and globally.

This chapter explores the reconciliation of the conflict of Jeju 4.3 through an analysis of the Jeju 4.3 Peace Park. I argue that the state strategically intervened in the construction process of the park to present itself as a mature democracy while advancing national unity and harmony. To facilitate this, the state mediated between those who supported the narrative of "communist rebellion" and those who supported alternative narratives such as a "people's uprising" and "state violence." Moreover, it actively played a role as a peacemaker, shifting the discourse of Jeju 4.3 into peace for future generations. This pivot, I argue, entailed a strategic displacement of the state's role as a facilitator of violence into one of its future prevention. These cumulative shifts were both constituted by and constitutive of South Korea's democratic transition.

THE JEJU 4.3 TRANSITIONAL JUSTICE PROCESS
AND THE DEVELOPMENT OF DEMOCRACY

Transitional justice is embedded in larger processes of democratic state building. According to the United Nations, transitional justice refers to "the full range of processes and mechanisms associated with a society's attempts to come to terms with a legacy of large-scale past abuses in order to ensure accountability and justice, and achieve reconciliation."[7] Scholars of transitional justice further remark that the "introduction of transitional justice measures is regarded to be an important part of state building and political transition efforts."[8] From the 1980s onward, many countries, including South Korea, have implemented transitional justice measures as part of their transitions to democracy and democratic consolidation.[9] The relationship between transitional justice and democratic state building is mutually constitutive. According to Tilly, "a regime is democratic to the degree that political relations between the state and its citizens feature broad, equal, protected and mutually binding consultation."[10] Tilly argues that "democracy gives popular voice (however grudging) a significant influence over a ruler's performance."[11] Indeed, the extent of transitional justice of Jeju 4.3 has been associated with the degree of democracy in South Korea.

South Korea experienced democracy for the first time after the resignation of Rhee Syng-man in the wake of the 1960 mass protests against the fraudulent election for president and vice president. Immediately following Rhee's resignation, victims of civilian massacres that had occurred under the Rhee regime, such as the massacre of National Guidance Alliance members, and their families, demanded that the new government of Jang Myeon restore the honor of the victims. These petitions were met with initial success when the Congressional Special Committee for Investigation of Civilian Deaths was set up by the National Assembly in May 1960 to investigate the civilian massacres.[12] As part of this process, Jeju college students, journalists, and local assembly members took the initiative in investigating Jeju 4.3 and submitted an investigation report to the special committee in the National Assembly. However, these efforts came to an abrupt halt when Park Chung-hee seized power by military coup on May 16, 1961. Immediately following the coup, the Jeju students and journalists were arrested for fomenting social unrest, and two months later the military government established the Anti-Communism Law to punish offenders who opposed its anticommunist policies.[13] State repression was highly effective, as victims of civilian massacres on Jeju and the mainland remained silent throughout Park's tenure. Writers and artists were no exception and had good reasons to stay reticent. For example, when Hyun Gi-yeong described the mass killing of innocent people of Jeju 4.3 in his 1978 novel *Suni Samchon*, he was jailed and severely tortured, while publication of his book was prohibited.[14]

The landscape began to shift, however, following South Korea's 1987 democratic transition. The transition may have appeared sudden to outside observers, but it was a result of economic development, the expansion of the middle class, international pressure, and a particularly long struggle for democracy by prodemocracy forces, including intellectuals, students, workers, and human rights organizations.[15] Concerning the latter forces, this process was incubated in the early years of the Park regime's Yusin dictatorship. In 1972, Park enacted the Yusin Constitution, which removed direct elections for the president, effectively turning his presidency into a legal dictatorship for life. The Park government exercised more violent and arbitrary power in suppressing civil rights, but this exacerbated resistance. Student protests were enough of a threat for the regime to issue a presidential Emergency Decree to outlaw progressive student associations in 1974.[16] Amid political instability, Park was assassinated by Kim Jae-kyu, the director of the Korean Central Intelligence Agency, in October 1979. South Korean people had expected democratization in the wake of Park's death, but General Chun Doo-hwan's launched a military coup in December 1979. Chun strengthened authoritarianism and economic development while strictly controlling the media and suppressing workers' strikes.

In spite of the persistent repression, a prodemocracy movement began. Students and citizens in Gwangju in South Jeolla Province protested against Chun's military rule in May 1980. In response, the regime ordered the military to open fire on civilians. As a result, the estimated number of victims was at least 5,189, including 163 civilian deaths, 166 disappearances, 3,139 injuries, and 1,589 arrests and detentions, according to the 2009 investigation by Gwangju City.[17] After regrouping for a few years, prodemocracy forces resumed protests nationwide in May 1985, demanding that the government apologize for the Gwangju massacre while criticizing the United States for its support of Chun's government. The protests resulted to the 1987 June Democratic Struggle—a decisive turning point in South Korea's democratization—when many people, including middle-class citizens, rose up nationwide to end the coercive rule. Chun finally accepted the protestors' demand for a direct presidential election system and other reforms to the South Korean constitution on June 29.

With democratization, many Jeju people were released from the guilt-by-association system that discriminated against family members of alleged communists in employment, promotion, and even international travel for over four decades. Now provided with an expanded political and ideological space, the Jeju 4.3 advocacy movement began in earnest. Local journalists, students, artists, and activists from various civic organizations played leading roles in the movement.[18] They began to establish a public memorial service, perform art festivals, collect testimonies of the survivors, disseminate information and testimonies through local media, and engage in other Jeju 4.3–related advocacy.[19]

However, the initial conditions for these efforts were far from ideal. The Roh Tae-woo government (1988–1993), which was established largely due to a split in the vote between the two leading opposition figures, Kim Young-sam and Kim Dae-jung, continued suppressing activists by ordering their arrest and prohibiting their publications.[20] A critical turning point was when the civilian-led Kim Young-sam government (1994–1998) was established, and with this the Jeju 4.3 advocacy movement advanced along with democratic consolidation. Under the civilian government, the Jeju local council organized a special committee to investigate Jeju 4.3 and distributed its own report across the country, attracting national attention. Jeju people from various circles also submitted a signed petition several times to the National Assembly for the establishment of a special act to account for the Jeju 4.3 events.[21]

It was the Kim Dae-jung government (1998–2003), however, that finally established the special law for Jeju 4.3. In December 1999, the Jeju 4.3 Special Act passed the National Assembly, and, in January 2000, President Kim Dae-jung, an awardee of the Nobel Peace Prize in 2000, signed the bill to approve it. Though "persistent local activism was the single strongest foundation for the truth commission process," as Hun Joon Kim, who studied the Jeju 4.3 National Committee, argued,[22] the enactment of the special act was also an expression of South Korea's democratic transition—one that entailed the presence of the state as a key mediator. President Kim Dae-jung signaled as much upon signing the bill, when he said that "the Special Act will be a monumental landmark in the development of human rights and democracy in our society."[23] His statement implied that the South Korean state was able to resolve the conflicts of the past, even cases that involved South Korea's complex history of national division and communism.

CONSTRUCTION OF THE ISLAND OF WORLD PEACE

This novel and expanded role for the state was forged throughout the construction of the memorial park for the 4.3 mass killings, as acrimonious negotiations between groups with different memories of the massacre and agendas hindered its creation from the first planning stage in 2000 through to its opening in 2008.[24] Similar to other national museums in the world, the peace park became the focus of a power struggle between competing ideological groups over its primary narratives.[25] While local activists emphasized restorative justice and truth seeking, conservative groups, such as the *Seonguhoe* (the Korea Retired Generals and Admirals Association), objected to the entire transitional justice process, including the creation of the park.[26] According to the *Seonguhoe*, the Jeju Incident was a communist rebellion and therefore illegitimate. In 2000 they requested that the Constitutional Court rule on whether the Jeju 4.3 Special Act was constitutional. According to the request, the "Jeju 4.3 Special Act denied the legality and legitimacy of the suppression by the military and police. The special act also did not distinguish as victims among civilians, the police and army, and the rebels."[27] This request was promptly dismissed. However, the ante was upped when forty-three conservative groups submitted a constitutional petition in July 2004 objecting to the report, this time on the basis that the report damaged the legitimacy of the Republic of Korea. This petition was likewise dismissed. Finally, in response, ninety-four conservative groups, more than double those in the last petition, made a public statement preceding the opening of the peace park. The statement declared that "Jeju 4.3 was a communist rebellion led by the South Korean Labor Party. The Jeju 4.3 Peace Park transformed the rebels into the victims. The fabricated and distorted Jeju April Third Incident Investigation Report should be revised, and the opening of Jeju 4.3 Peace Park should be postponed."[28] The statement was also published as an advertisement in major conservative national newspapers, including the *Donga Ilbo* and *Chosun Ilbo*. As these various conservative dissents indicate, a seemingly irreconcilable split existed in the public representation of the once-repressed history of 4.3. On the one side, local activists and bereaved families sought to expunge the stigma of communism and honor the memories of their loved ones. One the other side, conservative forces argued that the premise on which the process of transitional justice was predicated was a threat to the legitimacy of the Republic of Korea. Under these circumstances, the Kim Dae-jung and Roh Moo-hyun governments sought to mediate these issues in such a way as to legitimize the democratic state.

Conflict Resolution

The South Korean state's compromise between the conflicting groups began with the enactment of the 2000 Special Act. The role was apparent in the official definition and time line of the event itself. The act defined the scope as an "incident causing civilians' sacrifices in the course of armed conflicts, and the suppression operations beginning March 1, 1947 to April 3, 1948 through September 21, 1954."[29] The definition incorporated the narrative of a people's uprising by adopting the start date as March 1, 1947, the day of the March First Shooting Incident, when tens of thousands of Jeju people participated in a rally to denounce the U.S. military government's policies and to protest the local police's fatal shooting of six people. However, the act primarily focused on "civilian sacrifices," such as killings and injuries, without specifying the state violence, thus tacitly consenting to potential objections that it may threaten the legitimacy of the state itself.[30]

An even more fraught issue was who fit the criteria of a legitimate victim. The act defined a victim as someone who was deceased, missing, or permanently injured as a result of Jeju 4.3. (In a revised act in 2007, political prisoners of Jeju 4.3 were also included among the victims.) With this, the definition could conceivably include police officers, soldiers, armed insurgents, rightist groups, political prisoners, and civilians as victims.[31] This expansive and radically inclusive scope elicited considerable controversy. Predictably, conservative groups protested the inclusion of "rioters" within the scope of victimhood and filed a constitutional appeal on the status of victimhood as soon as the Jeju 4.3 National Committee was organized.[32] These groups also issued a statement that "the political prisoners should not be selected as legitimate victims of Jeju 4.3."[33] On the other hand, the Jeju 4.3–related civic organizations insisted that those so-called rioters and the political prisoners should be recognized as official victims of the state violence.[34] The inclusion of soldiers, police officers, and rightists who had been treated as persons of national merit within the scope of victimhood further complicated matters. Some members of the Jeju 4.3 National Committee argued that it was not legally valid for these people of national merit to regain their honor following the Jeju 4.3 Special Act through a form of double rehabilitation, while others claimed that the inclusion of not only people of national merit but also soldiers and police officers accorded with the purpose of the act.[35] The latter members argued that people of national merit, solders, and police officers who had been reported as victims to the committee by their family members were mostly Jeju Islanders.[36]

Presented with these intersecting dilemmas, the Jeju 4.3 National Committee sought to forge a workable compromise through consultation with the state. In 2002, based on guidelines recommended by the Constitutional Court, the committee decided to exclude only those who were opposed to "the basic order of liberal democracy and the national identity of the Republic of Korea" from the scope of victimhood.[37] The committee then made a new stipulation that "the key executive members of the Jeju SKLP" and "ringleaders of the armed insurgents" were the principal members of this category.[38] Finally, in 2006, the committee considered all other victims, including political prisoners, soldiers, police officers, and rightists, the official victims. This decision was arrived at after many discussions and consultations with the Ministry of Government Legislation.[39] In other words, the committee decided to include both state agents, the primary perpetrators of the civilian massacre, and local civilians, the primary victims, within the range of official victims. As the progressive scholar Sungman Koh notes, this compromise by the committee contributed to providing state agents with immunity from punishment while also strengthening the state ideology of "national unity."[40] In this sense, it reflected a strategic compromise.

While the criteria for victimhood reflected a political strategy of reconciliation, so did the choice of terminology. In the Special Act, the word "*huisaengja*" was chosen instead of "*pihaeja*." While both words translate to mean "victim" in English, they have subtle—albeit in this context, crucial—differences in Korea. The word "*huisaengja*" in Korea has two meanings. First, it literally means "the sacrificed" who dedicated their lives, property, or honor to a good cause such as a patriotic movement. It also means someone who has regretfully been hurt, damaged, or killed due to a natural disaster or events. On the other hand, the word "*pihaeja*" is typically used when an offender exists. To cite a few examples, Korean people often say "*huisaengja* for national independence," "typhoon *huisaengja*," "crime *pihaeja*," or "road accident *pihaeja*." Although the victims and the bereaved on both sides usually identified a perpetrator, the Special Act opted for the cautious term, *huisaengja*—emphasizing the multilayered notion of sacrifice rather than implying a perpetrator. In other words, the state framed the events as "civilian sacrifices" while obscuring the politicide it had initially authored. At the same time, the state demonstrated its role in promoting democracy and human rights by raising the patriotic status of *pihaeja* of Jeju 4.3 to *huisaengja* and publicly honoring these *huisaengja*.[41]

The ideology of national harmony was furthered through the material construction of the 4.3 Peace Park and the historical narratives embedded within its landscape. The construction of the park began in 2000 under the supervision of the national government while the Jeju 4.3 National Committee carried deliberations throughout.[42] During the first phase of the construction, the Jeju 4.3 National Committee adopted its design through a competition. It borrowed elements of its model from the Korean National Cemetery, including a large-sized *taegeuk* mark (the yin-yang symbol displayed on the South Korean national flag) on the ground of Memorial Square in front of the Memorial Tablets Enshrinement Room.[43] As sociologist Kim Min-hwan notes, the design with the *taegeuk* mark was perhaps selected to appease strong opposition from the conservative groups and, at the same time, to present a landscape in which the state embraces every victim in its territory.[44] Indeed, the Jeju Government and its affiliated Jeju Development Institute had recommended not to adopt this design as it was not representative of the natural features of Jeju Island and did not provide a bereaved-centered memorial space.[45] In other word, a narrative of national unity took primacy over more Jeju-specific and victim-centric conceptions.

This emphasis on national cohesion is furthered through the Memorial Tablets Enshrinement Room, the Headstone Monument Engraved with Names of the Deceased, and the Tombstone Park for the Missing, which cumulatively work to inscribe every name of the victims, including local civilians and counterinsurgents, at the site. The Memorial Tablets Enshrinement Room, located at the top of the park, contains 14,114 memorial tablets of the victims, including 130 of those of police officers and soldiers.[46] The black memorial tablets of the victims organized by villages fill the whole wall of the oval room (figure 6.1). Meanwhile, in the style of a folding screen that embodies Jeju's volcanic cones, the Headstone Monument Engraved with Names of the Deceased is engraved with the names of the victims, their gender and age, and the date they were killed (figure 6.2). Finally, the Tombstone Park for the Missing has a total 3,891 tombstones of the victims who were disappeared in Jeju or in prisons on the mainland (figure 6.3).[47] The headstones are divided into sections according to the regions where they were disappeared.

This latter feature of the park is not merely a static representation of a historical past; rather, it performs a ritualistic and cathartic function. Every year on April 3, the families of the victims bring food, flowers, and incense with them and perform a memorial service in front of the memorial tablet, the monument, or the tombstone engraved with the name of their family member (figure 6.4). On a memorial ceremony day, a woman I met at the park told me, "I feel a sense of release when I see my father's name in the Tombstone Park for the Missing."[48] Her feelings are not isolated ones. For the families, the name of the victims being honored here means that it is no longer a wrongful death, and accordingly, the soul can finally rest in peace. Further, the inclusion of the names in a nationally recognized site means that the families are now free from the stigma of being family members of the rebels.[49] In addition, all of the victims, in particular local civilian victims, have become publicly

Figure 6.1   Memorial Tablets Enshrinement Room

Figure 6.2   Headstone Monument Engraved with Names of the Deceased

recognized as *huisangja* who would be memorialized by future generations. It has been the highlight of the memorial ceremony of Jeju 4.3 that visitors, including the president of South Korea, appease the deceased with tributes of flowers and incense in the Memorial Service Altar in front of the Memorial Tablets Enshrinement Room. All these memorial structures and public rituals, therefore, make an impression to the bereaved and visitors that South Korea is moving toward harmony and national unity.

Figure 6.3　Tombstone Park for the Missing

Figure 6.4　A Memorial Service at the Memorial Tablets Enshrinement Room

The contents of the Jeju 4.3 Peace Memorial Hall at the park also reflect the desire for political compromise and mature democracy. In December 2004, the Jeju 4.3 National Committee formed a special team of exhibition managers that was composed of cultural activists of the Jeju 4.3 advocacy movement and progressive historians to work on exhibition presentations.[50] The team was reorganized as the Advisory Committee of Exhibition Presentation in May 2007, and investigation experts involved in producing the official report were included in this new team. Under the team's plan, visual artists, who were mostly activists from the advocacy movement, helped present the history of the massacre in pictures, statues, and other artifacts. These artists presented the events as a people's uprising against suppression by the U.S. military and the Rhee government. The investigation experts involved in the official report, including those on the advisory committee, also participated by organizing the writing of museum panels.[51] They, too, attempted to present the massacre as state violence on the basis of the 4.3 report. However, conservative groups once again protested the narrative of state violence.

According to Kim Min-hwan, under this pressure from conservative groups, rather than presenting a people's uprising against the U.S. military and the Rhee government, the first section of the exhibition in the Memorial Hall described people's actions as self-defense and resistance to oppression by the police and right-wing youths.[52] Further, evidence related to the responsibility of the U.S. military and the Rhee government for the massacre was modified or excluded before the opening of the exhibit by the Jeju 4.3 National Committee.[53] For example, a cartoon called "The Truth of U.S. Occupation" was dropped because it portrayed the Truman administration as the orchestrator of the events. However, conservative groups failed to directly intervene in the overall exhibition-presentation work, and the exhibition describes the background of the "self-defense," such as brutal behaviors of the police and the NWYA. The advisory committee also expressed the full range and brutality of the state's counterinsurgency operations, though the state violence is mainly represented as an isolated case rather than as part of the systematic violence against political leftists during the period of state formation.[54] Similar to the official apology by the president of South Korea, the description of state violence in this national museum indicates that South Korea's democracy is mature enough to acknowledge its past wrongdoings.

This notion that South Korea's acknowledgment of its dark past is predicated on the maturation of its democracy is furthered through the committee's incorporation of the transitional justice process into the exhibition itself. For example, in the final section, the committee concludes with a story of the truth-finding activities and the national government's transitional justice processes. The story starts with the publication of Hyun Gi-yeong's novel of *Suni Samchon* and then shows activities of the advocacy movement and the transitional justice process, such as the collection of testimonies, the enactment of the Jeju 4.3 Special Act, and the establishment of the Jeju 4.3 Peace Park. This section has since been expanded when the Jeju 4.3 Peace Foundation (which had been established in 2008 to operate the park on the basis of the special act) renovated the permanent exhibition in 2017.[55] The foundation added updates of the story, such as the designation of April 3 as a national memorial day and the excavation of remains. The detailed description of the transitional justice process shows the increased capacity of the government in dealing with past liquidation.

The narrative of unity and democratic consolidation, however, imposes certain limits, and a more complex picture emerges in the *Baekbi*, or "Unnamed Monument," installation. The coffin-shaped monument, which is erected in the Memorial Hall to symbolize the victims of the conflict, is deliberately left with no inscription. This lack of inscription vividly represents the unhappy impasse among the different groups fighting over Jeju 4.3's legacies and the state's incapacity to satisfactorily resolve this conflict. If the state defines Jeju 4.3 as either a "people's uprising" or "state violence," the state would not recognize its own agents—namely, the police and army—as official victims or people of national merit. At the same time, it could not include both rebels and its agents in the category of victimized citizens. As a result of this impasse, the state has left the naming of the monument to future generations.

Peace Building

To further buttress its claims to legitimacy over the 4.3 past and future, the state has adopted a discourse of peace building. A clear manifestation of this is the name of the memorial park itself: the Jeju 4.3 Peace Park, which was initially going to be named the Jeju 4.3 Memorial Park.[56] The discourse of peace began to acquire prominence with President Roh's official apology in 2003, where he stated that "by applying the valuable lessons that we have learned from the Jeju 4.3 Incident, we should try to promote universal human values such as peace and human rights. . . . The future of Jeju will be a symbol of human rights and a cornerstone of peace."[57] Roh's speech represented a turning point of sorts in the discourse surrounding 4.3 transitional justice as terms such as "reconciliation," "mutual prosperity," and "peace," rather than the "investigation of historical truth" and "accountability," became the key themes in ceremonies, forums, and academic conferences related to Jeju 4.3. This pivot was not merely discursive but also entailed a greater claim for the state over the meaning of 4.3. As scholars Cho Myung-ki and Jang Se-yong remark, this claim was dramatically asserted when President Roh declared Jeju an Island of World Peace in 2005.[58] Governmental officials and members of the Committee for Preparation and Execution of the Jeju 4.3 Memorial Ceremony have echoed this discourse by calling the 4.3 victims "creator deities of the island of peace" in their yearly memorial address.[59] Finally, the name of the memorial museum was also changed from the "Jeju 4.3 Historical Museum" to the "Jeju 4.3 Peace Memorial Hall" before its opening in 2008, in turn reflecting a symbolic shift in emphasis from truth seeking to peacemaking.[60]

The discourse of peace does crucial ideological and temporal work that interrelatedly functions to shore up the state. For example, through the discourse of peace, the South Korean state obscures its past systematic massacre against political leftists by positioning itself as the agency for reconciliation and peace building for the future. According to Roh's apology, peace and reconciliation involve "cessation of all conflicts and dissents" and "turning a new page in the nation's history."[61] That is, the discourse of peace tended to redirect Jeju's trajectory from the past into the future, thus burying its violent birth.[62] Even the Jeju 4.3 Peace Park, which has the multiple purposes discussed above, is partially grounded in this sensibility. According to its own brochure, the Jeju 4.3 Peace Park was established "to begin a new era of reconciliation and mutual prosperity based on human rights and peace."[63]

Educating future generations is a key component of the peace-building ideology, and the Jeju 4.3 Peace Foundation has played a key role in this endeavor. After opening the park, it has provided diverse peace education programs for Korea's youth, including the National Youth 4.3 Literary Awards, the National Youth 4.3 Peace Camp, National Teacher Training on Jeju 4.3, the 4.3 Academy for Korean Undergraduates, the 4.3 Academy for International Undergraduates, and the Student 4.3 Literary and Drawing Contest. The winner of the National Youth 4.3 Literary Award has often recited her or his winning work in the memorial ceremony at the park. Further, in 2016, the foundation built the Peace Education Center at the park, which consists of a multipurpose auditorium and the 4.3 Children Experience Center. In 2017, the foundation opened the 4.3 Children Experience Center, where children could understand the history of Jeju 4.3 and realize the importance of peace. The foundation has also established peace networks with domestic and overseas institutions, such as the Gwangju Memorial Foundation, the Taiwanese National Human Rights Museum, the Okinawa Prefectural Peace Memorial Museum, and the Hiroshima Peace Memorial Museum.[64] Through these global networks, the foundation has aimed for the "globalization of the spirit of peace learned from Jeju 4.3."[65]

As the movement toward education indicates, the place of 4.3 in the national past was dramatically altered with the arrival of democracy. Once focused on repressing past, the state adopted a guiding role in its representation and reconciliation. More than anything else, the Jeju 4.3 Peace Park is a physical manifestation of this intervention. While this represents a clear maturation and consolidation of the state-building process, latent tensions within this process continue to cast an ominous shadow.

NOTES

1. Jeju 4.3 Research Institute, *Ijesa malhaemsuda 1*; Jeju 4.3 Research Institute, *Ijesa malhaemsuda 2*.

2. The park is located in Bonggae village, in northeastern Jeju Island, about ten kilometers (6.2 miles) from Jeju City's City Hall. The village is a historical site that was burned down and seriously damaged during the period of the Jeju 4.3 events.

3. For more details about the facilities of the peace park, see the website of the Jeju 4.3 Peace Foundation (http://jeju43peace.org/).

4. Jeju 4.3 Peace Foundation, "40-manmyeong dolpa" [The Number of Visitors Exceeding 400,000], *News Letter* 5 (2018), https://jeju43peace.or.kr/kor/newsletter/preview.do?idx=7.

5. Eun-Jung Kang and Timothy Jeonglyeol Lee, "The Dark Tourism Experience: Visitors to the April Third Peace Park, South Korea," *Gwangwang Leisure Yeongu* [Tourism and Leisure] 23, no. 7 (2011): 558.

6. Ibid., 547–66.

7. United Nations Secretary-General, "The Rule of Law and Transitional Justice in Conflict and Post-conflict Societies," Report of the Secretary-General, August 23, 2004, 4.

8. Dorota Heidrich, "Transitional Justice in State-Building Processes in Kosovo: Social Constructivism Perspective," *International Conference on Political Science* 9 (2015): 63.

9. Kim, *Massacres at Mt. Halla*, 1.

10. Charles Tilly, *Democracy* (Cambridge: Cambridge University Press, 2007), 13–14.

11. Charles Tilly, "Grudging Consent," *American Interest* 3, no. 1 (2007): 18.

12. For more details, see Kim, *Massacres at Mt. Halla*, 45–53.

13. Ibid., 50–53; Wright, "Raising the Korean Dead."

14. *Suni Samchon* was first published in the journal *Changjakgwa Bipyeong* (Quarterly Changbi) in 1978 and published as a book by Changbi the next year. The novel, however, became a trigger for transitional justice for the victims of the Jeju massacre. The first time many South Korean mainlanders, including children of the Jeju 4.3 victims, became aware of the massacre was through reading or hearing about the novel. Most importantly, it inspired some children of survivors to get involved in the movement to reveal the truth about the massacre and obtain justice. For more details, see Kim, *Massacres at Mt. Halla*, 55–56.

15. Brazinsky, *Nation Building in South Korea*, 223–50.

16. Paul Chang and Byung-soo Kim, "Differential Impact of Repression on Social Movements: Christian Organizations and Liberation Theology in South Korea (1972–1979)," *Sociological Inquiry* 77, no. 3 (2007): 339.

17. *Kyunghyang Sinmun*, May 17, 2009. The exact number of victims is still unknown. The May 18 Democratization Movement Truth Commission, established in December 2020, reported in 2021 that the number of civilian deaths during the movement was estimated to be 166. The commission also reported that it was investigating the scale of missing people and forty-nine cases of sexual violence. May 18 Democratization Movement Truth Commission, *2021nyeon habang-gi josahwaldong bogoseo* [A Report on

Investigation of the May 18 Democratization Movement Carried Out in the Second Half of 2021] (Seoul: Seonin, 2021), 67, 80–85. For more details on the Gwangju movement, see Katsiaficas, *South Korean Movements in the 20th Century*, 162–220.

18. Hun Joon Kim, "Seeking Truth after 50 Years: The National Committee for Investigation of the Truth about the Jeju 4.3 Events," *International Journal of Transitional Justice* 3 (2009): 406–23.

19. Kim, *Massacres at Mt. Halla*, 65–75; Jong-min Kim, "Seventy Years after the Jeju April 3," in *The Jeju 4.3 Mass Killing: Atrocity, Justice, and Reconciliation*, ed. Jeju 4.3 Peace Foundation (Seoul: Yonsei University Press, 2018), 127–32.

20. Kim, *Massacres at Mt. Halla*, 63.

21. Ibid., 84–102; Kim, "Seventy Years after the Jeju April 3," 132–33.

22. Kim, *Massacres at Mt. Halla*, 5.

23. *Jemin Ilbo*, January 12, 2000.

24. Min-hwan Kim, "Jeonjang-i doen Jeju 4.3 pyeonghwagongwon: Pokdongronui 'areungeorim'gwa bunyeolden yeondae" [Jeju 4.3 Peace Park That Became a Battlefield: The "Absent Presence" of the Riot Interpretation and Divided Solidarity], *Gyeongjewa Sahoe* [Economy and Society] 102 (2014): 74–109.

25. Sharon Macdonald, "Theorizing Museum: Introduction," in *Theorizing Museum,* ed. Sharon Macdonald and Gordon Fyfe (Oxford: Blackwell, 1996), 1–20.

26. Jeju 4.3 National Committee, *Hwahaewa sangsaeng*, 100–102, 123–25.

27. Ibid., 124.

28. *KONAS.net*, March 27, 2008; *Dailian*, March 28, 2008.

29. Jeju 4.3 National Committee, *Jeju April Third Incident Investigation Report*, 688.

30. The amendment on Jeju 4.3 adopted by parliament on February 26, 2021, redefined the events by further clarifying Jeju people's resistance and the suppression operations. It defines Jeju 4.3 as "the incident causing civilians' sacrifices in the course of armed conflicts and the suppression operations, beginning with the protest of Jeju people and the suppression triggered by the police shooting on civilians on the March First Independence Movement Anniversary in 1947, to the uprising on April 3, 1948, through reopening Mt. Halla on September 21, 1954."

31. Jeju 4.3 National Committee, *Hwahaewa sangsaeng*, 162–77; Sungman Koh, "Trans-border Ritual for the Dead: Experiential Knowledge of Paternal Relatives after the Jeju 4.3 Incident," *Journal of Korean Religions* 9, no. 1 (2018): 85–86.

32. Jeju 4.3 National Committee, *Hwahaewa sangsaeng*, 167.

33. Ibid., 169.

34. Ibid., 159–60.

35. Ibid., 173.

36. Ibid.

37. Ibid., 149–50, 167–68.

38. Ibid.

39. Ibid., 158–77.

40. Koh, "Trans-border Ritual for the Dead," 86–89, 94–99; Jeong-sim Yang, "Jeju 4.3 teukbyeolbeopgwa yangmin haksal damnon, geugeoseul ttwieoneomeo" [Beyond the Jeju 4.3 Special Act and the Discourse of Civilian Massacre], *Yeoksa Yeongu* [Journal of Historical Studies] 7 (2000): 278–79.

41. Yang, "Jeju 4.3 teukbyeolbeopgwa yangmin haksal damnon," 278–79.

42. Jeju 4.3 National Committee, *Hwahaewa sangsaeng*, 192–93.

43. Kim, "Jeju 4.3 pyeonghwagongwon," 88–93.

44. Ibid., 90–91.

45. Jeju Government and Jeju Development Institute, *Jeju 4.3 pyeonghwagongwon joseong gibongyehoek* [The Basic Plan for Building the Jeju 4.3 Peace Park] (Jeju: Jeju Government, 2001), 255.

46. Jeju 4.3 Peace Foundation, "Jeju 4.3 Peace Park Memorial Sites," http://jeju43peace.org/jeju-4-3-peace-park/jeju-4-3-peace-park-_-memorial-site/.

47. Ibid.

48. I met this woman on the 2010 memorial ceremony day of Jeju 4.3 at the peace park.

49. Kwon, *After the Korean War*, 172–73.

50. Jeju 4.3 National Committee, *Hwahaewa sangsaeng*, 206–11.

51. Ibid., 210. According to Kim Jong-min, an investigation expert involved in the report, the advisory committee asked him to take responsibility for the contents of the panels at the final stage, one year before the opening of the park. He tried to do his best when selecting photographs and illustrating the Jeju 4.3 events. Interview with Kim Jong-min on December 10, 2013, on Jeju.

52. Kim, "Jeju 4.3 pyeonghwagongwon," 97–98.

53. Jeju 4.3 National Committee, *Hwahaewa sangsaeng*, 211; Kim, "Jeju 4.3 pyeonghwagongwon," 99–103.

54. Brendan Wright, "Politicidal Violence and the Problematics of Localized Memory at Civilian Massacre Sites: The Cheju 4.3 Peace Park and the Kŏch'ang Incident Memorial Park," *Cross-Currents: East Asian History and Culture Review* 14 (2015): 215–16.

55. Jeju 4.3 National Committee, *Hwahaewa sangsaeng*, 316–17. From September 19 to November 30, 2017, the Jeju 4.3 Peace Foundation renovated the permanent exhibition, mainly to present underillustrated histories of the advocacy movement and the transitional justice process after the construction of the hall.

56. Hye-gyeong Hyun, "Jeju 4.3 sageon ginyeomuiryeui hyeongseonggwa gujo" [The Formation and Structure of Memorial Ceremonies for the Jeju 4.3 Incident] (PhD diss., University of Jeonnam, 2008), 123–25.

57. *Jejusori*, October 31, 2003.

58. Myung-ki Cho and Se-yong Jang, "Jeju 4.3 sageongwa gukgaui rokeol gieok poseop gwajeong" [State Transference and Subsumption of Local Memory of Jeju 4.3], *Yeoksawa Segye* [History and the World] 43 (2013): 217–19.

59. Hyun, "Jeju 4.3 sageon ginyeomuiryeui hyeongseonggwa gujo," 128–29; Cho and Jang, "Jeju 4.3 sageongwa gukgaui rokeol gieok poseop gwajeong," 217.

60. Jeju 4.3 National Committee, *Hwahaewa sangsaeng*, 206; Cho and Jang, "Jeju 4.3 sageongwa gukgaui rokeol gieok poseop gwajeong," 217.

61. *Jejusori*, October 31, 2003.

62. Cho and Jang, "Jeju 4.3 sageongwa gukgaui rokeol gieok poseop gwajeong," 218–19.

63. See the Korean and English information brochure for the Jeju 4.3 Peace Park.

64. Jeju 4.3 Peace Foundation, "Key Projects," http://jeju43peace.org/foundation/key-projects-2/.

65. Ibid.

Conclusion: The Island
of World Peace

Throughout this book, I have explored the history of Jeju 4.3 and its after-math in relation to South Korean state-building processes. In its initial stage, the state was an active political actor in exterminating political leftists and civilians on Jeju in the midst of creating an anticommunist regime. Following these massacres, it sought to discipline Jeju residents and compel them to voluntarily participate in national movements as a means of establishing national identity and hegemony. These processes, which involved military recruitment and gendered development projects, entailed considerable agency on behalf of the islanders, even as they were ultimately integrated into the state-building project. Finally, in the wake of South Korea's hard-earned con-solidation of democracy, the state set up multiple instruments of transitional justice to clarify the truth of the 4.3 events and recover the honor of victims. Though the verdict on these efforts has been mixed, the state has persistently leveraged them to legitimize itself as an agent of national unity and recon-ciliation. Throughout this multidecade state-building processes, Jeju has been referred to as an "Island of Reds," an "Island of Strong Working Women," and an Island of World Peace. These changes in nomenclatures are indicative of the complicated historical relationship that exists between Jeju Island and the modern South Korean state.

In declaring Jeju an Island of World Peace in January 2005, the South Korean state sought to demonstrate its maturity and democratic legitimacy. However, as intimated in the previous chapter, it exposed some cracks and limitations of the state's endeavors. In this concluding chapter, I will first elaborate on some of these fissures—particularly the issue of the definition of "victim," the place of women in the public representation of 4.3, and the inability of the state to reconcile the 4.3 past at the local level. In the second section, I will explore the democratic regime's support for the development of a naval base in Gangjeong village on Jeju, which has exposed contradic-tions in fulfilling the vision of an Island of World Peace. In March 2005, just two months after the declaration of Jeju as an Island of World Peace, the nominally progressive government of Roh Moo-hyun announced its plan to construct a new South Korean naval base on Jeju. Immediately, a strong antibase movement emerged that has challenged the compatibility of the base with the notion that Jeju was an Island of World Peace. These conflicts over the naval base (which was completed in 2016), which are often called "the second Jeju 4.3," are still ongoing and reflect the ambivalent relationship between the state and civil society in South Korea today.

LIMITATIONS OF THE STATE-LED RECONCILIATION PROCEDURE

Unofficial Victims: Blank Memorial Tablets

As discussed in the previous chapter, the issue of how to categorize left-wing insurgents has been a persistent problem in the reconciliation process of 4.3. This issue is visible in the Jeju 4.3 Peace Park. In the Memorial Tablets Enshrinement Room, among the thousands of tablets contained within, there are some blank black tablets (see figure 6.1). In most of these cases, the place-ment of these blank tablets resulted from a correction of mistakes, such as duplicate applications for the status of victim. However, twelve of these blank tablets were set up based on the Jeju 4.3 National Committee's final criteria guidelines for the status of victimhood, symbolically reflecting an irreconcil-able conflict within the transitional justice process. Following the passage of the 2000 Special Act, the Practical Committee for the Investigation of Jeju 4.3 and Honoring Victims (which had been established to deliver decisions of the Jeju 4.3 National Committee and act on entrusted items of the com-mittee) received applications for the status of victim from the victims and the bereaved families. Initially, when the practical committee previewed the applications, they recognized leaders of armed insurgents as legitimate victims.[1] However, based on the Jeju 4.3 National Committee's final crite-ria guidelines for the status of victimhood in 2002, the memorial tablets of "key executive members of the Jeju SKLP" and "ringleaders of the armed insurgents" were removed and replaced by blank tablets in that place as a temporary expedient. During the final deliberation and decision on the status of victim by the Jeju 4.3 National Committee, the memorial tablets of the victims recognized by the practical committee were set up in the Memorial Tablets Enshrinement Room. Though the Jeju 4.3 National Committee rec-ommended that applications for bereaved who fell within "exceptions to the range of victims" be withdrawn in order to give them a second chance of application at the right time, instead of notifying of the nonrecognition of victim status, the committee decided to remove the memorial tablets of those who were not eventually recognized as official victims.[2]

These blank tablets in the enshrinement room underline the incoherence within the state's various efforts for reconciliation of the historical conflict. Since the Jeju 4.3 Special Act broadly defined who were genuine victims, the issue over the selection criteria of victimhood raised acrimonious disputes nationwide. After all, the Constitutional Court of South Korea recommended not recognizing as official victims those who violated the basic tenet of liberal democracy.[3] Though the recommendation was not legally binding, the Jeju 4.3 National Committee followed it to bypass predictable conservative groups' interruptions of the committee's activities, such as lawsuits based on unconstitutionality.[4] This same eligibility criteria of the official victims has been in use without modification until today. As a result, some of the bereaved families of individuals who fell within the "exceptions to the range of victims" category gave up applying for the status of victim, while others ended up withdrawing before the examination at the unofficial request of the committee.[5] However, the purpose of the Jeju 4.3 Special Act was proclaimed to be "the promotion of human rights, the progress of democracy, and the unity of the nation" through the investigation of Jeju 4.3 and the honoring of its victims and its bereaved,[6] but the Jeju 4.3 National Committee eventually did not include leaders of the Jeju SKLP and the armed insurgents as victims. As the scholar Koh Sungman insists, the denial of victimhood defeats the purpose of the act.[7]

Later attempts to further investigations into Jeju 4.3 have been hampered by the same issue. For example, the 2021 Amendment on Jeju 4.3 paved the way for additional investigation into Jeju 4.3 and sought to recover former prisoners' honor through a class action lawsuit. It also aimed to provide legal grounds for systematic compensation for the victims and their bereaved families. Finally, the amendment also redefined the events themselves, adding contents of Jeju people's resistance and suppression operations into the official narrative.[8] However, it failed to redefine the term "victim" despite such advances of restorative justice and reparations. As a result, there is little room to change the selection criteria of victim.

The process of transitional justice was in part stalled by a restoration of conservative power for a decade. Indeed, the previous conservative regimes of Lee Myung-bak (February 2008–February 2013) and Park Geun-hye (February 2013–March 2017) restricted the truth-seeking activities of Jeju 4.3 by reducing the Jeju 4.3 National Committee's budget and personnel.[9] However, the more progressive Moon Jae-in government (May 2017–May 2022)[10] also did not challenge the selection criteria even if it was more open to resolving past political conflicts. In 2018, Moon apologized for state violence again as president of South Korea during the seventieth memorial ceremony of Jeju 4.3. In his speech, he asked for the overcoming of internal disputes caused by ideological labeling and a movement toward harmony in the country as a whole.[11] Yet he did not acknowledge the leaders of armed insurgents as citizens for national harmony even while he interpreted the Jeju people's uprising as a movement for national unification. Again, in the seventy-second memorial ceremony on Jeju, he stated that "Jeju envisioned a genuine independence beyond mere liberation and aspired to peace and unification that transcended the nation's division. Jeju residents were only trying to preserve national self-esteem and to rebuild the reclaimed nation in its entirety."[12] The next year, he made a similar speech, emphasizing the "merciless suppression against Jeju residents by state power."[13] This spirit of reconciliation was extended to other institutions. On the same day as the seventy-third memorial ceremony, both the minister of defense and the chief of the National Police Agency acknowledged their past crimes for the first time. However, the Jeju 4.3 National Committee under the Moon government still examined and judged victimhood by the same standard. The leaders of the Jeju SKLP and armed insurgents have been classified as "exceptions to the range of victims," or exceptions to the range of national reconciliation, until today despite various efforts to facilitate transitional justice. It is doubtful that the conservative government of Yoon Suk-yeol (May 2022–May 2027) will seek to change these criteria.

Marginalization of Women's Voices at the Jeju 4.3 Peace Park

Another limitation of the state's reconciliation efforts is with the representation of Jeju women's history at the Jeju 4.3 Peace Park. As previously discussed, the Jeju 4.3 Peace Memorial Hall at the park provides the history of Jeju 4.3 from Korea's liberation to the ongoing process of transitional justice. However, the voices of Jeju's women are marginalized and underrepresented, while Jeju women are not even presented as a distinct social group. Instead, they are either portrayed as weak figures or are highly objectified and dramatized in images and art as helpless women. In spite of many findings about women's experiences during the advocacy movement, the memorial museum and park did not adequately portray women's experiences. In this sense, the park has reproduced dominant tropes of patriarchal history.[14]

This marginalization in part reflects specific shortcomings that are inherent to the process of transitional justice in general and South Korea in particular. As scholars have noted, transitional justice by its nature "will inevitably produce and reproduce already existing hierarchies, norms and perceptions regarding the recognition of gendered (and other) crimes."[15] In South Korea, the gendered landscape compounded these problems. During the years of official investigation of Jeju 4.3, Korean society remained male centered, particularly in the political and legal spheres. As of 2000, women comprised only 13.7 percent of the national congress members. Similar to the under-representation of women in the political and legal fields, their participation in the transitional justice process of Jeju 4.3 was meager. In fact, there were no women among the first twenty Jeju 4.3 National Committee members, and no women were chosen to help write the reports.[16] The gender composition of the committee was never raised as an issue, and gender issues were seldomly considered in the negotiation process of legislating the Jeju 4.3 Special Act.

Given these circumstances, it is hardly surprising that the patriarchal discourse prevailed in the process of transitional justice. In the clauses of the Jeju 4.3 Special Act, the definitions of "Jeju 4.3" and "victim," in particular, limited the scope of the official investigation from its inception. The 2000 act primarily framed killings and injuries in the events as examples of "civilian sacrifices." It also defined "victim" as someone who was deceased, missing, or permanently injured as a result of Jeju 4.3. This definition did not include the vast majority of women who could conceivably be identified as victims. Efforts to amend problems within the criteria for victims further reproduced this discourse. For example, in a revised act in 2007, political prisoners of Jeju 4.3 were also included among the victims, but women who suffered from forced marriages, rape, and sexual violation were still not included. Following the act's definition of Jeju 4.3 and its victims, the investigators paid more attention to killings, injuries, and disappearances than they did to other human rights violations. They focused on the systematic massacre of people, the disappearance of Jeju residents, torture, and summary executions—all of which were more common among male victims. Due to these exclusions, among the 14,028 victims reported in the official investigation by the Jeju 4.3 National Committee in 2001, men (11,043) were killed, missing, or permanently injured in much greater numbers than women (2,985).[17]

The investigators also selected men as witnesses of Jeju 4.3 over women.[18] This further marginalized women's experiences within the official history.[19] Though a relatively small archive of testimony, documents, and research about women was created by the advocacy movement, these materials were not widely utilized in writing the official report. Moreover, women were denied a separate status as victims who suffered gender-specific abuse. Instead, they were often simply grouped among "the weak and the elderly" or the "unarmed civilians," while crimes that were specifically committed against them as women—such as sexual violence—were recorded as a category of torture or an example of an atrocity against civilians. In sum, the truth seeking embodied in the report entailed multiple acts of gendered erasure.

Absence of Jeju Women's Histories

Given the gendered imbalances that were endemic to the transitional justice process, it is unsurprising that the Memorial Hall does not offer the full range of women's experiences, particularly their active struggles in each stage of the course of Jeju 4.3. Throughout the hall, an implicit gender binary structures the historical narrative: men are represented mainly as Jeju people who struggled against the oppression of the South Korean police and paramilitary, while women are portrayed as traumatized victims. Although the gender-neutral term "Jeju people" is used in the texts of displays, the exhibitions throughout the Memorial Hall predominantly show the histories of men. In fact, there are no photographs or exhibition commentaries about women's participation in the uprising. This stands in contrast to the concrete history of postliberation Jeju. As witnesses have recalled, Jeju women, including middle school students, played a significant role in propagandizing, collecting information, and liaising both before and during the uprising.[20] For example, the Women's League, or *Bunye Dongmaeng* (established in January 1947), published and distributed leaflets to villagers and mobilized them for a rally to celebrate the anniversary of the March First Korean Independence Movement in 1947—commonly seen as the starting point of the 4.3 events.[21] The league and various other women also liaised between the insurgents, delivered food and supplies to them, and helped provide a shelter in the mountains for refugees who had escaped the counterinsurgents' violence during the events.[22] Their omission from the Memorial Hall is revealing.

Reconstruction efforts by women after the massacre, including those described in chapter 5, are likewise absent, despite the plethora of testimony describing women's substantial contributions to these efforts. Instead, male staff members of official organizations for reconstruction are shown as those in command in the exhibition's photographs. Men are also converted into the symbolic leaders of the advocacy movement and transitional justice process. For example, while the 2017 renovated exhibition on the history of the advocacy movement includes more photographs of women when compared to the initial exhibition, the photographs are mainly men, with related illustrations, newspapers, and books. However, Jeju women, both as individuals and as members of civic organizations, also contributed to the advocacy movement by collecting testimonies, producing literary works, and organizing public commemoration rites and art festivals.[23] As a result of these cumulative omissions, visitors to the Jeju 4.3 Peace Park barely learn about Jeju women's role in the initial protests against the U.S. military government, the economic reconstruction that followed the uprisings and massacres, and the advocacy movement.

*Women as Generic Representatives of the Weak and the
Permanent Victim*

The agency of women during the 4.3 and post-4.3 periods is further undermined in the Memorial Hall through their symbolic representation as objects
of pity and trauma. Similar to the official report, women are grouped among
the weak and the elderly, and both groups are reduced to permanent victims
of the massacre. The following text accompanying a photograph of refugees
is an illustrative example: "The elderly, women, and children suffered from
freezing and starving on the mountain." Here, women are lumped into an
amorphous group of helpless victims. The text of the "casualties" display in
the exhibition further indicates women's function in the Memorial Hall. The
subtitles of the text read, "Some 30,000 people were killed," and "One-third
of the victims were the elderly, women, and children."[24] A graph then shows
the number of casualties by age, indicating the high proportion of the elderly
and children who were killed. However, there is no information about casualties by gender. As such, visitors do not learn how many women were killed
or how women were victimized in specific ways.

Admittedly, specific representations of female victimhood do exist.
However, these portrayals reduce women to broader gendered symbols in
a larger story of atrocities—a common trope found in Holocaust photographs and other representations of traumatic pasts.[25] An example of this is
the sculpture called *Woman's Death*, which is part of an installation by the
prominent male painter and sculptor Ko Gil-cheon titled *Jeju, an Island of
Death*. This installation portrays fourteen types of killing committed during
Jeju 4.3 through plaster sculptures on the wall. The methods include burial
at sea, strangulation, decapitation, and suffocation. *Woman's Death* is the
only exhibit of a death on the wall that is described as a woman's death and
portrays a face full of horror, with the woman half naked, while her bosom is
half exposed in a crumpled skirt and bare feet. It thus represents women as
double victims of both rape and murder. As this is the only female-specific
piece in the exhibit, it works to represent the totality of women's experiences
and suffering.

Another prominent image of women that is found in the hall and park is
that of a grieving mother.[26] For example, *Biseol*, or "Pile of Snow Scattered by
Strong Wind," is the only statue the park commissioned at the basic planning
stage to "definitively represent the tragedy of the massacre"[27] (figure C.1). It
commemorates the death of twenty-five-year-old Byeon Byeong-saeng and
her two-year-old daughter, who were both killed at the site of the park. *Biseol*
occupies the largest space among the images of the sculptures in the Korean

brochure on the park, and it is flagged as one of the most important places at the park, as indicated by the numerous signs directing visitors to it.

This statue captures a mother who is falling down on the snow-covered ground with her baby girl in her arms. The sign in Korean and English in front of the site of the statue suggests that the mother desperately fled barefoot in the snow while holding her daughter but was shot by suppression forces. A trail of footprints showing her frantic flight, the mother's bare feet, her posture holding her baby, and the tendon that is clearly visible on the mother's wrist communicate the mother's desperate attempt to save her baby. The words of a lullaby in Jeju dialect are written on snail-shaped stone walls. Its lyrics, "*wongi zalang wongi zalang*," or "hushaby, hushaby," also express the mother's love and suffering. The image is undoubtedly heart-rendering and works to create an emotional bond between the visitor and the historical past through the trope of the paternal bond between mother and child. This aesthetic strategy is common in genocide remembrance. As Janet Jacobs argues about commemorations of the Holocaust, the image of mother and child promotes "the construction of an empathic-based collective memory that facilitates an emotional connection to the horrors of the past."[28] Whatever merit there may be to this depiction, it reproduces elements of patriarchal discourse by focusing on this universal image of female suffering and motherly sacrifice, rather than on the diverse experiences of Jeju women. Similar to Ko Gil-cheon's exhibit, it does not portray women as individuals in other roles, such as insurgents, farmers, civilian guards, or school students. As such, the two main portrayals at the park of women reproduce archetypical images of women as maternal agents and voiceless victims.

Figure C.1   Biseol

Reconciliation among Jeju Islanders at the Local Level

Lingering issues over the definition of victimhood or the place of women in 4.3 lay bare the limitations of the state's ability to reconcile the 4.3 past in official places of memory. However, the state has likewise been unable to reconcile many conflicts among islanders themselves, leading many islanders to take the initiative in forging intercommunal harmony. Among other things, the 4.3 massacres brought on a collapse of community on the island, which was catastrophic for a culture that revolved around kinship relationships. The political divisions between villagers and villages during the massacre created sharp tensions that sometimes even harmed relations between family members, other relatives, or clans in the same village. The counterinsurgency's troops stoked these tensions by labeling people communists and villages "red villages," compiling lists of enemies, and torturing villagers to extract names of rebels and collaborators. When tortured villagers named someone as a communist in their village, they were tarnished as an informant by their fellow villagers, which sometimes mushroomed into bigger conflicts between relatives or clans in neighboring villages. These tensions were also fed by the coercion of villagers by counterinsurgency forces to participate in their attacks on insurgents (including on residents of their own villages), become members of the Civilian Guard or rightist organizations, assault or kill communist suspects from the same or neighboring villages, or even kill their own relatives. Finally, the psychological pain of the victims and their families did not go away and was even transmitted to the children of the massacre's survivors.[29] Cumulatively, these scars led to long-term enmity among the islanders. They also marred the transitional justice process and efforts at reconciliation, as many people were conflicted as to who had been mainly at fault.

The Hagui village in northwestern Jeju was one of the communities that was fractured by 4.3. During the massacre, government forces labeled people in one part of the village rebels, who then blamed people in the other part of the village for making false and secret accusations against them. Throughout the massacre, more than three hundred out of 2,800 villagers were killed, mostly by the counterinsurgency forces, and relations between the two groups subsequently deteriorated. Because of its high death toll, the village was by the end of Jeju 4.3 called a red village, similar to Bukchon village. The surviving villagers were discriminated against in employment in public sectors due to the village stigma, which inflamed further grievances between the two groups. Some villagers began to worry about how this discrimination would impact the young generation's social and political advancement, and the villagers eventually changed the names of the two parts of the village into

Dong-gui and Gui-il at the end of 1953. After the name change, the relationship between the two villages worsened, and the two villages often clashed over regional development and intervillage events.[30]

Given the intimacy of this conflict, the state was limited in its capacity to forge reconciliation. Therefore, villagers eventually took the initiative. During the early period of the advocacy movement, the village assemblies of the two villages agreed to revive the original name of Hagui and began to create a committee, the Committee for Village Development, for reconciliation between the two groups. The two village heads, who both had moved to the village from other villages on Jeju, drove to revive the village name and received wide support from the villagers and nonresidents. The village natives who had lived on the mainland or Japan had felt like displaced persons since the name change and wanted to revive the name of their hometown. In 1993, the villagers finally revived not only their original name of Hagui but also their sense of pride for the hometown as a key center of the Korean independence movement on Jeju.

Beyond the change in name, villagers utilized the moral practice of paying tribute to the dead as a form of intercommunal reconciliation.[31] In Korean Confucian culture, it is customary to pay tribute to a deceased person's soul by erecting a shrine and a stone monument and performing an ancestor ceremony. These funeral rites are more deeply rooted in Jeju society than on the mainland because the practice of ancestor worship in Confucian culture was incorporated strongly into established indigenous beliefs and practices involving the deceased.[32] In 2000, the Committee for Village Development decided to erect a local ancestral shrine to promote reconciliation and coexistence in the community. It raised funds for the erection by using the Jeju traditional community band music, dance, and ritual called *geolgung* and other methods. Significantly, the committee never asked the local or national government for funding because it did not want involvement of administrative organizations in its own project.[33] To build community integration and solidarity, the committee decided that all village souls of the deceased from Jeju 4.3, the resistance to Japanese colonialism, the Korean War, and the Vietnam War would be memorialized together. In May 2003, the committee finished constructing the local ancestral shrine, *Yeongmowon*, or "Shrine for the Commemoration of Beautiful Souls." From this time onward, the villagers have performed ancestral rites for all of the souls—regardless of identification as victim or perpetrator—at the shrine five times a year.[34] Through emphasizing the moral practice of paying tribute to the "wandering souls" and forgiveness toward each other, the villagers in Hagui have achieved reconciliation independent from the state.

The moral practice of paying tribute to the dead was also used to mediate conflicts between members of the Jeju 4.3 Bereaved Family Association (an association of victims' families founded in 2001 to memorialize the victims) and the Jeju Police Veterans Association (the Jeju branch of the association of police veterans in Korea established in 1963). Given the history of 4.3, the groups were long hostile toward each other. Indeed, even prior to the establishment of both associations, Jeju native policemen and the victims and their bereaved families had chilly relationships. The Jeju native policemen played a role in taking villagers off to a police station or other places during the counterinsurgency campaign by following orders from their superiors, who were mostly mainlanders.[35] For the victims and their families, it was therefore the Jeju native police officers who caused the victims to be tortured or killed, and they bore a grudge against the policemen. Meanwhile, Jeju native policemen blamed the insurgents for the killing of fellow police officers and their families. The hostile relationship continued into the period of advocacy movement and transitional justice. While the Jeju 4.3 Bereaved Family Association had testified about the atrocities of former police officers during the official investigation of the massacre, the Jeju Police Veterans Association had criticized the description of the police as a major oppressor in the official report and at the Jeju 4.3 Peace Park. The disputes between the two Jeju groups devolved into mutual hatred and contempt.

The national government embraced both victims of civilians and police officers as the official victims at the park, but this reconciliation strategy at the national level hardly solved the deeply rooted hostility between the two groups. In an attempt at reconciliation in August 2013, the two associations announced an agreement to resolve sixty-five years of antagonism. According to Hyun Chang-ha (the president of the Jeju Police Veterans Association) and Jeong Moon-hyeon (the president of the Jeju 4.3 Bereaved Family Association), both had felt the need for reconciliation between the two associations in order not to pass their mutual hatred on to future generations.[36]

Initially, the efforts did not go well. At an open debate titled "Isn't There a Way for Reconciliation and Coexistence of Jeju 4.3?" hosted by the Jeju branch of Donga Broadcasting System in March 2013, the panelists and members of the two associations on the floor bitterly argued with each other.[37] As a result, both Hyun and Jeong recognized the seriousness of conflicts and decided to have conversations about the resolution of the conflicts after the debate.[38] According to them, it was not easy to reach an agreement for harmony. After seven or eight meetings between the presidents and executive members from each association, they finally agreed with the basic premise of "we all are *huisaengja* [victims]" and decided to declare their agreement for reconciliation in a news conference. That June, the Jeju 4.3 Bereaved Family Association visited the cemetery for the Korean War dead on Memorial Day, and on the Memorial Day of Jeju 4.3 the following year, the Jeju Police Veterans Association participated in the memorial service for the massacre's victims at the Jeju 4.3 Peace Park. Up to the present, they continue to visit the two sites together. Their reconciliation, therefore, was based on a moral ethics of paying respect to souls of the victims and of not passing on mutual hatred to the next generation, rather than on the state ideology of national unity.

CONSTRUCTION OF A NEW NAVAL BASE
ON THE ISLAND OF WORLD PEACE

The contradictions of the state's position as an agent of reconciliation have been most glaringly present throughout the naval base controversy that has raged on Jeju since the early 2000s. In 2002, the South Korean navy proposed the construction of a naval base on the island, but the Jeju government requested that the Maritime Affairs Ministry delay the construction due to its unpopularity. However, in 2005, the Korean navy again proposed constructing a new naval base, measuring about four hundred thousand square meters, or the equivalent of about fifty-six football fields, to moor twenty sophisticated warships, including 7,600-ton Aegis-equipped KDX-III destroyers on Jeju Island. According to the navy, the naval base would strengthen South Korea's national security by monitoring potential threats from China or Japan while protecting the route for shipment of oil near Jeju. The Jeju government this time supported the proposal because of the regional economic advantages that the naval base would generate.[39] In May 2007, based in part on a public opinion poll, the Jeju government and the Ministry of Defense finally selected Gangjeong village as the base's site from three proposed locations.[40] Immediately, however, the antibase islanders and their supporters nationwide pointed out the contradiction between the construction of a new military base and the state's vision of Jeju as an Island of World Peace. Those protestors also criticized the state for its lack of democratic transparency and the excessive use of force in the construction process. From the time when the Korean navy proposed a Jeju naval base until the present, the state has been coping with these challenges.

Contradictions between Militarization and the Notion
of an Island of World Peace

The proposed opening of the naval base ushered in a debate in which each respective side sought to mobilize the language of peace to advance its case. Antibase islanders, including civic organizations, college professors, and artists, issued a statement that the construction of a new naval base on Jeju was an "obvious challenge" to the vision of Jeju Island as a mecca for the

Northeast Asian peace community and world peace.[41] In response, the navy argued in December 2006 that "the notion of peace does not refer to demilitarization. For peace is not mere absence of war but refers to a society where individual freedom and social justice can be realized. The proclamation of peace does not ensure peace. To achieve peace, we should provide deterrence against external aggression on the basis of military power."[42] However, after Gangjeong was selected as the site of a new naval base on Jeju, more people, including civic organizations and Catholics nationwide, once again objected to remilitarization on an island "where the residents had suffered from the Jeju massacre."[43] The protestors emphasized that military tension and conflict caused by the construction of the naval base would prevent future cooperation between Northeast Asia nations. They were also concerned that Jeju Island would become an outpost against China for the United States and its military allies. Under these pressures, President Roh Moo-hyun tried to explain the need for the construction by utilizing his theory of the state. He stated during his visit to Jeju in June 2007 that "to maintain a state of peace, we need militarization. We cannot have peace without the protection of the state. We also cannot operate the state without the military."[44]

In spite of his remarks, the issue of compatibility continued into the following administrations. The conservative Lee Myung-bak and Park Geun-hye governments continued to highlight the importance of sovereignty over waters and the prevention of wars to preserve peace. In an attempt to quell opposition, the Lee government decided to construct an "eco-friendly" naval base as well as a commercial port for tourism.[45] However, the protestors proposed that the best way to keep peace was through peaceful means, which inspired national and international support throughout the construction. Internationally recognized public intellectuals and human rights activists, including Noam Chomsky and the 2012 Nobel Peace Prize candidate Angie Zelter, echoed the sentiment of antibase activists by emphasizing the importance of demilitarization on Jeju Island as the key to realizing the vision of an Jeju as an "Island of World Peace" and hub for human rights.[46]

However, the progressive President Moon Jae-in, who had promised in an election pledge to solve the conflicts around the Jeju naval base, once again leveraged the discourse of peace to defend the base. In a 2018 address at the ceremony of the International Fleet Review at the naval base in Gangjeong, he argued that the base was "a foothold for peace, not a foothold for war."[47] He stated that "Jeju Island has become a place of harmony and friendship for navies throughout the world. The waters of Jeju have become a symbol of cooperation for the sea of peace. . . . I will help further fortify the Republic of Korea Navy so that it will be able to contribute to peace not only on the Korean Peninsula but also in Northeast Asia and the world."[48] Through this, the Moon government sought to mediate the conflicting ideas of peace that existed between the opposing camps and position the state as a peacemaker.

Lack of Procedural Legitimacy

From the inception of construction for the naval base, various national governments also have had to deal with procedural problems. When the naval base was proposed, the Ministry of Defense promised to respect the residents' opinion and uphold proper legal procedures on the construction.[49] However, the antibase residents immediately raised the question of procedural justice. Principally, they criticized the procedure for the selection of the site. According to the protestors, only eighty-seven out of 1,050 eligible voters in Gangjeong requested that the village be a candidate site at a temporary meeting for regional development. Meanwhile, the first of two surveys was done in just a week prior to the decision, and the rest of Gangjeong villagers did not get a chance to judge the situation. Given the small population and rushed pace, Gangjeong villagers held a plebiscite vote to ascertain opinions of residents in August 2007, and a majority (94 percent or 680 villagers out of a total of 725 participants) voted against the base construction. Given this discrepancy, the antibase residents called the selection of the site "wrong from the beginning" and demanded that it be reversed.[50]

The antibase residents also protested against manipulation of the law by the local and national governments. According to the protestors, in December 2009, members of the ruling party of the Lee government in the Jeju local assembly approved the cancellation of the Absolute Preservation Zone in Gangjeong, an area where development is limited to protect endangered species and coastal waters, without the villagers' consent.[51] This lack of consent was problematic as the relevant ordinance requires villagers' consent to make changes to an Absolute Preservation Zone.[52] In addition, according to the protestors, the Ministry of Defense had approved the construction plan for military facilities in Gangjeong in January 2009, which was before the completion of the environmental impact assessment, an important measure to analyze the environmental impact of a national project.[53] Only after the residents filed an administrative litigation against this illegal procedure in April 2009 was an assessment done in September 2009, and the ministry reapproved the amendment of the plan in March 2010.[54] (In July 2010, however, the Seoul Administrative Court ruled that the final approval of the construction plan was not illegal, though the court agreed that there were "some procedural problems.")[55] The antibase residents said that these were only a few examples of unjustified procedures during the construction. For example, the antibase residents and their supporters insisted on the authorization of the Cultural

Heritage Administration as a violation of the cultural protection law because the administration approved the construction without taking steps to conserve buried relics that were discovered at the construction site.[56] In May 2011, the opposition political parties also acknowledged these procedural problems and asked the Lee government to halt construction and reexamine the construction plan.[57] However, the government denied this request.

Given the negative optics that these procedural indiscretions produced, the successive governments of Roh (2003–2008), Lee (2008–2013), and Park (2013–2017) all used various persuasion tactics to secure procedural legitimacy. In May 2007, just after Gangjeong was selected as the site of construction, the Ministry of Defense announced that it would spend roughly seventy billion won (sixty-one million U.S. dollars) for the villagers and regional development and consult with the villagers about how to spend the funds.[58] The navy also established a public relations center at the port in Gangjeong and sent an information pamphlet to every house in the village in July of the same year.[59] The pamphlet included a detailed plan for regional development and advertised rewards to villagers, such as fishing workers and land owners within the boundaries of the construction site, who were harmed by the construction. The navy and the national government often held presentations about regional development, compensation, environmental impact assessments, and building apartments for soldiers' families.[60] The protesters, however, criticized these as mere formalities. In August 2011, the Ministry of Defense remarked at a press interview that it had already held about ten presentations for the residents and considered their opinions when building public facilities for the soldiers and the residents in the village.[61] Through these presentations and hearings, the national government attempted to demonstrate that it was carrying out the construction "in accordance with the proper legal process."[62]

However, these efforts at appeasement were undermined by the conservative administrations' tendency to use repression against the protesters. According to a report by the opposition political parties to the Park regime in October 2013, 202,626 police officers were stationed in Gangjeong between August 2011 and August 2013.[63] During the same period, the national police dispatched 27,193 police officers from the mainland to enforce public order.[64] This was the first time since the outbreak of Jeju 4.3 that such a large number of police officers from the mainland had been sent to the island. Jang Ha-na, a member of the National Assembly, said, "It was like Gangjeong village was in a state of emergency under martial law for the last two years. . . . The police were obsessed with arresting the antibase residents and peace activists, rather than maintaining public order."[65] As a result, according to the Gangjeong Village Committee, roughly seven hundred people had been arrested from 2007 to July 2015.[66] Physical repression was dovetailed by financial punishment, as villagers were obliged to pay fines imposed by police officers for obstructing the police from carrying out their duties, hindering construction work, violating laws of assembly and demonstration, and as compensation for damages caused by the antibase movement. By July 2015, the fines had reached 400 million won (354,000 U.S. dollars).[67] Moreover, in Mach 2016, just after the opening of the naval base, the navy exercised its indemnity for construction delays by suing 116 antibase residents and peace activists and five antibase organizations, including the Gangjeong Village Committee, for 3.45 billion won (three million U.S. dollars)—a sum that the defendants could never afford to pay.[68]

Unsurprisingly, the use of these coercive means did little to quell the underlying problems in the construction of the naval base. In a news conference, the antibase residents said, "It is ironic that Jeju people again suffer from state violence in a democratic society that our people have achieved with blood and sweat."[69] They added, "We have not been treated as citizens of the Republic of Korea."[70] Though the conflicts in Gangjeong over the construction period suggest the growth of civil society in South Korea, they also indicate that democracy in South Korea may not be mature enough to fulfill procedural justice and legitimacy.

Resolution of Conflict over the Jeju Naval Base

Beyond the strains between the protestors and the national governments, the construction of the naval base damaged relations within Gangjeong village. Gangjeong was a typical farming village with a population of 1,900 that valued its face-to-face social networks and a sense of kinship. Relationships between its residents were strained and even severed by their divisions over the base.[71] According to the residents, 80 percent of two hundred informal social groups and a traditional private village fund had been severed. Some family members stopped talking to each other, and probase and antibase residents shopped at different stores and ate at different restaurants in the village. The two groups sometimes even engaged in verbal and physical fights in the street. These intercommunal conflicts were reminiscent of the island's dark past as villagers began to call their conflicts over the base "the second Jeju 4.3" due to the widespread breakdown within the community.[72]

In this context, the Moon administration sought to legitimize itself by assuming the role of conflict mediator. As the first move of conflict resolution, the Moon government decided to withdraw the indemnity trial by accepting a court-mediated offer in December 2017.[73] The Moon government further attempted to solve the conflicts in Gangjeong by accepting responsibility on behalf of the state for some of the friction. After participating in the 2018 International Fleet Review at the naval base in Gangjeong, Moon expressed his regret at the lack of democratic transparency and the breakdown of community in Gangjeong and Jeju society.[74] He also promised national support for a project of community recovery that the local government and Gangjeong villagers had already initiated in March 2017 to promote harmony among the villagers.[75] As he promised, in February 2019, the Ministry of the Public Administration and Security decided to financially support the project, which included building an agricultural processing plant, constructing a South Korean navy museum, and the promotion of a wind power generation industry.[76] In addition, the National Police Agency apologized for the abuses of power that were inflicted in Gangjeong, such as illegal collection of evidence and compulsory dissolution of the protests.[77] The navy also apologized for "the inconveniences and conflicts caused by the construction of the naval base in Gangjeong" and made a cooperation agreement with the Gangjeong Village Committee in August 2020.[78] However, the protestors have requested that the national government should investigate human rights violations and improper administrative procedures in the construction to realize a genuine reconciliation between the state and the residents.[79] The state's attempt to mediate and facilitate reconciliation, therefore, remains an unfinished project—in part due to its own involvement in the initial crisis. In this sense, the aftermath of the conflict over the naval base bares a troubling resemblance to that of 4.3. It remains unclear how the legacies of these two events will shape future relations between islanders and the state.

NOTES

1. Jeju 4.3 National Committee, *Hwahaewa sangsaeng*, 136–46; Kim, "Jeju 4.3 pyeonghwagongwon," 93.

2. According to Cho Jeong-hee, director of the Commemoration Division at the Jeju 4.3 Peace Foundation, the Jeju 4.3 National Committee found ten cases of "exceptions to the range of victims" just after its final decision making of the status of victim and two more cases after the Park Geun-hye administration started. Phone interview with Cho Jeong-hee on August 27 and 29, 2022. For more details on this issue, see Sungman Koh, "4.3 'huisaengja'ui byeonyonggwa hwaryong: Mujangdae chulsinjaui gwageocheongsan gyeongheomeul saryero" [Transformation and Utilization of 4.3 "Victims": A Case Study of the Government's Clean-Up of Past Acts Perpetrated by the Armed Rebels], *Sahoewa Yeoksa* [Society and History] 129 (2021).

3. Jeju 4.3 National Committee, *Hwahaewa sangsaeng*, 167.

4. Koh, "4.3 'huisaengja'ui byeonyonggwa hwaryong," 270.

5. Phone interview with Cho Jeong-hee, director of the Commemoration Division at the Jeju 4.3 Peace Foundation, on August 27 and 29, 2022; *Hankyoreh*, March 22, 2021.

6. Jeju 4.3 National Committee, *Jeju April Third Incident Investigation Report*, 688.

7. Koh, "4.3 'huisaengja'ui byeonyonggwa hwaryong," 269.

8. See note 30 in chapter 6 for this redefiniton.

9. Hun Joon Kim, "Returned Suppression and the Jeju 4.3: Struggles in the Dark Times," in *The Jeju 4.3 Mass Killing: Atrocity, Justice, and Reconciliation*, ed. Jeju 4.3 Peace Foundation (Seoul: Yonsei University Press, 2018), 179–200.

10. Moon Jae-in was elected in the May 2017 presidential election after the impeachment and dismissal of Park Geun-hye. Park's impeachment followed a sprawling corruption scandal involving bribery, abuse of power, and the leaking of government secrets.

11. *Hankyoreh*, April 4, 2018.

12. *Jejusori*, April 3, 2020.

13. *Headline Jeju*, April 3, 2021.

14. Joan Ringelheim, "Genocide and Gender: A Split Memory," in *Gender and Catastrophe*, ed. Ronit Lentin (New York: Zed Books, 1997), 18–33.

15. Susanne Buckley-Zistel and Magdalena Zolkos, "Introduction: Gender and Transitional Justice," in *Gender in Transitional Justice*, ed. Susanne Buckley-Zistel and Ruth Stanley (Hampshire, UK: Palgrave Macmillan, 2011), 13.

16. Jeju 4.3 National Committee, *Hwahaewa sangsaeng*, 47–49.

17. Jeju 4.3 National Committee, *Jeju April Third Incident Investigation Report*, 458–59.

18. Ibid., 60–61.

19. Gwisook Gwon, "Jeju 4.3ui jinsanggyumyeonggwa gendeo yeongu" [Truth-Seeking and Gender Research on Jeju 4.3], *Tamla Munhwa* [Tamla Culture] 45 (2014): 179–86.

20. Jeju 4.3 Research Institute, *Ijesa malhamsuda 1*, 16–17, 43–44, 105; *Jemin Ilbo*, June 8, 2004.

21. Jeju Police Agency, *Jeju gyeongchalsa* [The History of the Jeju Police] (n.p., 1990), 281; *Jeju Sinbo*, May 12, 1947.

22. Hq. USAFIK, G-2 Periodic Report, No.857, June 11, 1948, in Jeju 4.3 National Committee, *Jeju 4.3 sageon jaryojip 7*, 318–19; Han and Kim, "Jeju Women's Lives in the Context of the Jeju April Third Uprising," 30; Gyeong-in Yang, *Seonchangeun eonjena naui moksieotda*, 42–56.

23. Yeong-beoum Kim, "Gieok tujaeng-euroseoui 4.3 munhwaundong seoseol" [Introduction to the Jeju 4.3 Cultural Movement as a Struggle for Memory], in *Gieok tujaenggwa munhwaundongui jeongae* [A Struggle for Memory and the Development of the Cultural Movement], ed. Kan-chae Na, Keun-sik Jung, and Chang-il Kang (Seoul: Yeoksa Bipyeongsa, 2004), 26–68.

24. The exhibit "Casualties of the Jeju Incident" was slightly changed with the 2017 renovation. The new "Casualties of the Jeju Incident" includes a map illustrating the casualty distribution across Jeju Island and a text showing the number of refugees and destroyed houses. However, the main text of the casualties display described in

this section was not changed. Only the graph illustrating the number of casualties by age was switched from a bar graph to a pie chart. There is still no information about casualties by gender in the text or the map.

25. Barbie Zelizer, "Gender and Atrocity: Women in Holocaust Photographs," in *Visual Culture and the Holocaust*, ed. Barbie Zelizer (New Jersey: Rutgers University Press, 2001), 247–60.

26. The image of helpless woman or grieving mother has often been presented as a symbol of the trauma the Jeju massacre inflicted since the advocacy movement began. Gwisook Gwon, *Gieokui jeongchi: Daeryanghaksarui gieokgwa yeoksajeok jinsil* [The Politics of Memory: Social Memory and Historical Truth of Massacre] (Seoul: Munji Publishing, 2006), 211–41.

27. Jeju Government and Jeju Development Institute, *Jeju 4.3 pyeonghwagongwon joseong gibongyehoek*, 257.

28. Janet Jacobs, *Gender, Genocide, and Collective Memory* (London: I. B. Tauris, 2010), 35–36.

29. Eun-shil Kim, "The Politics of the Jeju 4.3 *Holeomeong* Bodies: 'Speaking' and Emotion as Embodied Language," *Korean Anthropology Review* 2 (2018): 1–41; Ae-duck Im, "Searching for Jeju 4.3 Trauma Model: Collective Stigma and Jeju 4.3 Historical Trauma," *World Environment and Island Studies* 7, no. 3 (2017): 151–57.

30. Interviews with Ko Chang-seon and Bae Gwang-si, the cochairs of the Committee for Village Development at the time of constructing the local shrine, on June 28, 2020, on Jeju.

31. Kwon, *After the Korean War*, 162–67.

32. Seong-nae Kim, "Work of Memory," 229–31.

33. Interviews with Ko Chang-seon and Bae Gwang-si on June 28, 2020, on Jeju.

34. According to my two interviewees above, they have paid tribute to the souls on January 3 of the lunar calendar, March First Independence Day, Jeju 4.3 Memorial Day, Korean National Memorial Day, and Korean National Liberation Day until today.

35. Interview with Hyun Chang-ha, the president of the Jeju Police Veterans Association at the time of the reconciliation, on June 27, 2020, on Jeju.

36. Ibid.; interview with Jeong Moon-hyeon, the president of the Jeju 4.3 Bereaved Family Association at the time of the reconciliation, on June 2, 2017, and June 30, 2020, on Jeju.

37. Interview with Hyun Chang-ha on June 27, 2020, on Jeju; interview with Jeong Moon-hyeon on June 30, 2020, on Jeju.

38. Ibid.

39. *Jejusori*, May 31, 2007.

40. Gwisook Gwon, "Remembering 4.3 and Resisting the Remilitarisation of Jeju," in *Under Occupation: Resistance and Struggle in a Militarized Asia-Pacific*, ed. Daniel Broudy, Peter Simpson, and Makoto Arakaki (London: Cambridge Scholars, 2013), 239.

41. *Jemin Ilbo*, August 1, December 20, and December 21, 2006.

42. *Jejusori*, December 14, 2006.

43. *Jejusori*, June 20 and June 25, 2007; *Jemin Ilbo*, July 25 and July 27, 2007.

44. *Jejusori*, June 22, 2007.

45. *Headline Jeju*, August 4, 2011, and February 22, 2012.

46. *Kyunghyang Sinmun*, July 12, 2011; *BBC News*, September 3, 2011; *Columban Fathers*, January 4, 2013; *Yonhap News*, August 1, 2014; *Headline Jeju*, August 6, 2015; *Hankyoreh*, October 11, 2018.

47. *Asia Times*, October 11, 2018.

48. Ibid.

49. *Jemin Ilbo*, December 14, 2006; *Chosun Ilbo*, December 21, 2006.

50. For more details of this issue, see Gwon, "Remembering 4.3 and Resisting the Remilitarisation of Jeju," 247.

51. *Sequipo Sinmun*, December 18, 2009.

52. In August 2018, the chair of the local assembly finally apologized for this approval. *Nocut News*, July 9, 2019.

53. *Jejusori*, January 30, 2009.

54. *Jejusori*, April 20, 2009; *Ohmynews*, September 25, 2009.

55. *Sequipo Sinmun*, July 15, 2010.

56. Bronze-period relics and late Joseon-period relics were discovered at the construction site in early September 2011. *Headline Jeju*, September 4, 2011; *Jejusori*, September 20, 2011; *Headline Jeju*, September 29, 2011; *Jejudomin Ilbo*, November, 6, 2011.

57. *Ohmynews*, August 4, 2011.

58. *Jejusori*, May 31, 2007.

59. *Jejusori*, July 26, 2007.

60. *Jejusori*, September 6, 2007; December 13, 2008; and April 24, 2009; *Halla Ilbo*, December 3, 2010; *Headline Jeju*, June 15, 2012.

61. *Headline Jeju*, August 4, 2011.

62. *Joongang Ilbo*, August 31, 2011.

63. *Kyunghyang Sinmun*, October 29, 2013.

64. Ibid.

65. Ibid.

66. *Headline Jeju*, July 27, 2015; *Jejusori*, August 6, 2015.

67. *Headline Jeju*, July 27, 2015; *Jejusori*, November 4, 2015.

68. *Hankook Ilbo*, March 30, 2016.

69. *Headline Jeju*, August 15, 2011.

70. *Sequipo Sinmun*, January 21, 2010; *Jejusori*, December 24, 2010. During my fieldwork in Gangjeong, I often heard similar remarks from antibase residents.

71. Gwon, "Remembering 4.3 and Resisting the Remilitarisation of Jeju," 238–70.

72. Ibid., 249.

73. *Jejusori*, December 12, 2017.

74. *Jejusori*, October 11, 2018.

75. *Jejusori*, March 10, 2017.

76. *Jejusori*, February 11, 2019.

77. *Jejusori*, July 26, 2019.

78. *Headline Jeju*, August 31, 2020.
79. *Seoguipo Sinmun*, September 1, 2020; *Jejusori*, June 30, 2021, and July 27, 2022.

Bibliography

An, Ho-sang. *Ilminjuui-ui bonbatang* [The Basis of One People Principle]. Seoul: Ilminjuui Research Institute, 1950.

Anderson, Benedict. *Imagined Communities: Reflections on the Origin and Spread of Nationalism.* London: Verso, 1983.

Araújo Nocedo, Ana Micaela. "The 'Good Wife and Wise Mother' Pattern: Gender Differences in Today's Japanese Society." *Critica Contemporanea: Revista de Teoria Politica* 2 (2012): 156–69.

Association of Bereaved Families Engaging in Fact-Finding Research concerning Jeju 4.3, eds. *4.3ui jinjeonghan huisaengjaneun!* [Who Are the Genuine Victims of Jeju 4.3?]. Jeju: Sinmyeong, 2015.

Baekjoilson Bereaved Family Association. *Baekjoilson yeongnyeong 60nyeonsa* [The Sixty Year History of the Baekjoilson Victims]. Jeju: Baekjoilson Bereaved Family Association, 2011.

Brazinsky, Gregg. *Nation Building in South Korea: Koreans, Americans, and the Making of Democracy.* Chapel Hill: University of North Carolina Press, 2007.

Bu, Chang-ok. *Hangukjeonjaeng sucheop: Eoneu hakdobyeongui chamjeon ilgi* [A Note of the Korean War: A Diary of a Student Soldier]. 3rd ed. Goyang: Dongmunchaekbang, 2014.

Bu, Man-geun. *Gwangbok Jeju 30nyeon* [The Thirty-Year History of Jeju after Korea's Liberation]. Seoul: Munjosa, 1975.

Buckley-Zistel, Susanne, and Magdalena Zolkos. "Introduction: Gender and Transitional Justice." In *Gender in Transitional Justice*, edited by Susanne Buckley-Zistel and Ruth Stanley, 1–36. Hampshire, UK: Palgrave Macmillan, 2011.

Center for Supporting Those Related to the Jeju April 3 Incident and Jeju 4.3 Research Institute, eds. *Jaeiljejuin 4.3 jeungeon chaerokjip* [A Collection of Testimonies of Jeju 4.3 from Jeju Natives in Japan]. Jeju: Center for Supporting Those Related to the Jeju April 3 Incident and Jeju 4.3 Research Institute, 2003.

Chang, Jieun. "National Narrative, Traumatic Memory and Testimony: Reading Traces of the Cheju April Third Incident, South Korea, 1948." PhD diss., New York University, 2009.

Chang, Paul, and Byung-soo Kim. "Differential Impact of Repression on Social Movements: Christian Organizations and Liberation Theology in South Korea (1972–1979)." *Sociological Inquiry* 77, no. 3 (2007): 326–55.

Cho, Hae-jeong. *Hangukui yeoseonggwa namseong* [Korean Women and Men]. Seoul: Munji Publishing, 1988.

Cho, Jeong-hee. "Hangukjeonjeang balbal jikhu Jeju jiyeok yebigeomsokgwa jipdanhaksarui seonggyeok" [The Characteristics of the Preventive Detention and Massacre in Jeju Island Right after the Outbreak of the Korean War]. MA thesis, Jeju National University, 2013.

Cho, Myung-ki, and Se-yong Jang. "Jeju 4.3 sageongwa gukgaui rokeol gieok poseop gwajeong" [State Transference and Subsumption of Local Memory of Jeju 4.3]. *Yeoksawa Segye* [History and the World] 43 (2013): 205–34.

Cho, Nam-su. *4.3 jinsang* [The Truth of Jeju 4.3]. Jeju: Wolgan Gwangwangjeju, 1988.

Cho, Seong-yoon, Yeong-im Ji, and Ho-joon Heo. *Ppaeatgin sidae, ppaeatgin sijeol: Jejudo minjungdeurui iyagi* [Robbed of Their Era and Time: Stories of the People of Jeju Island]. Seoul: Seonin, 2007.

Choi, Ho-geun. *Jenosaideu: Haksalgwa eunpyeui yeoksa* [Genocide: History of Massacres and Cover-Up]. Seoul: Chaeksesang, 2005.

Choi, Hyaeweol. "Wise Mother, Good Wife: A Transcultural Discursive Construct in Modern Korea." *Journal of Korean Studies* 14, no. 1 (2009): 1–33.

Chung, Yong Wook. "6.25 jeonjaenggi migunui simnijeon jojikgwa jeongae yangsang" [How the U.S. Military Organized and Carried Out Psychological Warfare during the Korean War]. *Hanguksaron* [Korean History Studies] 50 (2004): 369–404.

———. "Leaflets, and the Nature of the Korean War as Psychological Warfare." *Review of Korean Studies* 7, no. 3 (2004): 91–116.

Committee for Promotion of Academic and Cultural Projects in Commemoration of the Fiftieth Anniversary of Jeju 4.3, ed. *Ireobeorin maeureul chajaseo* [Searching the Lost Villages]. Seoul: Hakminsa, 1998.

Conway, Martin. "The Inventory of Experience: Memory and Identity." In *Collective Memory of Political Events*, edited by James Pennebaker, Dario Paez, and Bernard Rime, 21–45. Mahwah: Lawrence Erlbaum Associates Publishers, 1997.

Cumings, Bruce. "American Responsibility and the Massacres in Cheju Conference on Overcoming the Past: Healing and Reconciliation—Cheju and the World in Comparison." *World Environment and Island Studies* 6, no. 4 (2016): 203–9.

———. *The Korean War: A History.* New York: Random House, 2010.

———. *The Origins of the Korean War.* Vol. 1: *Liberation and the Emergence of Separate Regimes, 1945–1947.* Seoul: Yeoksa Bipyeongsa, 2002.

———. *The Origins of the Korea War.* Vol. 2: *The Roaring of the Cataract, 1947–1950.* Seoul: Yeoksa Bipyeongsa, 2002.

———. "The Question of American Responsibility for the Suppression of the Chejudo Uprising." Paper presented at the Conference to Celebrate the 50th Anniversary of the April 3, 1948, Chejudo Rebellion, Tokyo, March 14, 1998.

De Wit, Jerôme. "The Representation of the Enemy in North and South Korean Literature from the Korean War." *Memory Studies* 6, no. 2 (2013): 146–60.

Digital Jeju Grand Culture. "Byeonso gaeryang undong" [Toilet Improvement Movement]. http://jeju.grandculture.net/jeju/toc/GC00700882.

———. "Gamgyul" [Tangerine]. http://jeju.grandculture.net/jeju/toc/GC00700046.

———. "Jeju Sinbo." http://jeju.grandculture.net/jeju/toc/GC00702072.

Fein, Helen. *Imperial Crime and Punishment.* Honolulu: University of Hawaii Press, 1977.

Foucault, Michel. *Discipline and Punish: The Birth of the Prison.* Translated by Alan Sheridan. New York: Vintage Books, 1995.

Gamson, William. "Hiroshima, the Holocaust, and the Politics of Exclusion." *American Sociological Review* 60 (1995): 1–20.

Gwon, Gwisook. "Daeryanghaksarui sahoesimni: Jeju 4.3 sageonui haksal gwajeong" [Sociopsychology of Genocide: The Process of Massacre during the Jeju 4.3 Incident]. *Hanguk Sahoehak* [Korean Journal of Sociology] 36, no. 5 (2002): 171–200.

———. *Gieogui jeongchi: Daeryanghaksarui gieokgwa yeoksajeok jinsil* [The Politics of Memory: Social Memory and Historical Truth of Massacre]. Seoul: Munji Publishing, 2006.

———. "Jeju 4.3ui jinsanggyumyeonggwa gendeo yeongu" [Truth-Seeking and Gender Research on Jeju 4.3]. *Tamla Munhwa* [Tamla Culture] 45 (2014): 171–99.

———. "Remembering 4.3 and Resisting the Remilitarisation of Jeju." In *Under Occupation: Resistance and Struggle in a Militarized Asia-Pacific*, edited by Daniel Broudy, Peter Simpson, and Makoto Arakaki, 252–84. London: Cambridge Scholars, 2013.

Gwon, O-heon. "Yushin chejeui Shin Saimdang ginyeomgwa hyeonmoyangcheo mandeulgi" [The Yushin Regime's Attempt to Set Shin Saimdang as a Role Model and Encourage Women to Be a "Wise Mother and Good Wife" after Her]. *Journal of Korean Culture* 35 (2016): 61–91.

Hahm, In-hee. "Hangukjeonjaeng, gajok, geurigo yeoseongui dajungjeok geundaeseong" [The Korean War, Families and Women's Multilayered Modernity]. *Sahoewa Iron* [Society and Theory] 9 (2006): 159–89.

Han, Rimhwa, and Soonhee Kim. "Jeju Women's Lives in the Context of the Jeju April Third Uprising." *Asian Women* 17 (2003): 21–37.

Hauben, Jey. "People's Republic of Jeju Island, 1945–1946." *Papers, Essays and Reviews* 3, no. 3 (2011): 277–84.

Heidrich, Dorota. "Transitional Justice in State-Building Processes in Kosovo: Social Constructivism Perspective." *International Conference on Political Science* 9 (2015): 62–66.

Heo, Eun. "'5.16 gunjeonggi' jaegeongungminundongui seonggyeok" [The Characteristics of the National Reconstruction Movement under the Military Government That Seized Power through a Coup in May 1961]. *Yeoksamunje Yeongu* [Critical Studies of Modern Korean History] 11 (2004): 11–51.

Heo, Ho-joon. *American Involvement in the Jeju April 3 Incident.* Translated by David Carruth and Colin Mouat. Jeju: Jeju 4.3 Research Institute, 2021.

———. "Jeju 4.3e isseoseoui minganin haksal nolli" [Logics of Civilian Massacre Perpetrated during Jeju 4.3]. *4.3gwa Yeoksa* [4.3 and History] 8 (2008): 103–61.

————. "Jeju 4.3 hangjaenggwa jenosaideu" [The Jeju 4.3 Uprising and Genocide]. *4.3gwa Yeoksa* [4.3 and History] 4 (2004): 178–215.

Heo, Yoon. "Hangukjeonjaenggwa hiseuteriui jeonyu: Jeonjaeng mimanginui seksyueollitiwa jeonhu gajokjilseoreul jungsimeuro" [The Korean War and the Appropriation of Hysteria: With a Focus on War Widows' Sexuality and Postwar Family Order]. *Yeoseongmunhwak Yeongu* [Feminism and Korean Literature] 21 (2009): 93–124.

Hong, Gui-Young. "Becoming a 'Legitimate' Ancestor: A Sociocultural Understanding of a Sonless Jamnyeo's Life Story." *Forum: Qualitative Social Research* 5, no. 3 (2004). http://dx.doi.org/10.17169/fqs-5.3.565.

Hong, Seong Choul. "Propaganda Leaflets and Cold War Frames during the Korean War." *Media, War, and Conflict* 11, no. 2 (2018): 244–64.

Hong, Yang-hee. "Hyeonmoyangcheoui sangjing, Shin Saimdang: Singminjisigi Shin Saimdang-ui jaehyeongwa jendeo jeongchihak" [Shin Saimdang, the Symbol of the "Wise Mother and Good Wife": Shin Saimdang's Images and Gender Politics during the Japanese Colonial Period]. *Sahak Yeongu* [Review of Korean History] 122 (2016): 155–90.

Hwang, Su-kyoung. *Korea's Grievous War*. Philadelphia: University of Pennsylvania Press, 2016.

Hyun, Gi-yeong. *Suni Samchon* [Aunt Suni]. Seoul: Changbi, 1979.

————. *Suni Samchon*. Translated into English by Jung-hee Lee. Seoul: Asia Publishers, 2012.

Hyun, Hye-gyeong. "Jeju 4.3 sageon ginyeomuiryeui hyeongseonggwa gujo" [The Formation and Structure of Memorial Ceremonies for the Jeju 4.3 Incident]. PhD diss., University of Jeonnam, 2008.

Im, Ae-duck. "Searching for Jeju 4.3 Trauma Model: Collective Stigma and Jeju 4.3 Historical Trauma." *World Environment and Island Studies* 7, no. 3 (2017): 151–57.

Im, Chong-Myung. "The Making of the Republic of Korea as a Modern Nation-State, August 1948–May 1950." PhD diss., University of Chicago, 2004.

Institute for Military History Compilation, Ministry of National Defense (MND). *6.25 jeonjaeng: Yeogun chamjeonsa* [The Korean War: The History of Female Soldiers Engaging in the War]. Seoul: Ministry of National Defense, 2012.

————. *Hangukjeonjaengsa 1: Haebanggwa geongun* [The Korean War History 1: Liberation and Foundation of the Armed Forces]. Seoul: Institute for Military History Compilation, Ministry of National Defense (MND), 1967.

Jacobs, Janet. *Gender, Genocide, and Collective Memory*. London: I. B. Tauris, 2010.

Jeju 4.3 National Committee. *Hwahaewa sangsaeng: Jeju 4.3 wiweonhoe hwaldong baekseo* [Reconciliation and Coexistence: White Paper on the Activities of the Jeju 4.3 National Committee]. Seoul: Jeju 4.3 National Committee, 2008.

————. *Jeju 4.3 sageon jinsang josa bogoseo* [The Jeju April Third Incident Investigation Report]. Seoul: Jeju 4.3 National Committee, 2003.

————. *The Jeju April Third Incident Investigation Report*. Translated by Jeju 4.3 Peace Foundation. Jeju: Jeju 4.3 Peace Foundation, 2013.

————, ed. *Jeju 4.3 sageon jaryojip 7: Miguk jaryo pyeon 1* [Jeju 4.3 Incident Sourcebook, vol. 7: U.S. Documents, vol. 1]. Seoul: Geumseong Munhwasa, 2003.

———, ed. *Jeju 4.3 sageon jaryojip 9: Miguk jaryo pyeon 3* [Jeju 4.3 Incident Sourcebook, vol. 9: U.S. Documents, vol. 3]. Seoul: Geumseong Munhwasa, 2003.

Jeju 4.3 Peace Foundation. "40-manmyeong dolpa" [The Number of Visitors Exceeding 400,000]. *News Letter* 5 (2018). https://jeju43peace.or.kr/kor/newsletter/preview.do?idx=7.

———. "Jeju 4.3 Peace Park Memorial Rites." http://jeju43peace.org/jeju-4-3-peace-park/jeju-4-3-peace-park-_-memorial-site/.

———. *Jeju 4.3 sageon chuga jinsang josa bogoseo 1* [The Jeju April Third Incident Additional Investigation Report, vol. 1]. Jeju: Gak, 2019.

Jeju 4.3 Peace Foundation and Jeju 4.3 Research Institute, eds. *Amuri eoryeowodo saljago hamyeon saneunbeop* [Those Willing Can Survive However Hard the Situation Is]. Jeju: Hangeuru, 2010.

———, eds. *Galchiga galchi kkollaeng-i kkeuneomeogeotda hal subakke* [A Cutlassfish Eats Up the Other Cutlassfish's Tail]. Jeju: Hangeuru, 2010.

———, eds. *Jigeumkkaji sarajin geosi yongheongeora* [It Is a Miracle That I've Survived]. Jeju: Hangeuru, 2011.

———, eds. *Saneseodo museopgo araeseodo museopgo geunyang sallyeogoman* [We Just Tried to Survive, Scared of Both Guerillas in the Mountain and Counterinsurgents Sent by the Government]. Jeju: Hangeuru, 2011.

Jeju 4.3 Research Institute, ed. *4.3gwa yeoseong: Geu saranaen naldeurui girok* [Jeju 4.3 and Women: A Record of the Hard Days They Went Through]. Jeju: Gak, 2019.

———, ed. *Billemotgul, geu kkeuteomneun eodum sogeseo* [Billemot Cave, in That Never-Ending Darkness]. Seoul: Hanul Academy, 2013.

———, ed. *Dasi hagui junghagwoneul gieokhamyeo* [Recollecting the Days of Hagui Middle School]. Seoul: Hanul Academy, 2013.

———, ed. *Eotteoke hyeongsaga geomsareul?* [How Dare a Detective Arrest a Prosecutor?]. Jeju: Jeju 4.3 Peace Foundation, 2015.

———, ed. *Garibangeuro gieokhaneun yeoldu sal sonyeonui 4.3* [A Twelve-Year-Old Boy's Memory of Jeju 4.3 Left in Mimeograph]. Seoul: Hanul Academy, 2015.

———, ed. *Geuneul sogui 4.3* [In the Shadows of 4.3]. Seoul: Seonin, 2009.

———, ed. *Gudeong-i pare bihaengjang-e gatda wan* [We Went to the Airport to Dig a Hole]. Jeju: Jeju 4.3 Peace Foundation, 2015.

———, ed. *Ijesa malhaemsuda 1* [Now We Speak Out, vol. 1]. Seoul: Hanul, 1989.

———, ed. *Ijesa malhaemsuda 2* [Now We Speak Out, vol. 2]. Seoul: Hanul, 1989.

———, ed. *Jeju 4.3 jaryojip II: Migukmuseong jejudo gwangye munseo* [Jeju 4.3 Sourcebook II: The U.S. State Department Documents Related to Jeju Island]. Jeju: Gak, 2001.

———, ed. *Jeo saram pokdo aniudage geunyang bonaejupseo* [That Person Is Not a Rioter. Please Let Him Go]. Jeju: Jeju 4.3 Peace Foundation, 2015.

———, ed. *Manbengdui-ui nunmul* [Tears of Manbengdui Cemetery]. Seoul: Hanul Academy, 2015.

Jeju Business and Professional Women's Club. "Jeju-ui jeonmunjik yeoseong seongakja-ege baeunda" [Lessons to Learn Jeju Professional Women, Pioneers]. *Women's Network* 10 (2006): 24–58.

Jeju Defence Command. *Jejuwa haebyeongdae* [Jeju and the Korean Marine Corps]. Jeju: Jeju Defence Command, 1997.

Jeju Government and Jeju Development Institute. *Jeju 4.3 pyeonghwagongwon joseong gibongyehoek* [The Basic Plan for Building the Jeju 4.3 Peace Park]. Jeju: Jeju Government, 2001.

Jeju Government and Jeju Special Committee for Women, eds. *Gusullo mannaneun Jeju yeoseongui sam geurigo yeoksa* [An Oral Story of the Life and History of Jeju Women]. Jeju: Jeju Government, 2004.

———, eds. *Jeju yeoseongui saengae: Saramsinan saratju* [Life Stories of Jeju Women: We've Barely Survived]. Jeju: Jeju Government, 2006.

———, eds. *Sidaereul apseo gan Jeju yeoseong* [Jeju Women Who Were Way ahead of Their Time]. Jeju: Gak, 2005.

Jeju Munhwa Broadcasting Corporation TV. "4.3 jeungeon" [Testimonies about Jeju 4.3]. April 22, 2001.

Jeju Police Agency. *Jeju gyeongchalsa* [The History of the Jeju Police]. N.p., 1990.

Jeju Special Self-Governing Provincial Office of Education. *Geunhyeondae Jeju gyoyuk 100nyeonsa* [The One-Hundred-Year History of (Early) Modern Education in Jeju]. Jeju: Gyeongsin Inswaesa, 2011.

Jemin Ilbo 4.3 Reporting Team. *4.3eun malhanda 1* [4.3 Speaks, vol. 1]. Seoul: Jeonyaewon, 1994.

———. *4.3eun malhanda 2* [4.3 Speaks, vol. 2]. Seoul: Jeonyaewon, 1994.

———. *4.3eun malhanda 3* [4.3 Speaks, vol. 3]. Seoul: Jeonyaewon, 1995.

———. *4.3eun malhanda 4* [4.3 Speaks, vol. 4]. Seoul: Jeonyaewon, 1997.

———. *4.3eun malhanda 5* [4.3 Speaks, vol. 5]. Seoul: Jeonyaewon, 1998.

Jeon, Gap-saeng. "Hangukjeonjaeng jeonhu daehancheongnyeondanui jibangjo-jikgwa hwaldong" [The Daehan Youth Association's Local Branches and Their Activities in Pre- and Post–Korean War Periods]. *Jenosaideu Yeongu* [Genocide Studies] 4 (2008): 11–82.

Jeong, Shin-ji. "Georeumeong bomeong deureumeong" [Walking, Looking, and Listening]. *Jejusori*, August 11, 2012.

Jeong, Su-hyeon, ed. *6.25 jeonjaenggwa Jeju yeongungdeul* [The Korean War and the Heroes from Jeju]. Jeju: Yeollimmunhwa, 2009.

———, ed. *6.25 jeonjaenggwa Jeju yeongungdeul 3* [The Korean War and the Heroes from Jeju, vol. 3]. Jeju: Yeollimmunhwa, 2011.

———, ed. *6.25 jeonjaenggwa Jeju yongsadeul 7* [The Korean War and the Heroes from Jeju, vol. 7]. Jeju: Jeju Veterans Association, 2015.

———, ed. *Jageun yeongungdeurui iyagi* [The Story of Little Heroes]. Jeju: Cultural Center of Southern Jeju, 2006.

Jeong, Yeong-hun. "Hanminjogui jeongcheseonggwa Dangun minjokjuui" [Korean National Identity and Dangun Nationalism]. *Minjokmunhwa Nonchong* [Korean Cultural Studies] 55 (2013): 93–137.

Jin, Gwan-hun. "Iljeha Jeju gyeongjewa haenyeo nodong-e gwanhan yeongu" [A Study on Female Divers' Labor and the Local Economy of Jeju Island during Japanese Colonial Control]. *Jeongsin Munhwa Yeongu* [Korean Studies Quarterly] 27, no.1 (2004): 149–78.

Kang, Dae-won. *Haenyeo yeongu* [A Study of Female Divers]. Seoul: Hanjin Munhwasa, 1973.

Kang, Eun-jung, and Timothy Jeonglyeol Lee. "The Dark Tourism Experience: Visitors to the April Third Peace Park, South Korea." *Gwangwang Leisure Yeongu* [Tourism and Leisure] 23, no. 7 (2011): 547–66.

Kang, Jun-man. *Hanguk hyeondaesa sanchaek: 1950nyeondae pyeon 1* [A Trip through Modern Korean History: The Period of the 1950s, vol. 1]. Seoul: Inmulgwa Sasangsa, 2004.

———. *Hanguk hyeondaesa sanchaek: 1940nyeondae pyeon 2* [A Trip through Modern Korean History: The Period of the 1940s, vol. 2]. Seoul: Inmulgwa Sasangsa, 2006.

Kang, Seong-hyeon. "'Aka'-wa 'ppalgaengi'ui tansaeng: Jeok mandeulgiwa bigung-minui gyebohak" [The Birth of "Aka (meaning Reds in Japanese)" and "Ppalgaengi (the Reds)": The Making of the Enemy and the Genealogy of Those Unqualified as Good Citizens]. *Sahoewa Yeoksa* [Society and History] 100 (2013): 235–77.

Katsiaficas, George. *Asia's Unknown Uprisings Volume 1: South Korean Movements in the 20th Century.* Oakland, CA: PM Press, 2012.

Kaurin, Pauline. "Identity, Loyalty and Combat Effectiveness: A Cautionary Tale." 2006 Conference of the International Society for Military Ethics (ISME). http://isme.tamu.edu/JSCOPE06/Kaurin06.html.

Kelman, Herbert. "The Policy Context of Torture: A Social-Psychological Analysis." *International Review of the Red Cross* 87 (2005): 123–34.

Kim, Bong-hyun, and Min-ju Kim. *Jejudo inmindeurui 4.3 mujang tujaengsa* [A History of the Jeju People's 4.3 Armed Struggle]. Osaka: Munusa 1963.

———. "Jejudo inmindeurui 4.3 mujang tujaengsa" [A History of the Jeju People's 4.3 Armed Struggle]. In *Jeju minjung hangjaeng 1* [Jeju People's Uprising, vol. 1], edited by Arari Research Institute, 199–277. Seoul: Sonamu, 1988.

Kim, Bong-jin. "Paramilitary Politics under the USAMGIK and the Establishment of the Republic of Korea." *Korea Journal* 43, no. 2 (2003): 289–322.

Kim, Byeng-tak. *Jeju yesurui sahoesa* [Social History of Art and Literature in Jeju]. Jeju: Research Institute for Tamla Culture, 2010.

Kim, Chang-hu. "Jaeiljejuinui hangil undong" [Jeju Islanders' Anti-Japanese Movement in Japan]." *Jejudosa Yeongu* [Review of Jeju History] 4 (1995): 258–73.

Kim, Choong Nam. "The Impact of the Korean War on the Korean Military." *International Journal of Korean Studies* 5, no. 1 (2001): 159–82.

———. "State and Nation Building in South Korea: A Comparative Historical Perspective." *Review of Korean Studies* 12, no. 1 (2009): 121–50.

Kim, Deuk-jung. *'Ppalgaengi'ui tansaeng* [The Birth of the "Reds"]. Seoul: Seonin, 2009.

Kim, Dong Choon. *Jeonjaenggwa sahoe* [War and Society]. Seoul: Dolbegae, 2000.

———. "The Social Grounds of Anticommunism in South Korea: Crisis of the Ruling Class and Anticommunist Reaction." *Asian Journal of German and European Studies* 2 (2017): 1–25.

Kim, Dong-gyu. "Jaegeon cheong/buinhoe-e baraneun geot" [What I Would Like the National Reconstruction Youth Association and the Women's Association to Do]. *Jejudo* [Jeju Province] 5 (1962): 32–36.

Kim, Dong-man. "Haebang jikhu jibang jeongchi yeongu: Jeju jibang geongukjun-biwiwonhoe inminwiwonhoeui jojikgwa hwaldong" [A Study on Postliberation Local Politics: The Organization and Activities of the Jeju Branch of the Committee for the Preparation of Korean Independence and of the Committee for the Korean People's Republic]. *Yeoksa Bipyeong* [Critical Review of History] 14 (1991): 191–207.

Kim, Dong-ro. "Hangukjeonjaenggwa jibae ideollogi" [The Korean War and the Ruling Ideology]. *Asia Munhwa* [Asian Culture] 16 (2000): 279–309.

Kim, Eun-ha. "Jeonhu gukga geundaehwawa wiheomhan mimanginui munhwa jeongchihak" [A Study on Cultural Politics of Postwar Modernization and Dangerous Widows]. *Hangukmunhwa Irongwa Bipyeong* [Korean Literature Theory and Criticism] 14, no. 4 (2010): 211–29.

Kim, Eun-hee. "Jeju 4.3sigi 'jeollyakchon'ui hyeongseonggwa jumin saenghwal" [The Formation of the "Strategic Village" and the Life of the Villagers during Jeju 4.3]. *Yeoksa Minsokhak* [Journal of Korean Historical Folklife] 23 (2006): 181–210.

Kim, Eun-kyung. "1950nyeondae moseong damnongwa hyeonsil" [Motherhood Discourse and the Reality in the 1950s]. *Yeoseonghak Yeongu* [Journal of Women's Studies] 21, no.1 (2011): 123–59.

———. "Hangukjeonjaeng hu jaegeon yulliroseoui 'jeontongnon'gwa yeoseong" ["Tradition" and Women in the Process of Reconstruction after the Korean War]. *Asia Yeoseong Yeongu* [Journal of Asian Women] 45, no. 2 (2006): 7–48.

Kim, Eun-shil. "The Politics of the Jeju 4.3 *Holeomeong* Bodies: 'Speaking' and Emotion as Embodied Language." *Korean Anthropology Review* 2 (2018): 1–41.

Kim, Gyeong-hwan. "Jeju yeoseongui jiyeokjeok gwaeop" [The Role of Jeju Women in the Community Development]. *Jejudo* [Jeju Province] 13 (1964): 149–54.

Kim, Hun Joon. *The Massacres at Mt. Halla: Sixty Years of Truth Seeking in South Korea.* Ithaca, NY: Cornell University Press, 2014.

———. "Returned Suppression and the Jeju 4.3: Struggles in the Dark Times." In *The Jeju 4.3 Mass Killing: Atrocity, Justice, and Reconciliation*, edited by Jeju 4.3 Peace Foundation, 179–200. Seoul: Yonsei University Press, 2018.

———. "Seeking Truth after 50 Years: The National Committee for Investigation of the Truth about the Jeju 4.3 Events." *International Journal of Transitional Justice* 3 (2009): 406–23.

Kim, Hyun Sun. "Life and Work of Korean War Widows during the1950s." *Review of Korean Studies* 12, no. 4 (2009): 87–109.

Kim, Ik-ryeol. "4.3ui jinsil" [The Truth of Jeju 4.3]. In *4.3eun malhanda 2* [4.3 Speaks, vol. 2], edited by Jemin Ilbo 4.3 Reporting Team, 273–357. Seoul: Jeonyaewon, 1994.

Kim, Inhan. "Land Reform in South Korea under the U.S. Military Occupation, 1945–1948." *Journal of Cold War Studies* 18, no. 2 (2016): 97–129.

Kim, Jeong-gon. *Hangukjeonjaenggwa nodongdang jeollyak* [The Korean War and the South Korean Labor Party's Strategy]. Seoul: Bakyeongsa, 1973.

Kim, Jong-min. "4.3 ihu 50nyeon" [Fifty Years after 4.3]. In *Jeju 4.3 yeongu* [A Study on the Jeju 4.3], edited by Jeju 4.3 Research Institute, 338–424. Seoul: Yeoksa Bipyeongsa, 1999.

————. "Early Cold War Genocide: The Jeju 4.3 Massacre and U.S. Responsibility." *Korea Policy Institute*, April 4, 2020. https://www.kpolicy.org/post/early-cold-war -genocide-the-jeju-4-3-massacre-and-u-s-responsibility.

————. "Seventy Years after the Jeju April 3." In *The Jeju 4.3 Mass Killing: Atrocity, Justice, and Reconciliation*, edited by Jeju 4.3 Peace Foundation, 115–52. Seoul: Yonsei University Press, 2018.

Kim, Jung-hee, ed. *Jeonmol haebyeongui sugi* [Memoirs of Korean Marines Killed in Action]. Seoul: Office of Information and Education of Headquarters, Korean Marine Corps (KMC), 1965.

————. "Ugukgangyeon [A lecture of patriotism]." In *Hanbeon haebyeongeun yeongwonhan haebyeong* [Once a Marine, Always a Marine], edited by Seon-ho Lee, 389–91. Seoul: Jungudang, 1997.

Kim, Jung Han, and Jeong-Mi Park. "Subjectivation and Social Movements in Post-Colonial Korea." In *The History of Social Movements in Global Perspective: A Survey*, edited by Stefan Berger and Holger Nehring, 297–324. London: Palgrave Macmillan, 2017.

Kim, Mi-hyang. "1950nyeondae jeonhu soseore natanan gajok hyeongsanghwawa geu uimi" [Family Configuration and Its Meaning Contained in Postwar Novels in the 1950s]. *Hyeondaesoseol Yeongu* [Modern Fiction Studies] 43 (2010): 227–53.

Kim, Min-hwan. "Jeonjang-i doen Jeju 4.3 pyeonghwagongwon: Pokdongronui 'areungeorim'gwa bunyeolden yeondae" [Jeju 4.3 Peace Park That Became a Battlefield: The "Absent Presence" of the Riot Interpretation and Divided Solidarity]. *Gyeongjewa Sahoe* [Economy and Society] 102 (2014): 74–109.

Kim, Monica. *The Interrogation Rooms of the Korean War: The Untold History.* Princeton, NJ: Princeton University Press, 2019.

Kim, Mun. *Janggunui bimangnok 2* [Memorandum of Korean Generals, vol. 2]. Seoul: Byeolmang, 1998.

Kim, Mu-yong. "Yeosu-Suncheon sageon jinabeul wihan daehang guerilla jakjeongwa minganin huisaenghwa jeollyak" [Counterguerilla Operations and Civilian Victimization Strategies during the Suppression of the Yeosu-Suncheon Incident]. *Yeoksa Yeongu* [Journal of History] 31 (2016): 245–302.

Kim, Myeong-gu. "Hanmal iljegangjeom chogi Sin Chae-ho-ui minjokjuui sasang" [Sin Chae-ho's Nationalism in the Late Jeoseon Period and the Early Period of Japanese Colonial Rule]. *Baeksanhakpo* [The Baek-San Hakpo] 62 (2002): 229–64.

Kim, Ryeo-sil. "Nyuseuril jeonjaeng: Hangukjeonjaeng chogi migukui nyuseurilgwa <ribeoti nyuseu>ui tansaeng" [Nyuseuril War: U. S. War Newsreels and the Birth of *Liberty News* during the Early Days of the Korean War]. *Hyundai Yeonghwa Yeongu* [Modern Film Studies] 25 (2016): 70–105.

Kim, Sang-heun, *Namsarok* [Travel Diary of Namsa]. Translated by Hui-dong Kim. Seoul: Yeonggamunhwasa, 1992.

Kim, Seong-eun. *Naui jani neomchinaida* [My Cup Runneth Over]. Seoul: Itemple Korea, 2008.

Kim, Seong-nae. "Gukgapongnyeokgwa yeoseong cheheom" [Women's Experiences of State Violence]. In *Dongasiaui pyounghhawa ingwon* [Peace and Human Rights in East Asia], edited by Jeju 4.3 Research Institute, 154–72. Seoul: Yeoksa Bipyeongsa, 1999.

———. "Memory Politics and the Emergence of a Women's Sphere to Counter Historical Violence in Korea." In *Gender, Transitional Justice and Memorial Arts*, edited by Jelke Boesten and Helen Scanlon, 75–96. New York: Routledge, 2021.

———. "Placing the Dead in the Postmemory of the Cheju Massacre in Korea." *Journal of Religion* 99, no.1 (2019): 80–97.

———. "Sexual Politics of State Violence: On Cheju April Third Massacre of 1948." In *Traces 2: Race Panic and the Memory of Migration*, edited by Meagan Morris and Brett de Bary, 259–92. Hong Kong: Hong Kong University Press, 2001.

———. "Shamanic Epics and Narrative Construction of Identity on Cheju Island." *Asian Folklore Studies* 63 (2004): 57–78.

Kim, Seong-nae, Chul-in Yoo, Eun-shil Kim, Chang-min Kim, Chang-hoon Ko, and Suk-joon Kim. "Jeju 4.3ui gyeongheomgwa maeul gongdongcheui byeonhwa" [The Experience of Jeju 4.3 and Changes in a Village Community]. *Hangukmunhwa Illyuhak* [Journal of Korean Cultural Anthropology] 34, no. 1 (2001): 89–137.

Kim, Soo-ja. "Rhee Syng-man-ui ilminjuui-ui jechanggwa nolli" [The Advocacy and Logic of Rhee Syng-man's One People Principle]. *Hanguk Sasangsahak* [Korean History of Thought] 22 (2004): 437–71.

Kim, Soojin. "Jeontongui changangwa yeoseongui gungminhwa: Shin Saimdang-eul jungsimeuro" [The Invention of Tradition and the Nationalization of Women in Postcolonial Korea: Making Shin Saimdang an Image of the "Wise Mother and Good Wife"]. *Sahoewa Yeoksa* [Society and History] 80 (2008): 215–55.

———. "Vacillating Images of Shin Saimdang: The Invention of a Historical Heroine in Colonial Korea." *Inter-Asia Cultural Studies* 15, no. 2 (2014): 274–90.

Kim, Suzy. *Everyday Life in the North Korean Revolution, 1945–1950.* Ithaca, NY: Cornell University Press, 2013.

Kim, Yeong-beoum. "Gieok tujaeng-euroseoui 4.3 munhwaundong seoseol" [Introduction to the Jeju 4.3 Cultural Movement as a Struggle for Memory]. In *Gieok tujaenggwa munhwaundongui jeongae* [A Struggle for Memory and the Development of the Cultural Movement], edited by Kan-chae Na, Keun-sik Jung, and Chang-il Kang, 26–68. Seoul: Yeoksa Bipyeongsa, 2004.

———. "Yeonjwajeui yeoksajeok jeongaewa geu uimimang: Joseon sidaereul jungsimeuro" [The Historical Development of the Guilt-by-Association System and Its Semantic Network in the Joseon Dynasty]. In *Sahoesa yeonguui irongwa silje* [Theory and Practice in Social History Studies], edited by Korean Social History Research Group, 324–47. Seoul: Munji Publishing, 1990.

Kim, Yeong-don. "Jejudominui geunmyeonseong" [Diligence of Jeju Residents]. *Jejudo* [Jeju Province] 43 (1970): 190–95.

Ko, Chang-hun. "4.3 minjung hangjaengui jeongaewa seonggyok" [The Process and Characteristics of the 4.3 People's Uprising]. In *Haebang jeonhusaui insik 4* [A

View of the History of the Pre/Post-Liberation Periods, vol. 4], edited by Jang-jip Choi, 245–340. Seoul: Hangilsa, 1989.

Ko, Du-hui. "Yeoseonggwa sinang" [Women and Belief]. *Jejudo* [Jeju Province] 13 (1964): 145–48.

Ko, Mun-seong. *Jeju saramdeurui seorum* [The Sorrows of Jeju People]. Jeju: Sinamunhwasa, 1991.

Ko, Si-hong. "Ko Su-seon." In *Jeju yeoinsang* [An Image of Jeju Women], edited by Jeju Cultural Center, 339–422. Jeju: Hwasinmungo, 1998.

Ko, Su-seon. "Naega saraon gil" [The Way I Lived]. *Jeju Sinmum*, June 19, 1978.

Koh, Sungman. "4.3 'huisaengja'ui byeonyonggwa hwaryong: Mujangdae chulsinjaui gwageocheongsan gyeongheomeul saryero" [Transformation and Utilization of 4.3 "Victims": A Case Study of the Government's Clean-Up of Past Acts Perpetrated by the Armed Rebels]. *Sahoewa Yeoksa* [Society and History] 129 (2021): 263–92.

———. "Trans-border Ritual for the Dead: Experiential Knowledge of Paternal Relatives after the Jeju 4.3 Incident." *Journal of Korean Religions* 9, no.1 (2018): 71–103.

Korea Institute for Military Affairs. *Hangukjeonjaeng jiwonsa: Insa, gunsu, minsa jiwon* [The History of Defense Support for the Korean War: Personnel, Military, and Civil Support]. Seoul: Korea Institute for Military Affairs, 1997.

Kraft, Diane B. "South Korea's National Security Law: A Tool of Oppression in an Insecure World." *Wisconsin International Law Journal* 24, no. 2 (2006): 627–59.

Kwon, Heonik. *After the Korean War: An Intimate History.* Cambridge: Cambridge University Press, 2020.

Kwon, Ja-kyung. "Hangukjeonjaeng, jeonhu bokguwa jawon dongwon" [The Korean War, Postwar Rehabilitation, and Resource Mobilization]. *Hanguk Geobeoneonseu Hoebo* [Korean Governance Review] 18, no. 2 (2011): 275–301.

Lee, Chang-ki. *Jejudoui inguwa gajok* [Population and Families of Jeju Island]. Daegu: Youngnam University Press, 1999.

Lee, Eun-ju, and Ok-hwa Oh. "Yeoseongui sahoechamyeo hwakdae bangan" [Ways of Expanding Women's Social Participation]. In *21segi modureul wihan jejudo* [Jeju Island for All in the Twenty-First Century], edited by Jeju Development Research Institute, 203–56. Jeju: Jeju Development Research Institute, 1998.

Lee, Im Ha. "Hangukjeonjaenggwa yeoseong nodongui hwakdae" [The Korean War and the Expansion of Women's Labor]. *Hanguksa Hakbo* [Journal for the Studies of Korean History] 14 (2003): 251–78.

———. "The Korean War and the Role of Women." *Review of Korean Studies* 9, no. 2 (2006): 89–110.

———. *Yeoseong, jeonjaengeul neomeo ireoseoda* [Women Rise beyond the War]. Seoul: Seohaemunjip, 2004.

Lee, Jong Won. "The Impact of the Korean War on the Korean Economy." *International Journal of Korean Studies* 5 (2001): 97–118.

Lee, Sang-ho, and Yeong-sil Park. *6.25 jeonjaeng: Sonyeonbyeong yeongu* [The Korean War: A Study of Child Soldiers]. Seoul: Institute for Military History Compilation, Ministry of National Defense (MND), 2011.

Lee, Steven. *The Korean War.* New York: Routledge, 2001.

Lee, Un-bang. "4.3 sageonui jinsang" [The Truth of the Jeju 4.3 Incident]. In *Ijesa malhaemsuda 1* [Now We Speak Out, vol. 1], edited by Jeju 4.3 Research Institute, 201–33. Seoul: Hanul, 1989.

Lee, Yeong-gwon. "15–17segi Jeju yuminui sahoesajeok yeongu" [A Social History Study of Drifting People in Jeju between the Fifteenth and the Seventeenth Centuries]. PhD diss., Jeju National University, 2013.

Lee, Yeong-il. "Yeo-Sun sageon jinsanggyumyeongwiwonhoeui siljewa gwaje" [The Reality and Challenge of Commission for the Investigation of the Truth of the Yeosu-Suncheon Incident]. Paper presented at the Symposium to Celebrate the 68th Anniversary of the Yeosu-Suncheon Incident, Yeosu, October 21, 2016.

Lim, Dae-sik. "Jeju 4.3 hangjaenggwa u-ik cheongyeondan" [The Jeju 4.3 Uprising and the Rightist Youth Association]. In *Jeju 4.3 yeongu* [A Study on Jeju 4.3], edited by Jeju 4.3 Research Institute, 205–37. Seoul: Yeoksa Bipyeongsa, 1999.

Macdonald, Sharon. "Theorizing Museum: Introduction." In *Theorizing Museum*, edited by Sharon Macdonald and Gordon Fyfe, 1–20. Oxford: Blackwell, 1996.

May, Hope. "The United States, the United Nations and the Jeju April 3rd Incident: A Story of Responsibility." In *The Jeju 4.3 Mass Killing: Atrocity, Justice, and Reconciliation*, edited by Jeju 4.3 Peace Foundation, 33–63. Seoul: Yonsei University Press, 2018.

May 18 Democratization Movement Truth Commission. *2021nyeon habang-gi josahwaldong bogoseo* [A Report on Investigation of the May 18 Democratization Movement Carried Out in the Second Half of 2021]. Seoul: Seonin, 2021.

Merrill, John. "The Cheju-do Rebellion." *Journal of Korean Studies* 2 (1980): 139–97.

———. "Reflections of the Jeju 4.3 Incident: Korea's 'Dark History' and Its Implications for Current Policy." In *The Jeju 4.3 Mass Killing: Atrocity, Justice, and Reconciliation*, edited by Jeju 4.3 Peace Foundation, 325–50. Seoul: Yonsei University Press, 2018.

Ministry of Patriots and Veterans Affairs. *Bohun 50nyeonsa: 1961–2011* [The Fifty-Year History of Patriots and Veterans Affairs: 1961–2011]. Seoul: Ministry of Patriots and Veterans Affairs, 2011.

National Bureau of Statistics of Economic Planning Board. *1960 ingu jutaek guk-sejosa bogo* [1960 Population and Housing Census Report]. Seoul: Economic Planning Board, 1963.

———. *1980 ingu mit jutaek census bogoseo* [1980 Population and Housing Census Report]. Seoul: Economic Planning Board, 1982.

Nobu, Takahashi. *Joseonbandoui nongbeobgwa nongmin: Jejudo* [Farming Techniques and Peasantry in Joseon: Jeju Island]. Jeju: Woodang Library, 2000.

Oh, Seong-chan, ed. *Hallaui tonggoksori: Jeju daehaksarui jeungeon* [The Wailing of Halla: Testimonies about the Jeju Massacre]. Seoul: Sonamu, 1988.

Park, Chan-sik. *4.3gwa Jeju yeoksa* [4.3 and the History of Jeju]. Jeju: Gak, 2008.

———. *1901nyeon Jeju millan yeongu* [A Study of the Jeju Uprising in 1901]. Jeju: Gak, 2013.

Park, Jung Ho, and Young Hag Kim. "A Study on the Influence of Land Institution on State-Building in South Korea: Human Resources." *Land Use Policy* 69 (2017): 106–11.

Park, Myung-lim. "Jejudo 4.3 minjung hangjaeng-e gwanhan yeongu" [A Study on the Jeju 4.3 Popular Uprising]. MA thesis, Korea University, 1988.

———. "Minjujuui, iseong, geurigo yeoksa yeongu: Jeju 4.3gwa hanguk hyeondaesa" [Democracy, Reason, and a Study of History: Jeju 4.3 and Modern History of Korea]. In *Jeju 4.3 yeongu* [A Study on Jeju 4.3], edited by Jeju 4.3 Research Institute, 425–60. Seoul: Yeoksa Bipyeongsa, 1999.

———. "Towards a Universal Model of Reconciliation: The Case of the Jeju 4.3 Incident." *Journal of Korean Religions* 9, no. 1 (2018): 105–30.

Park, Seo-dong. *Yeongwonhan urideurui apeum, 4.3* [Our Never-Ending Pains of Life, 4.3]. Jeju: Wolgan Gwangwangjeju, 1990.

Ramsey, Robert, III. *Advising Indigenous Forces: American Advisors in Korea, Vietnam, and El Salvador.* Fort Leavenworth, KS: Combat Studies Institute Press, 2006.

Rhee, Syng-man. *Daetongnyeong Rhee Syng-man baksa damhwajip* [A Collection of President Rhee Syng-man's Speeches]. Seoul: Public Information Agency, 1953.

———. *Ilminjuui gaesul* [Outline of One People Principle]. Seoul: Committee for the Promotion of Ilminjuui, 1949.

Riley, John, and Leonard Cottrell. "Psychological Warfare in Korea." *Public Opinion Quarterly* 15, no. 1 (1951): 65–75.

Sim, Jae-woo. "Joseonsidae yeonjwajeui silsang" [The Realty of the System of Guilt by Association in the Joseon Dynasty]." *Hanguk Munhwa* [Korean Culture] 55 (2011): 87–112.

Son, Kyeongho. "The 4.3 Incident: Background, Development, and Pacification, 1945–1949." PhD diss., Ohio State University, 2008.

Third and Fourth Groups of the Korean Marines Corps, ed. *Chamjeonsillok* [A True Record concerning Those Who Fought in the Korean War]. Seoul: Munchang Yeongusa, 2002.

Tilly, Charles. *Democracy*. Cambridge: Cambridge University Press, 2007.

———. "Grudging Consent." *American Interest* 3, no. 1 (2007): 17–23.

———. *The Politics of Collective Violence.* Cambridge: Cambridge University Press, 2003.

———. "War Making and State Making as Organized Crime." In *Bringing the State Back*, edited by Peter Evans, Dietrich Rueschemeyer, and Theda Skocpol, 169–87. Cambridge: Cambridge University Press, 1985.

United Nations Secretary-General. "The Rule of Law and Transitional Justice in Conflict and Post-conflict Societies." Report of the Secretary-General, August 23, 2004.

Wright, Brendan. "Civil War, Politicide, and the Politics of Memory in South Korea, 1948–1961." PhD diss., University of British Colombia, 2016.

———. "Kinship Killings, Taesal and Biologized State Violence during the Korean Civil War." *Journal of Genocide Research* (October 2021): 1–15.

————. "Politicidal Violence and the Problematics of Localized Memory at Civilian Massacre Sites: The Cheju 4.3 Peace Park and the Kŏch'ang Incident Memorial Park." *Cross-Currents: East Asian History and Culture Review* 14 (2015): 204–33.

————. "Raising the Korean Dead: Bereaved Family Associations and the Politics of 1960–1961 South Korea." *Asia-Pacific Journal: Japan Focus* 13, issue 41, no. 2 (2015): 1–19.

Yang, Gyeong-in. *Seonchangeun eonjena naui moksieotda: Yeoseonghaebangui kkumeul kkun Jeju 4.3 yeoseong undonggaui saengae* [I Always Led the Others When Singing in a Team: The Life of a Jeju 4.3 Female Activist Who Dreamed of Women's Liberation]. Seoul: Eunhaengnamu, 2022.

Yang, Han-gwon. "Jejudo 4.3 pokdongui baegyeong-e gwanhan yeongu" [A Study on the Historical Background of the Jeju 4.3 Rebellion]. MA thesis, Seoul National University, 1988.

Yang, Jeong-sim. "Jeju 4.3 teukbyeolbeopgwa yangmin haksal damnon, geugeoseul ttwieoneomeo" [Beyond the Jeju 4.3 Special Act and the Discourse of Civilian Massacre]. *Yeoksa Yeongu* [Journal of Historical Studies] 7 (2000): 271–82.

————. *Jeju 4.3 hangjaeng: Jeohanggwa apeumui yeoksa* [The Jeju 4.3 Uprising: A History of Resistance and Pain]. Seoul: Seonin, 2008.

————. "The Jeju 4.3, Memories of Massacre and Times of Uprising." In *The Jeju 4.3 Mass Killing: Atrocity, Justice, and Reconciliation*, edited by Jeju 4.3 Peace Foundation, 153–78. Seoul: Yonsei University Press, 2018.

————. "Judoseryeogeul tonghaeseo bon Jeju 4.3 hangjaengui baegyeong" [Background of the Jeju 4.3 Uprising: With a Focus on Leading Forces]." In *Jeju 4.3 yeongu* [A Study on Jeju 4.3], edited by Jeju 4.3 Research Institute, 51–96. Seoul: Yeoksa Bipyeongsa, 1999.

Yang, Jo-hoon. "The Truth of the April 3 Incident and the Role and Responsibility of the U.S." In *The Jeju 4.3 Mass Killing: Atrocity, Justice, and Reconciliation*, edited by Jeju 4.3 Peace Foundation, 65–112. Seoul: Yonsei University Press, 2018.

Yang, Young-ja. "Sesi pungsokgwa jeonseung minnyo" [Seasonal Customs and Folk Songs Handed down for Generations]. In *Jeju yeoseong jeonseung munhwa* [Traditional Culture Handed down among Local Women in Jeju], edited by Jeju Culture, Art, and History Compilation Committee, 16–100. Jeju: Jeju Government, 2004.

Yoo, Chul-in. *Munhwaillyuhakjaui jagi minjokji: Jejudo* [An Autoethnography Written by a Cultural Anthropologist: Jeju Island]. Seoul: Minsokwon, 2021.

Yoon, So-young. "Geundae gukga hyeongseonggi hanirui 'hyeonmoyangcheo'ron" [A Study of the Image of the "Wise Mother and Good Wife" of Korea and Japan in the Formative Period of Modern Nations]. *Hangukminjok Undongsa Yeongu* [Journal of Studies on Korean National Movement] 44 (2005): 77–119.

Zelizer, Barbie. "Gender and Atrocity: Women in Holocaust Photographs." In *Visual Culture and the Holocaust*, edited by Barbie Zelizer, 247–60. New Jersey: Rutgers University Press, 2001.

Index

The ABC of Communism (Bukharin and
Preobrazhensky), 12
Act on the Establishment of National
Defense Army (1950), 65n3
"After the Hen Cackles, Morning
Comes and an Enlightened Society
Arrives" (Ko Su-seon), 99
Ahn Jae-hong, 7
Ahn Se-hun, 11
American Public Opinion Bureau, 11
An, Ho-sang, 52–53, 61–62
ancestor ceremonies, 3, 102–3, 144
Anderson, Benedict, 79
anticommunism, xi–xvi, 8, 51–53;
bangong policy, 65, 79–80;
establishment of anticommunist
South Korea, 30–39; and imagined
community, 79, 83–84; *myeolgong*
obliteration policy, 65, 80; and One
People Principle, 52–53; public
acts of violence central to, 37; and
right-wing youth group atrocities,
25–26, 28; surveillance systems,
53–55; used by Rhee, 31, 32. *See
also* communism
Anti-Communism Law (1961), x, 121
Antinational Activist Punishment Law
(1948), 31

April 3, as national memorial
day, 130, 145
Armed Resistance Group (People's
Liberation Army, or Mountain
People), 22, 26–27, 31
army, as machine, 75
Asahi Shimbun, 16n26

Baekbi ("Unnamed Monument"),
ix, *x,* 129
belt *(chuninchim, sennimbari),* as
enlistment ritual, 64
Bentham, Jeremy, 54
Biseol ("Pile of Snow Scattered by
Strong Wind"), 141–42, *142*
blood applications, 56–57, 61–62
blood lineage *(minjok),* 52–53, 59, 79
Bonggae village (Jeju Island), 131n2
Bukchon village massacre (Jeju Island),
36, 40, 57, 83, 143
Byeon Byeong-saeng, 141–42

Capital (Marx and Engels), 12
Catholic Church, 2
Chang, Jieun, 38
Changdeok Palace, 96
Changwon county, 6
"The Cheju-do Rebellion" (Merrill), xii
China, and Korean War, 83–84

171

Cho, Hae-jeong, 110
Cho, Jeong-hee, 151n2
Cho Byeong-ok, 24–25, 28
Choi, Ho-geun, 22
Choi, Hyaeweol, 93
Choi Gyeong-jin, 24–25
Choi Jeong-suk, 114n55
Chomsky, Noam, 147
Cho Myung-ki, 130
Choong Nam Kim, 80
Chosun Ilbo (newspaper), 94
Christian mission schools and
    organizations, 93–94
Chun Doo-hwan, 121
citizens *(gungmin)*, 80–81, 85
Civilian Guard *(minbodan)*, 36, 37, 143
"civilian sacrifices," ideology of, xi,
    124–26, 139
Cold War, xii, 29, 31, 37
Committee for Preparation and
    Execution of the Jeju 4.3 Memorial
    Ceremony, 130
Committee for the Preparation for
    Korean Independence, xiv–xv
Committee for the Preparation for
    Korean Independence (CPKI),
    xiv–xv, 7–9. *See also* People's
    Committees (PC)
Committee for Village Development
    (Hagui village), 143–44
communism. *See also* anticommunism;
    Jeju PC (People's Committee);
    People's Committees (PC)
Communist Party of Japan, 4
Communist Party of Korea: blamed for
    1946 uprisings, 14; and education
    of children, 12; Jeju *Yacheika*
    (subgroup), 5, 9, 14
Concerning Interim Military and
    Security Matters Executive
    Agreement, 32
concubines, 12, 102–4
Confucianism, xvi, 2, 144; and Wise
    Mother, Good Wife ideology, 93, 94

Congressional Special Committee for
    Investigation of Civilian Deaths, 121
Constitutional Court of South Korea,
    123, 125, 137
counterinsurgency operations, xii–
    xv; Jeju Defense Headquarters,
    32; obedience to, 55; as political
    genocide, xiii; and universe of
    obligation, 28–29, 32–33, 36–37;
    weaponization of leftist politics, 27
Counterintelligence Corps (Korean army
    headquarters), 59
Cultural Heritage Administration, 148
Cumings, Bruce, xii–xiii, 1, 6, 8, 35

Daehan Women's Association (DWA),
    59, 68n69, 96
Daehan Youth Association, 25, 50, 51,
    55, 60–61, 69n88
Dae-jung, Kim, xi
dang (shamanic shrine), 103–4
"dark tourism," 120
dehumanization, 37, 73, 81
democracy, xii, 135, 150; as
    anticommunism, 53; lack of
    understanding about, 80; student
    movements, 121–22; and transitional
    justice process, 120–24
Democratic People's Front, 8, 14
Democratic People's Republic of Korea
    (North Korea): invasion of South
    Korea, 22, 49, 56; labor movement
    collaboration with, 80; not
    considered separate by South Korean
    people, 80; occupation of South
    Korea, 50; underground election
    (1948), 31
Departure Prohibition Order (1629), 2
displacement, 3–4, 35, 54
divers, female, 3, 4–5, 100–101, 103,
    106–10; boycott campaigns, 109;
    symbolic currency of, 108
Donga Ilbo (newspaper), 11, 80, 108
Donner, Francesca, 96

economic development, xii, xvi–xvii, 91–93, 104–9, 121–22
education: by Christian organizations, 93–94; elementary and middle school, 6–7, 11–12; high level of among Jeju marines, 77; and National Student Corps, 61–64; night schools, 12; *Our Pledge (Uri-ui maengse)* campaign, 52, 55; principals and student military enlistment, 62, 63; and Wise Mother, Good Wife ideology, 92, 93
Emergency Decree (1974), 121
ethnic nation *(minjok)*, 80–81, 83–84
"evils," 53
exclusion, political, 28–29, 35

face-saving culture, 74
farming, independent, 7
Fein, Helen, 28
Female Volunteer Army, 50, 65–66n8
First Republic of Korea, xv, 32
fishery activities, 4–5, 7. *See also* divers, female
Foucault, Michel, 55, 75
free-fire zone, 33, 34

Gamson, William, 29
Gangjeong village (Jeju Island), 146–51. *See also* naval base, Jeju Island
Gangjeong Village Committee, 149, 150, 151
gender: "good" and "bad" women discourse, 95, 97; and marriage customs, 12; Meiji gender ideology, 93; sexual violence, 37–38; and transitional justice process, 138–39; and Western modernity, 93–95. *See also* Wise Mother, Good Wife ideology; women
geolgung ritual, 144
"Ghost-Catching Marines" (Higgins), 76
Goryeo Dynasty, 2
group identity, 75–79

guilty by association *(yeonjwaje)*, 39–41, 48n167
Gujwa-myeon (town), 5
Gwangju massacre (May, 1980), 122
gwendang (kinship community), 102–3

Hagui village (Jeju Island), 143–44
"Hand back power to the People's Committee" slogan, 14, 23
Heo, Ho-joon, xiii
Hideyoshi invasions of 1592–1598, 62
Higgins, Marguerite, 76
Hodge, John, 1, 8
Hun Joon Kim, 123
Hwang, Su-kyoung, xiii, 24
Hwang, Su-Kyoung, 26
hyeonmoyangcheo. See "Wise Mother, Good Wife"
Hyun Chang-ha, 145
Hyun Gi-yeong, 83, 121, 129, 132n14

identification cards *(Yangminjeung)*, 30
Ijesa malhaemsuda ("Now We Speak Out") testimony, 119
Imagined Communities (Anderson), 79
imagined national community, xvi, 49, 71, 79–84
Im-ha Lee, 66n8
Incheon Landing Operation, xix, 49, 65n3, 75, 82, 84
Incident of Local Dignitaries *(Youji sageun)*, 69n82
internalization, xvi, 39, 40, 55, 65, 74, 100, 108
International Fleet Review ceremony, 147, 150
"Island of Reds," Jeju Island as, xv, 24–25, 28, 119, 135
"Island of the Reds": invention of, 23–30; March 1st shooting incident and general strike, 14, 23–24
"Island of World Peace" rhetoric: construction of park, 123–24, 126; contradictions with militarization,

146–47; used to sublimate atrocities, xi, xvii, 119, 130–31, 135
"Isn't There a Way for Reconciliation and Coexistence of Jeju 4.3?" debate, 145

Jang, Se-yong, 130
Jang Ha-na, 149
Jang Myeon government, 121
Japan, 64; fishery union, 4–5; liberation of Korean peninsula from, xiv, 6–7, 10; Meiji gender ideology, 93; mobilization of Jeju Islanders in World War II, 5; modernization drives, 3; surrender (1945), 1
Japanese colonialism, xvi, 3–4; "cultural rule," 94; divide and rule policy, 7; female ideal during, 92; industries operated by, 10; Korean blood lineage ideology rooted in, 56–57, 79; militarist legacy of, 56–57, 64
Japanese soldiers, repatriation status, 10, 13
Jeju, an Island of Death (Ko Gil-cheon), 141
Jeju 4.3 advocacy movement (1980s), x–xi, xiv, xviii, 122–23, 129
Jeju 4.3 Bereaved Family Association, 144–46
Jeju 4.3 massacre: Bukchon village massacre, 36, 40, 57, 83, 143; casualties, 14, 33, 141, 152n24; civilians, public execution of, 37; and combat police officers, 28; deaths of children and elderly, xv, 21, 34, 35, 141; duration of, xiii–xiv; entrapment of villagers, 36; guerrilla terrorism, 34; height of violence in 1948–1949, 39; martial law as justification for, 34, 51; mass killing of 1948–1949, xv; numbers killed, 21–22, 41n1; October 11, 1948 start of, 32; official definition of contested, ix, 123–25, 133n30, 151n2; political prisoners of, 41n6,

57, 68n60, 83, 124–25, 139; refugees massacred, 35–36; revenge killings, methodological nature of, 36, 40; "self-defense" rhetoric, 24, 129–30; shamanic practices to preserve memories of, 104; terrorism, 37; time periods of, 22; unarmed civilians as majority of victims, 21, 29
Jeju 4.3 National Committee, xi, xxii (note 25), 21, 119, 123–29, 136; compromises made by, 125; women not represented on, 139
Jeju 4.3 Peace Foundation, xxii (note 26), 129, 134n55
Jeju 4.3 Peace Park (Jeju Island), xi, xvii; 4.3 Children Experience Center, 131; Advisory Committee of Exhibition Presentation, 129; *Baekbi* ("Unnamed Monument"), ix, *x,* 129; blank tablets in memorial room, 136–37; casualties portrayed, 141, 152n24; construction of, 123, 126; contents of, 119–20, 126–29*; memorial ceremonies, 120, 130–31, 137–38; Memorial Hall, ix, 5, 120, 127–29, 130, 138, 140–41; Memorial Tablets Enshrinement Room, 119, 126, *127,* 136; Peace Education Center, 131; state intervention in, 120; Tombstone Park for the Missing, 126, *128*; visitors to, 120; visual artists' work, 141, *142*; women as generic representatives of the weak and the permanent victim, 141–42, *142,* 153n26; women's representation at, 136, 138–42. *See also* reconciliation; transitional justice processes
Jeju 4.3 Special Act of 2000, xi, 41n6, 119
Jeju 4.3 uprising (April 3, 1948), ix; elementary and middle school student participation in, 12; main cause of, 26; March 1, 1947 as beginning of, 14; and People's

Republic of Jeju, xiv–xv; as precursor to Korean War, xii–xiii; Rebellion of Lee Jae-su as precursor to, 2; and Youth League subgroups, 9–10

Jeju April Third Incident Investigation Report (2003), 21

Jeju Defense Headquarters, 32, 33

Jeju Development Institute, 126

Jejudo (periodical), 107

Jeju Emergency Defense Headquarters, 27–28, 32

Jeju-eup (Jeju City), 8; March First Movement commemoration (1947) incident, 23–24

Jeju Government, 126

Jeju Island, ix, *xi*; appropriation and resistance tradition, 1, 2–3; autonomous provincial status, 13; birthrate on, 92–93; collective work, 3; conscription of young girls from, 5, 16n26; de facto government established on, 9–12; estrangement from mainland, 2–3; food shortages and economic problems (1947), 23; free-fire zone, 33, 34; as "Island of Reds," xv, 24–25, 28, 119, 135; as "Island of Women," 92; as "Island of World Peace," xi, xvii, 119, 123–24, 130–31, 135; kinship system, 3, 14, 39, 73, 102–4, 143; male-female ratio, xvi, xxii (note 22), 92–93, 102, 107; map of, *x, xi,* 35; martial law declared (1948), 32, 33–34, 45n109, 51; natural disasters, 99–100; naval base construction (2005), xvii, 135–36, 146–51; police presence expanded on, 13, 23, 32; popular sentiment in postcolonial, 3–5; population at time of massacre, 21; reconciliation at local level, 143–46; self-determination tradition, 2, 14, 33; six peasant rebellions, 2; socialist and liberationist ideologies, 3; as Tamla, 2; taxation on, 2; tension with mainland, xviii, 3–4, 32–33; as "woman's island," xvi; women's political activity on, 99. *See also* People's Republic of Jeju

Jeju Martial Law Command, 60

Jeju New Village Women's Association, 109

Jeju PC (People's Committee): administrative activities, 10–11; background to establishment of, 7–9; consumer union, 11; de facto government established by, 9–12; Industry Department, 10; as mass organization, 9–10; weakening of, 13–14, 23

Jeju people: foundations for radicalization of, 3–5; indigenous belief system, xvii, 2; migration between Jeju and Osaka, 3–4

Jeju Police Inspection Agency, 24, 27–28, 32

Jeju Police Veterans Association, 145–46

Jeju Provincial Office, 24

Jeju Sinbo (newspaper), 62, 96–97, 99

Jeju Sinmun (newspaper), 10

Jeju Women's Association, 98, 114n55

Jeju Youth Union, 5

Jemin Ilbo 4.3 Reporting Team, xviii, 10

Jenam Nursery School for Jeju orphans, 98

Jeong Bi-seok, 112n33

Jeong-mi Park, 104

Jeong Moon-hyeon, 145

Jeong-sim Yang, 12

Jinhae Training Center, 81, 83

Joseon Dynasty (1392–1910), 2, 4, 39, 93, 94

June Democratic Struggle (1987), 122

Jung-han Kim, 104

Kaurin, Pauline, 75

Kelman, Herbert, 34

Kim, Dong Choon, 80, 81

Kim, Hun Joon, xiii, xiv

Kim, Hyun Sun, 115n74
Kim, Ik-ryeol, 26, 28
Kim, Jong-min, xiv, 133–34n51
Kim, Monica, 37
Kim, Sang-heon, 116n87
Kim, Seong-eun, 63, 77, 78
Kim, Seong-nae, 38, 104
Kim Dae-jung, 122, 123
Kim Dae-jung government (1998–
   2003), xi, 122–24
Kim Dal-sam, 11
Kim Dong-hwan, 11
Kim Gu, 31
Kim Gyu-sik, 31
Kim Hyeon-suk, 50
Kim Il-sung, 82
Kim Jae-kyu, 121
Kim Jeong-ho, 28
Kim Jung-kyo, 99
Kim Man-deok, 107
Kim Man-deok Memorial Hall, 107
Kim Min-hwan, 126, 129
Kim Myeong-suk, 99
Kim Young-sam, 122
Kim Young-sam government
   (1994–1998), 122
Kin Seong-su, 8
kinship system, Jeju Island, 3, 14, 39,
   73, 143; and Gangjeong village, 150;
   gwendang (kinship community),
   102–3; and Wise Mother, Good Wife
   ideology, 102–4
Ko, Chang-hun, xiii
Ko, Su-seon, 98, 99, 107, 114n55
Ko Gil-cheon, 141, 142
Koh, Sungman, 125, 137
Ko Mun-seong, xiii
Korean Army: Eleventh Infantry
   Division, 87n34; Seventeenth
   Regiment, 75
Korean Central Intelligence Agency, 121
Korean Constabulary, 13, 32
Korean Democratic Party, 8, 24
Korean Democratic Youth League, 9–10
Korean Housewife Club, 105

Korean Marine Corps (KMC): creation
   of, 55–56; military educational
   system, 74
Korean Marine Corps (KMC), from
   Jeju Island: educational levels, 77;
   as "Ghost-Catching Marines," 76; as
   "Invincible Marine Corps," xvi, 71,
   77; middle school students, 62–63;
   reciprocal bonds with state, 77;
   sacrifice, sense of, 75, 78, 81; U.S.
   soldiers' view of, 77–78; women in,
   63, 81, 83
Korean National Cemetery, 126
Korean National Police, 24
Korean peninsula: First Republic of
   Korea, xv; and international political
   situation, 26; liberation from
   Japanese rule, xiv, 6–7, 10; national
   independence movement, 4; rural
   political organization, 8; strikes and
   protests of 1946, 14, 23–24; two
   separate governments, xii; unification
   as goal of Korean people, 80
Korean People's Army, 75
Korean People's Republic (KPR),
   xiv–xv, 7–9
Korean War (1950–1953), ix, 38; and
   anticommunism, 51; armistice, 85,
   90n115; casualties, 77, 85; Chinese
   intervention in, 83–84; conscription
   by South Korea, 49–50; Dosol Battle
   (Yanggu, June 1951), 77; Incheon
   Landing Operation, xix, 49, 65n3,
   75, 82, 84; Jeju 4.3 as precursor
   to, xii–xiii; Jeju dialect as secret
   code, 78; and national identity, 49,
   51–53; and One People Principle,
   53; recruitment on Jeju, 51; refugees
   from North, 82–83; Seoul Recovery,
   75, 81–82; and South Korean
   national identity, 49, 51–53; start
   of, 49; Tongyeong Battle (August
   17–19, 1950), 76. *See also* military
   enlistment; reintegration policies,
   and Korean War

Korean Women's Association (KWA), 105–6, 110, 117n106
Korea Retired Generals and Admirals Association *(Seonguhoe)*, 123
Kwon, Heonik, xiii

labor cooperatives *(sunureum)*, 101, 115n82
landlord-tenant relationships, 7
leaflets, 81–82
Lee, Steven, 80
Lee, Un-bang, 18n100
Lee Deok-gu, 11
Lee Jae-su, 2–3
Lee Myung-bak government (February 2008–February 2013), 137, 147–49
leftists, xiii; police blacklist of, 22, 59–60; as *ppalgaengi,* "commies" or "the reds," 39; retraining of, 59; stigma of being "Reds," xv, xvi, 57, 58, 61, 64, 73–74, 83, 85; as targets of Jeju 4.3 massacre, 28

MacArthur, Douglas, 75
Madam Freedom (Jeong Bi-seok), 95, 112nn33, 44
manufacturing industry, 91
March 1st 1947 shooting incident and general strike, 14, 23–24, 124
March First Independence Movement Anniversary (1947), 12, 14, 23–24
March First Korean Independence Movement of 1919, 10, 23, 79
Maritime Affairs Ministry, 146
Marshall Plan (European Recovery Program), 26, 30
martial law, 15, 33, 34
mass organizations, 9–10, 49–50; Daehan Women's Association, 59, 68n69; hierarchical system of, 59; National Association, 59, 68n69; National Guidance League, 57, 59–60; and Rhee government, 58–64. *See also* Daehan Youth Association; National Student Corps

May 10 election (1948), 26–30
May 18 Democratization Movement Truth Commission, 132n17
Meade, Grant, 1
media: and state building, 80–81; and Wise Mother, Good Wife ideology, 96–97, 107
Merrill, John, xii
migration, between Jeju and Osaka, 3–4
military enlistment, xiii, xv–xvi, 135; blood applications, 56–57, 61–62; conscription during Korean War, 49–50; in Korean Constabulary, 13; by National Guidance League members, 60; and patriotism, 56–57; for personal safety reasons, 57–58, 62–63, 78; process and motivations for, 55–58; removing stigma of being "Reds," 57, 58, 64, 73–74, 83, 85; and surveillance, 55; by women, 50, 51. *See also* Korean War (1950–1953)
Military Service Law (1949), 49, 65nn1, 3
Ministry of Defense, 50, 148, 149
Ministry of Education, 52, 61, 92
Ministry of Government Legislation, 125
Ministry of Health and Social Affairs, 96, 105
Ministry of Home Affairs, 59
Ministry of the Public Administration and Security, 151
minjok-state, 79
Minjungsibo (People's Newspaper, Osaka), 4
modernization, 93–95, 104–6
Mongolia, 2
Moon Bong-je, 28
Moon Jae-in government (May 2017–May 2022), 137, 152n10; and naval base construction, 147, 150–51
Mother's Day, 95–96, 97, 105, 113n35
Mt. Halla (Jeju Island), xiv, 2, 26
Mt. Jiri, 56

museums, and power struggles, 123

name seals, 63
National Assembly, 31, 121
National Association, 59, 68n69
National Guidance League, 57,
    59–60, 121
national identity, 65, 79, 81, 91, 94,
    125, 135; and blood lineage, 52–53,
    59, 79; and Korean War, 49, 51–53;
    "One People Principle" *(Ilminjuui)*,
    49, 52–53, 59, 60, 65, 79
National Police Agency, 151
National Reconstruction
    Movement, 106, 107
National Security Act (December
    1948), x, 51–52
National Student Corps, 50,
    56, 58, 61–64
"national traitors," punishment
    of, 8, 10, 31
national unity, ideology of, 120, 125–
    26, 135, 146
National Youth 4.3 Literary Award, 131
nation,. as socially constructed
    community, 79
naval base construction (Jeju
    Island), xvii, 135–36, 146–51;
    Absolute Preservation Zone, 148;
    contradictions with "Island of World
    Peace" rhetoric, 146–47; lack of
    procedural legitimacy, 148–50; relics
    discovered at site of, 148, 154n56;
    resolution of conflict over, 150–51
New Life Movement *(Sinsaenghwal
    Undong)*, 98–99, 103, 107
New Village Movement, 106,
    107, 109, 110
Ninth Regiment, 13, 26, 34–35
Northeast Asian peace community, 146
North Korea. *See* Democratic People's
    Republic of Korea (North Korea)
Northwest Youth Association (NWYA),
    25–26, 28, 32, 34–38, 59

obedience, 55, 71–76
Oh Dae-jin, 5, 9
"One People Principle" *(Ilminjuui)*, 49,
    52–53, 59, 60, 65, 79
The Origins of the Korean War
    (Cumings), xii–xiii
orphans, 96, 97, 98
Osaka, Japan, 3–4
Our Pledge (Uri-ui maengse)
    campaign, 52, 55

panoptic style of building, 53–55, *55*
Parent's Day, 105–6
Park, Myung-lim, xiii
Park Chung-hee, xii, xvi, 104–5;
    assassination of, 121–22
Park Chung-hee government (1961–
    1979), xvi, 104–6; and Wise Mother,
    Good Wife ideology, 92
Park Geun-hye government (February
    2013–March 2017), 137, 147,
    149, 152n10
Park Heon-yeong, 9
Park Jin-gyeong, 28, 29
Park Myung-lim, 22
pass cards, 55
patriarchal ideology, xvii, 12, 91–96, 99;
    reproduced at Peace Park, 138–39
patriotism, 64–65, 79, 84–85; "country
    first," 56–57; gendered, 95–96; lack
    of sense of, 80
peace (world peace), 135; discourse of
    peace building, 130–31; rhetoric of
    used to sublimate Jeju 4.3 atrocities,
    xi, xvii, 119
peacekeeping units, 10
People's Committees (PC), xiv–xv, 1, 5;
    outlaws by U.S. military government,
    9; supporting groups, 6. *See also*
    Committee for the Preparation for
    Korean Independence (CPKI)
People's Republic of Jeju, xiv, 1, 27;
    background to establishment of, 7–9;
    formation of, 6–12; slogans, 12. *See
    also* Jeju Island

polarization, 14, 28, 30, 32–33
police: blacklist of leftists, 22, 59–60;
combat police officers, right-wing
youth as, 28; districts, 60; expansion
of, 13, 23, 32; and March 1, 1947
shooting incident, 23–24; native,
24, 145; and reconciliation, 144–46;
revenge against by soldiers, 59,
68n68; rice collection by, 23
political prisoners of Jeju 4.3, 41n6, 57,
68n60, 83, 124–25, 139
polygamy, 12, 102–4
ppatda punishment, 72–74
Practical Committee for the
Investigation of Jeju 4.3 and
Honoring Victims, 136
preventive detention, 57, 60, 69nn79, 82
psychological warfare, 81–82
Pyoseon Bunyeohoe (Pyoseon Women's
Society), 97

rational thinking. *See* New Life
Movement *(Sinsaenghwal Undong)*
Rebellion of Lee Jae-su (1901), 2–3
reconciliation, xi, xiii, xvii, 119; and
criteria for victimhood, 125–26,
136–37; limitations of state efforts,
136–42; at local level, 143–46; and
police, 144–46; terminology of,
125–26. *See also* Jeju 4.3 Peace Park
(Jeju Island); truth commissions
"red villages," 143
refugees, x; adverse conditions for
after war, 99–100; amnesty for,
38; massacre of, 35–36; North
Korean, 25, 83–84
reintegration policies, and Korean
War: military enlistment, 55–58;
national identity formation, 51–53;
national organizations, 58–64; "One
People Principle" *(Ilminjuui)*, 49,
52–53, 59, 60, 65, 79; rituals for
boosting morale, 64–65; surveillance
systems, 53–55, *54*

reintegration policies, Jeju Marines:
and creation of imagined national
community, 79–84; group identity
and solidarity, 75–79; obedience
training, 71–75; patriotism and pro-
Americanism, 84–85
Republic of Korea (ROK) (South
Korea): apology for state
violence, xi, xvii, 119, 130,
137–38; constitutions, 48n167;
democratization, xii, 120–24, 135,
150; economic development, xii,
xvi–xvii, 91–93, 104–9, 121–22;
election (1954), 99; establishment
of as anticommunist, 30–39; First
Republic, xv, 32; founding of, 30;
imagined national community, xvi,
49, 71, 79–84; May 10 election
(1948), 26–30; military coups,
121–22; Military Service Law
of August 6, 1949, 49; National
Security Act (December 1948), x,
51–52; National Security State, 22;
presidential election (1960), 92, 121;
as "small America," 91; U.S. military
government in, xiii, 8–10, 13–15;
Yusin Constitution, 121. *See also*
South Korea; state building
Restoration of the Honor of Victims
(2000), xi
revenge, 36, 40, 58, 68n68, 83
Rhee Syng-man, xii, xv;
anticommunism used by to gain U.S.
support, 31, 32, 44n95; *Ilminjuui
gaesul (Outline of One People
Principle)*, 52; "Invincible Marine
Corps" title bestowed on Jeju
marines, xvi, 71, 77; Liberation Day
address (1951), 80; national identity
promoted by, 51; and NWYA,
32; on ostracization of dissenters,
53; as president of Daehan Youth
Association, 60; resignation of, 92,
121; rightist youth group support

of, 25; speech on One People
    Principle, 53
Rhee Syng-man government, 23;
    martial law declared on Jeju Island
    (1948), 32, 33–34, 51; and mass
    organizations, 50; national security
    and economic recovery logics, 91;
    "One People Principle" *(Ilminjuui),*
    49, 52–53, 59, 60, 65, 79; and Wise
    Mother, Good Wife ideology, 92
Ridgway, Matthew, 74
right-wing groups: anticommunism
    and youth group atrocities, 25–26,
    28; police combat police officers,
    28. *See also* Daehan Youth
    Association; Northwest Youth
    Association (NWYA)
Roh Moo-hyun, xi, 119, 130; apology
    for state violence, xi, 119, 130
Roh Moo-hyun government, 124; and
    naval base construction, 135–36, 147
Russian Revolution (1917), 4

sacrifice: "civilian sacrifices," ideology
    of, xi, 124–26, 139; in Japanese
    colonial ideology, 92; marines'
    sense of, 75, 78, 81; motherhood
    as, 92, 94, 97, 98; and women's
    communal networks, 101; women's
    work as, 106
Saimdang Academy, 105
Samyang Police Station, 37
Second Regiment, 34, 35
Seiji Yoshida, 16n26
"self-defense" rhetoric, 24, 129–30
Seoul Administrative Court, 148
Seoul City, and awards, 105
Seventeenth Regiment, 75
sexual violence, 37–38; not represented
    in Special Act, 139; women forced
    into sexual slavery, 5, 16n26, 37–38
shamanism, 98, 99, 103–4, 110
Shin Hyeon-jun, 57, 81
Shin Saimdang, 94–95, 105
Shin Saimdang Day and Prize, 105

Shin Seong-mo, 50
shrines, 103–4, 144
Son, Kyeongho, xiii
"Song for Mother," 96
Song Jing-woo, 8
Song Yeong, 112n26
Song Yo-chan, 33, 34
South Jeolla Province, 9, 32
South Korea. *See* Republic of Korea
    (ROK) (South Korea)
South Korean Labor Party (SKLP)
    (central organization), 14, 31
South Korean Labor Party (SKLP) (Jeju
    branch), xiii, 13–14, 59; and Jeju 4.3
    uprising, 26, 28; March 1, 1947 rally
    and incident, 23–24; marginalization
    of, 25; not included in definition of
    victims, 125, 136–37; organizational
    structure, 14, 26
Soviet Union, 26, 81–82
Special Act for Investigation of Jeju 4.3
    (2000), xi, 41n6, 123–26, 129, 136–
    37; gender not considered by, 139
Special Act for the Draft (July 26,
    1950), 49, 50
Special Committee for Investigating
    Antinational Activities, 31
Stalin, Joseph, 2
state: as above ethnic nation
    (minjok), 80–81, 83–84; citizens
    (gungmin), 80–81, 85; definition
    of, xi–xii; *gukga,* 80; limitations
    of reconciliation efforts, 136–
    42; *minjok*-state, 79. *See also*
    reconciliation; state building;
    transitional justice processes
state building, xi–xii, 135; coercive and
    constructive aspects, 51; as embodied
    and gendered phenomenon, 38–39;
    and media, 80–81; and transitional
    justice processes, 120–24; violence
    as central to, xii, 34. *See also*
    reintegration policies, and Korean
    War; reintegration policies,
    Jeju Marines

state violence: apologies for, xi, 119, 130, 137–38; central to state building, xii, 34; displacement of by peace rhetoric, 120; and formation of South Korea, 22; guilty by association *(yeonjwaje)*, 39–41, 48n167; legal justification of, 34; by untrained youth police officers, 28; against women, 38. *See also* Jeju 4.3 massacre; violence
stone walls for surveillance, 53–55, *54*
Student Shock Force, 62
Student Volunteer Army, 50, 87n43
Suni Samchon (Hyun Gi-yeong), 83, 121, 129, 132n14
surveillance systems, 53–55, *54*; and internalization, 55; and National Guidance League, 59; sentry posts, 55, 61; villagers forced to join Daehan Youth Association, 61

Taegeukgi (national flag of South Korea), 76, 126
taegeuk mark (yin-yang symbol), 126
Tak Seong-nok, 38
tangerine industry, 108–9
teachers, 6, 11–12; and military enlistment, 56, 63; and National Student Corps, 62
terrorism, 37
the Kim Man-deok Prize, 107
Tilly, Charles, xi–xii, 34, 121
transitional justice processes, viii, xiv, xvii, 132n14, 134n55, 135–40; and development of democracy, 120–24; incorporated into Peace Park exhibition, 129, 130; limitations of, 136–38; and reconciliation at local level, 143, 145; reproduction of existing hierarchies, 138–39
Truman administration, 26, 129
Truman Doctrine, 26, 30
truth commissions, x–xi, xii, xiii, xiv, 132n17. *See also* reconciliation

"The Truth of U.S. Occupation" cartoon, 129

Udo (island), 11
UNESCO List of Intangible Cultural Heritage, 108
United Nations, 31, 75, 81, 120
United Nations Temporary Commission on Korea, 26
United States: American soldiers shoot "collaborators," 76; colonial bureaucracy reinstalled by, 8; confections imported from, 6–7; C-rations from, 84, 89n110; cultural influence in South Korea, 91; occupation of Korea, 7; People's Committee weakened by, 1; policy of empowering South Korean army (1946), 31–32; pro-Americanism and South Korea, 84–85; Protestant missionaries, 93–94
United States Armed Forces in Korea (USAFIK), 8
United States–Soviet Joint Commission, 26
universe of moral obligation, 28–29, 32–33, 36–37
uprisings: strikes and protests (1946), 14, 23–24. *See also* Jeju 4.3 uprising (April 3, 1948)
U.S. Army, 6, 31, 81–82
U.S. Counterintelligence Corps (CIC), 25
U.S. Marine Corps, 74–75, 84–85; Fifth Regiment, 77
U.S. military government: attempts to terminate insurgency, 28; labeling of islanders as leftists, 24; March 1, 1947 protest against, 14, 23–24, 124; and protests of fall 1946, 14; response to 1947 strikes, 24–26; rightist youth groups organized by, 25; support for massacre, 37, 40–41, 44n95; withdrawal of troops (1948), 30–31

victims of Jeju 4.3 massacre: children and elderly, xv, 21, 34, 35, 141; criteria for inclusion in official definition of, 125–26, 136–37, 151n2; men as primary targets, 21–22, 29, 40; official count, 21, 41n1; silencing of, 119; unarmed civilians, 21, 29; women, 13–14; women as generic representatives, 141–42, *142,* 153n26

villages, 3, 5; Jeju PC administration of, 10–11; New Village Movement, 106, 107, 109, 110; "red," 143

violence: centrality of to state-building process, xi; politicidal, xiii; sexual, 5, 16n26, 37–38; torture of detainees, 25. *See also* state violence

widows: as concubines, 103; deprived of pensions, 96; due to Korean War, 91; economic independence for, 98; as insurgents, 12; patriotic media portrayals of, 96–97; sexual violence against, 37–38

Wise Mother, Good Wife *(hyeonmoyangcheo),* xvi; in 1960s and 1970s, 104–6; and Confucianism, 93, 94; and elite women, 96, 97–99, 106; exemplary mother prize, 105–6; on the island of working women, 91–93; Japanese *ryousaikenbo* ideology, 93–94, 98; Jeju women as symbol of strong working women, 107–11; and kinship community, 102–4; and local media, 96–97, 107; and militant nation (1940s), 94; and modernization, 93–94, 104–5; Mother's Day, 95–96, 97, 105, 113n35; and Park Chung-hee regime, 92; in postwar years, 93–96; sexuality regulated by, 92–93, 95, 112n33; Strong Woman, Working Mother on Jeju Island, 101; women as responsible for "tradition," 91,

94–95; women's expansion of, 101–4, 108–10; working mothers on Jeju Island, 99–102; working women as, 104–6

Woman's Death (Ko Gil-cheon), 141

women: American culture copied by, 91; Americans, sexual relations with, 95; divers, 3, 4–5, 100–101, 103, 106–8; and economic development, xii, xvi–xvii, 92–93, 104–9, 121–22; elite, 96, 97–99, 106; forced into sexual slavery, 5, 16n26, 37–38; as generic representatives of the weak and the permanent victim, 141–42, *142,* 153n26; labor cooperatives *(sunureum),* 101, 115n82; marines, 63, 81, 83; military enlistment by, 50, 51, 63; in National Student Corps, 63; political activity of, 99; religious rituals of, 103–4; torture of, 37–38; as victims of 4.3 massacres, 13–14. *See also* gender; Wise Mother, Good Wife *(hyeonmoyangcheo)*

Women's Center (Seoul), 104

World War II, 5

Wright, Brendan, xiii, 22, 31

Yacheika (subgroup of the Communist Party of Korea), 5

Yeongmowon ("Shrine for the Commemoration of Beautiful Souls"), 144

Yeosu-Suncheon (Yeosun) revolt (1948), 33, 53, 55–56, 61

Yeo Un-hyeong, 7, 8

Yi Sun-shin, 62

Yoo Hae-jin, 25

Yoon Suk-yeol government (May 2022–May 2027), 138

youth associations, left-wing, 5, 9–10. *See also specific associations*

youth associations, right-wing, 25–26, 28. *See also specific associations*

Youth Defense Corps, 69n88

Yuk Young-soo, 105

Yuk Young-soo Memorial
    Committee, 106
Yusin Constitution, 121

Zelter, Angie, 147

About the Author

Gwisook Gwon is a research fellow at the Research Institute for Tamla Culture at Jeju National University. She taught sociology at Jeju National University from 1994 to 2016. Her work has long centered on state violence, collective memory, and gender. She has published books and articles on the Jeju Massacre in the Korean language since 2001. Her 2006 book, *Gieogui jeongchi* [The Politics of Memory], was designated an Excellent Book of the Year by the Korean National Academy of Sciences. Her recent works about the Jeju Massacre and the Korean peace movement in the English language have appeared in *Under Occupation* (ed. Daniel Broudy, Peter Simpson, and Makoto Arakaki, 2013) and in the *Asia-Pacific Journal*. Her article about the connection between the Korean War and Christianity on Jeju appeared in the *Journal of Korean Religions* in October 2015.